D0282395

URBAN LAND ECONOMICS

URBAN LAND ECONOMICS

Principles and Policy

GRAHAM HALLETT

Senior Lecturer in Economics
University College, Cardiff

1979
Archon Books

First published 1979 in England by
THE MACMILLAN PRESS LTD
and in the USA as an Archon Book
an imprint of
THE SHOE STRING PRESS, INC.
995 Sherman Avenue,
Hamden, Connecticut 06514

Library of Congress Catalog Card No. 79-65820

British Library Cataloguing in Publication Data

Hallett, Graham
  Urban land economics
  1. Land use, Urban
  I. Title
  333.7'7   HD111

Macmillan ISBN 0–333–26183–6

Archon ISBN 0–208–01834–4

Manufactured in Great Britain

To Isabel

Contents

Contents

List of Figures

List of Tables

Foreword

In this book, I have attempted to bring together simple economic theory, empirical data and a little history in such a way as to illuminate some current issues in urban policy. In this field, there is today a crying need for more dialogue between specialists, and between specialists and a wider audience. Economists, architects and town planners are now viewed by the public with considerable scepticism, which they have done much to deserve. The reaction against town planning is indicated by books with titles like *The Death and Life of Great American Cities; The Failure of Town Planning* or *After the Planners*. Even if their analysis is often questionable, these *critiques* reflect what many people would regard as failings in post-War town planning, especially in Britain where 'town planning', – and attacks on 'land speculation', and slum clearance – have been carried further than in most other countries. To accept these criticisms does not necessarily imply a rejection of town planning and other aspects of urban policy. (I can remember being deeply influenced by a war-time Penguin, *Town Planning* by Dr Thomas Sharp, and would not wish to throw out the baby with the bath-water). But the time seems ripe for the development of a new synthesis on urban development, which gives greater weight to practitioners' knowledge, takes a more historical perspective, is less pretentious, and less subject to blinkered specialisation.

When I taught urban economics, I found it difficult to find one comprehensive book which I could recommend to students, and so decided to try to write one myself. It reflects in part my own experience: for example, my references tend to be confined to the countries I know best – the UK, West Germany, the USA and Canada. I hope it will be useful for both professional and amateur students.

Graham Hallett

Acknowledgements

I am grateful to the following organisations for supplying statistical information: the *Financial Times* for the property share indices in Fig. 9, Alsopp & Co. for the property yields in Table 4, the Nationwide Building Society for the land price data in Fig. 8 and Table 10, and the Building Societies Association for the data in Table 2 and the City of Cologne for Fig. 6. I am grateful to the Royal Town Planning Institute for permission to quote the figures in Table 11, to the Cambridge University Press for permission to quote Table 6 from *Urban Development in Britain* by P. A. Stone and to Professor B. J. L. Berry for permission to quote the diagram in Fig. 12 from 'The Factorial Ecology of Calcutta', *American Journal of Sociology* (The University of Chicago Press).

The author and publishers wish to thank the following who have kindly given permission to reproduce material:

Associated Book Publishers Ltd (Methuen) for *Planning & Profit in the Urban Economy* by T. A. Broadbent.

Cambridge University Press for *Urban Development in Britain* by P. A. Stone.

Croom Helm Ltd for *Economics & Land Use Planning* by A. J. Harrison.

Secker & Warburg for *The City in History* by Lewis Mumford and *The Road to Wigan Pier* by George Orwell.

The University of Chicago Press for 'The Concentric Zonal Pattern of Urban Residential Areas as Applied to Chicago' by E. W. Burgess in *The Growth of the City: An Introduction to a Research Project* by R. E. Park and E. W. Burgess; *The Constitution of Liberty* by J. A. Hayek; *From Economic Theory to Policy* by E. R. Walker and 'Urban Areas' by E. W. Burgess in *Chicago: An Experiment in Social Science Research* (T. V. Smith & L. D. White, eds).

I am grateful to Julian Gough, Garel Rhys, Milton Wilkinson, Roger Harris, Harold Carter and Richard Williams for commenting on various chapters; they of course bear no responsibility for my opinions. Finally, I must express my gratitude to my wife, who has had this book hanging over her throughout our married life and has contributed so much to bringing it to a successful conclusion.

I Principles

1 Two Cheers for Economics

'Urban land economics deals with the processes and patterns of land utilisation', according to an older textbook,[1] which points out that it is part of land economics, which is in turn part of economics as a whole. However, land economics as a subject covering all forms of land use has not (probably unfortunately) developed in the way envisaged by the inter-War pioneers in the USA, so that 'urban economics' may be considered a preferable term to 'urban land economics'. The latter term is certainly misleading if it implies a merely two dimensional approach: the economics of buildings are an integral part of its subject matter. However, 'urban land economics' has come to indicate a certain type of emphasis. It is primarily concerned with the way in which buildings are developed, managed and used, and is associated with the institutional inclinations of the 'Wisconsin School'.[2] This approach does not disparage economic theory. But it tries to combine simple theory with an analysis of institutional factors; it does not, for example, regard as particularly useful the 'new urban economics' which constructs an elaborate but purely theoretical edifice, with no discussion of the laws or institutions of the 'real world' (Chap. 6). We will therefore retain the term 'urban land economics'.

IS THERE AN ECONOMIC CONSENSUS?

Any detailed examination of, for example, urban land pricing, the development process, and the economic consequences of town planning must rest on a basis of general economic theory. Is there such a basis today? Jokes about any six economists having seven opinions, two of them Lord Keynes's, contain an uncomfortable amount of truth. There is undoubtedly considerable confusion in macroeconomics, i.e. the problems of inflation and unemployment. But on the problems of resource allocation which, in the field of real property, are the concern of

3

this book, economists have more of a common approach than might sometimes be imagined. Even if they differ on 'concrete truth' they generally share a view of economics as 'an engine for the discovery of concrete truth'. (The main exception are the Marxists, whose views will be discussed below). But how can economists who share a methodological consensus differ on questions of policy? The stock – and largely correct – answer is that this reflects either differing value judgements (which can be analysed) or differing factual assumptions (which can be empirically tested). But there is a less creditable aspect – the consequence of serious imperfections in the market for economists' services.

> Both at the academic level and at that of public pronouncements, prizes are won by product differentiation. There is little doubt that leading economists can make a notable, if superficial, impact by making their pronouncements appear as different as possible from those of their colleagues, and by putting the emphasis on those points which they believe to be original rather than on the common elements on which most economists agree.[3]

ESSENTIALS OF ECONOMICS

The underlying theme of this book is the need for a 'political economy' of urban affairs. This involves both a defense of the economic approach and a criticism of a great deal of recent economics. On the one hand, the basic propositions of microeconomics, i.e. the principles of price formation and resource allocation, are still valid; they apply as much to urban development as to manufacturing industry; when they are ignored by governments the effect of policies is different from that intended and often extremely harmful. On the other hand, the author parts company with economists who try to force the spatial pattern of a city into the Procrustean bed of an all-embracing economic model or who assume that town planning 'maximises social welfare' without examining how it works in practice.

Microeconomics is based on a number of essentially simple concepts. Resources are limited in relation to human wants, so that if they are used for one purpose they cannot be used for another. Economics constantly stresses the 'trade-off' between desirable alternatives, and the need for choice. The problem of scarcity is not affected by bringing resources into state ownership or by supplying a service 'free': it is the inevitable corollary of limited resources and potentially greater human wants. Even today,

> . . . the desire of the conveniences and ornaments of building, dress, equipage and household furniture seems to have no limit or certain boundary.[4]

If housing or land is supplied free of charge by the state, and if the demand consequently exceeds the available supply, some kind of rationing must be introduced. A market system and rationing are alternative ways of solving an unavoidable problem, and economics examines the implications of these alternative systems.

The problem of resource allocation applies not only between different uses at one time but between different periods of time. Most of us prefer to enjoy something now rather than in one, ten or twenty years' time. This 'time preference' underlies the rate of interest; those who borrow money (i.e. bring consumption forward) pay a price to those who lend money (i.e. postpone consumption). The rate of interest acts as a yardstick for ranking investment projects. At any one time there is a range of projects which will give returns in the future (either goods, resulting from industrial investment, or services such as the use of buildings). But some investments will give higher returns than others (measured by actual, or imputed, market prices), and the rate of interest enables a choice to be made. Does it pay to renovate a house, and rebuild it later, or rebuild it now? If no rate of interest is taken into account, it would always seem cheaper to rebuild now, but this could be a serious misuse of resources.[5]

The essence of the economic approach is thus the comparison of the costs and benefits of alternative uses of resources. This comparison can be carried out by consumers, faced with prices reflecting these costs, or by a government using 'shadow' prices or other ranking devices. The emphasis is thus on the factors underlying consumer demand for, and the costs of, urban 'goods'; the factors affecting the suppliers of these goods; the extent to which prices reflect costs (including 'social' ones); and the most efficient form of correction when they do not.

CRITICISMS OF ECONOMICS

But can we accept 'the economic approach' to urban land policy or, some might say, anything else? The experience in recent years of economists in government – at least in Britain – has hardly raised public esteem for the subject. But criticisms of economics can be divided into three types: criticisms of economics as a subject; criticisms of current fashions in economics; criticisms of a market economy.

A radical criticism is echoed by Professor Max Beloff:

> Historically, the record of economists since the discipline became a recognised one has been uniformly dismal.[6]

Few who have actually *read* Smith, Malthus, Mill, or Keynes, would share this view – although some of these economists have admittedly been badly served by their popularisers. Another criticism is that what is 'economic' may be undesirable on aesthetic, environmental or social grounds. This is a semantic misunderstanding. Economics concerns itself with 'the relation between ends and scarce resources having alternative uses'.[7] It certainly stresses the importance of costs, and the desirability of selecting the cheapest way of obtaining a particular outcome. But the other side of the relationship is 'ends' – which can just as much be non-material as material. Economics provides no grounds whatever for saying, for example, that power lines should be carried overhead rather than underground, merely because the former is cheaper. Cheapness and an uncluttered sky are both desirable objectives with a 'trade-off' between them, and the responsible authority has to strike a balance.

Strong criticisms of economics, and of a market economy, especially in relation to housing and land policy, have come from the school of 'social administration' founded in Britain by the late Professor Titmuss. (Criticisms of the economic approach and of the market economy are often closely connected, just as there is an undeniable affinity between 'mainstream' economics, political liberalism, and a market economy). The Titmuss school has criticised economists for believing that urban processes are, or should be, operated by coldly calculating economic men. For example, 'social administrators' have variously argued that rent control would not reduce the supply of privately rented housing, as economists had suggested; that the elimination of private tenancy is an inevitable consequence of economic progress; and that its elimination is desirable. Rents and land prices should not be determined by 'blind economic forces' but by social considerations.

The answer of 'mainstream' economics begins by emphasising the distinction between 'positive' statements and 'normative' statements, or 'value judgements'. 'Positive' statements express causal relationships, explicable in theoretical terms and verified by empirical observation. Such statements are either true or false, they are not a subject for moral argument. In the case of rented housing, the traditional theory is that the quantity supplied will, in the long run (i.e. after sufficient time to build or sell) increase if the rent is at, or above, a 'cost-covering' level and decrease if the rent is below this level, and expected to remain there. (This 'cost-covering' level can be roughly estimated from current property 'yields' applied to either construction costs, or sale value, with vacant possession). By comparing the price/cost relationship with (lagged) supply charges, the effect of rent control can be assessed, given sufficient observations. We can, for example compare the supply of private rented housing since the War in Britain and West Germany, which have followed very different rent policies; the effects, in Britain, on the previously uncontrolled sector after the imposition of 'fair rents' in 1965; the effects of the extension of the 'unfurnished code' to furnished housing after 1974.[8] In all these instances, the evidence supports the conclusions of simple economic theory.

Positive economic propositions thus have to be taken into account if economic policies are to achieve their intended results. Value judgements are a different matter. On fundamental and irreconcilable differences in value judgements, men can in the last resort only fight. However, as Professor Milton Friedman points out, most differences are not of this type but rather differences about the likely effects of various policies.[9] Has the virtual elimination of private rented housing in Britain benefited potential tenants? How do the effects of rent control in Britain compare with the effects of its abolition in West Germany? Has 'comprehensive re-development' achieved the hoped-for results? Has the British system of development control produced a better urban environment than, for example, the very different American or West German systems? These are largely factual questions, on which comparative studies – of which there have been very few – could at the very least narrow the scope for disagreement.

But although the distinction between 'positive' and 'normative' propositions is fundamental to any rational analysis of economic questions, the attempt to make economics 'value free' has in some ways done it harm. Drawing a distinction – as Lord Robbins did in *The Nature and Significance of Economic Science* – between, on the one hand, considerations of morality, aesthetics, or 'quality of life', and, on the other, empirical hypotheses and logical analysis never implied that the former were unimportant, merely that they were not provable in the same way. Having correctly made this distinction, however, many economists – although they include neither Lord Robbins nor Professor Friedman – have tended to ignore all the questions of ultimate value which stir men's souls and to concentrate on a technical analysis which may seem to be an intellectual game. It is hardly surprising if some students conclude that economics is irrelevant to real problems, and that it is only the 'anti-economists' who care about the state of the world. It is, in fact, difficult to examine contentious questions without making at least implicit value judgements; far better – some economists argue – to bring them out into the open.

> The surest way of emphasising the distinction between positive and normative studies, as well as their mutual relations, is to place them in close juxtaposition to each other rather than to isolate them in logic-tight compartments.[10]

My discussion below of land policy and town planning will not conceal my desire to contribute to a re-interpretation of economic liberalism in these fields.

Many of the common criticisms of 'mainstream' economics may be misguided, but one must distinguish between the basic economic approach and recent fashions in the subject. It has recently been fashionable to exclude the institutional and historical elements which were so important in the works of the older economists. But pure theory without historical perspective or institutional knowledge can lead to dangerously unrealistic conclusions. This danger is illustrated by 'cost-benefit analysis'. In a general way, a comparison of costs and benefits is, and has always been, an essential part of policy-making. And in some cases 'shadow prices' can serve a useful purpose. But the tendency of the cost-benefit practitioners to quantify, or ignore, the unquantifiable can produce strange results. The saga of the Roskill Commission and the Third London Airport has underlined the defects in the approach of what Professor Self calls 'the econocrats'.[11]

In a broader sense, however, economics is still concerned with comparing the costs and benefits of alternative policies, and has to draw on other subjects for the necessary information. The economics of urban development draws on surveying for the costs of constructing buildings, on traffic engineers for the costs of alternative transportation systems. It draws on sociology and social psychology for information on the human consequences of life in high flats, 'ghettos', low density suburbs and council estates, or on people's attitudes to shopping or the use of cars or public transport. Moreover, many issues – such as policy towards the 'inner city' – involve questions of political science and public administration. It is unrealistic to discuss town planning or local housing policy in terms of pure ideals with no reference to the political factors which in fact influence councillors and planners.

THEORY AND PRACTICE

Economists are beginning to turn to the previously neglected fields of urban land policy, housing policy and the economics of town planning. But there is still a wide gap between academic economists, who often know little about the details of urban development, and the 'practical men' who actually build towns – architects, builders, surveyors and developers. University economics and what might be termed 'practical urban development economics' (e.g. the 'urban eonomics' syllabus of the Royal Institution of Chartered Surveyors) are conducted in almost complete separation. This has impoverished both. The occasional comments by university economists on urban development have often suffered from an innocence of any practical knowledge. On the other hand, 'estate management' has for too long been an inbred, technical subject divorced from the more fundamental economic questions. This is one of the reasons why many informed, perceptive comments by professional bodies have sometimes been presented in a way that attracts little attention, and have often been ignored. It is characteristic that the 'discounted cash flow' technique, developed by surveyors before the first World War, had to be 'discovered' by economists in the 1960s.

The 'practical men' can learn from the wider horizons of (some) academics, but the academics can also learn from the practical men. The dangers are, on the one hand, not seeing the wood for the trees and, on the other, describing the wood incorrectly through not knowing anything about trees. To apply theories inappropriately, without understanding the institutional context, can be worse than relying on commonsense. As one distinguished economist has written:

> Commonsense is sometimes bad theory, and then it may mislead. But it is often good, but crude, theory. Rough theory, or good commonsense is, in practice, what we need.[12]

REFERENCES

1. R. U. Ratcliff, *Urban Land Economics*, New York, 1949, p. v.
2. R. T. Ely & G. S. Wehrwein, *Land Economics*, University of Wisconsin Press, 1940
3. Samuel Brittan, *Capitalism and the Permissive Society*, Macmillan, 1975, p. 80.
4. Adam Smith, *The Wealth of Nations*, Everyman ed. p. 149, Vol. 1.
5. Even if the investment is undertaken by the state, and no price charged (e.g. for roads) it may still be desirable to make use of an assumed, or 'shadow' rate of interest, in order to decide rationally on economic priorities. The Marxist attack on the charging of interest (like that by Aristotle, the scholastic philosophers of the Middle Ages, and Mohammed) was developed before the modern analysis of the rate of interest. Marx – basing his reasoning on the labour theory of value of the 'classical' economists – regarded interest as being stolen from the workers. As a result, interest was orginally ignored in investment calculations in the USSR. This led to such obvious inefficiency in investment decisions that, Marxist doctrine notwithstanding, a 'shadow' rate of interest has been adopted for industrial investment.
6. *Encounter*, March 1968, p. 91.
7. L. Robbins, *The Nature and Significance of Economic Science*, p. 16.
8. Graham Hallett, *Housing and Land Policies in Britain and Germany*, Macmillan, 1977, Pt. 1; Duncan Maclennan, 'The 1974 Rent Act—Some Short Run Supply Effects', *The Economic Journal*, June 1978.
9. Milton Friedman, 'The Methodology of Positive Economics' in *Essays in Positive Economics*, Chicago, 1935.
10. E. R. Walker, *From Economic Theory to Policy*, Chicago, 1943, p. 227.
11. Peter Self, *Econocrats and the Policy Process*, Macmillan, 1975.
12. I. M. D. Little, *A Critique of Welfare Economics*, Oxford, 1952, p. 272.

2 Urban Problems and Economic Theory

Underneath all economic laws, the final basis of human action is psychological, so that the last stage of analysis of the problems of the structure of cities, the distribution of utilities, the earnings of the buildings which house them, and the land values resulting therefrom, turn on individual and collective taste and preference, as shown in social habits and customs.

Richard M. Hurd, *Principles of City Land Values*, 1903, p. 17

THREE WAYS OF ALLOCATING RESOURCES

The problems of allocating urban land uses are basically the same as those of allocating food, clothes, cars or anything else. Economic textbooks begin by pointing out that all societies, whatever their political and social organisation, have to answer three economic questions. *What* is to be produced? *How* is it to be produced? *For whom* is it to be produced?[1] In the urban field, this means such questions as: How many houses, shops, offices are to be built? Where and how are they to be built? Who is to obtain the use of the houses, shops and offices?

These questions can be answered in three ways: by means of a traditional economy, a market economy, or a command economy. Although logically distinct, these economic types can to some extent co-exist, and most economies are 'mixed' in various proportions. In a traditional economy, the questions of a resource allocation are decided by custom and convention, usually with a religious basis. The rural economy of medieval Europe, or of Africa before the opening up of the continent, might be classified as (mainly) a traditional economy. In such economies, land is not thought of as something to be bought and sold, but as something to be used communally, according to fixed con-

11

tentions, or to be allocated according to a strong hereditary class system.[2]

But neither a primitive communal economy, nor one based on a rigid social hierarchy has ever fitted well into an urban economy. With the growth of European towns in the later Middle Ages, a market economy began to emerge. To oversimplify a very complex development, we can say that the market economy came to predominate in real property with the Industrial Revolution in England (and somewhat later in other European countries) although elements of a traditional society persisted in the countryside up to within living memory. Later in the 19th century, but especially in the 20th century, a command economy began to emerge, with the growth of town planning.

A traditional society presupposes a slow rate of change in technology, incomes and ways of life; it is undermined by the growth of industry and technology. And yet there is a recurrent tendency, whenever a society is under stress, to hark back to an idealised vision of a primitive communal society. After the Industrial Revolution had led to a rapid growth of ill-planned and unsanitary industrial towns, the reaction of what Marx called the 'utopian socialists' was to advocate new ideal communities in which there would be no buying and selling, and in which simple benevolence would be a sufficient guide for action. The many attempts to set up such 'communes' in the 19th century failed, except where they were motivated by a strong religious faith. The 'utopian socialist' view has been resurrected in our own day by the 'New Left', which rejects both the market economy and the state bureaucracy of traditional socialism. This view has acquired some support from 'radical architects' who, reacting – only too justifiably – against tower blocks, 'urban renewal', and the general inhumanity of much modern architecture and town planning, have applied New Left ideas in the urban field.[3] On this view, town planning is a conspiracy of capitalists and officials, designed to maintain their position. The positive prescriptions are a little vague but boil down to letting people decide their own environment; this is to be achieved by 'squatting', refusing to pay rent, and other guerilla action against 'the system'. Some of the ideals behind this philosophy would command widespread approval – the idea that buildings should be made for man and not man for buildings, the groping towards more decentralised decision-making and 'the human scale'. But the basic weakness of this approach is that it has no answer to the three fundamental economic questions.[4] When a group of squatters take over a building, they are acting as parasites on the existing system. Insofar as this is tolerated for a time, it can only exist because it is quantitatively insignificant; if *everyone* decided to seize the house or office they fancied, the result would be a Hobbesian 'state of nature' and there would soon be an irresistible demand for the enforcement of law and order.

Thus the choice, in allocating real property resources, is between a market economy and a command economy, or a combination of the two, e.g. a market economy operating within a planning framework. Under a command economy, all decisions are taken by a central planning agency which decides, for instance, not only how many houses or flats are to be built, and of what type, but also how they are to be allocated – according to service to the Party, length of time on the waiting list, number of children, or accident and influence. The basic principle of a market economy, on the other hand, is that products have a price; consumers bid for them on the basis of the product's value to them, and producers supply what they find to be profitable. If the supply is fixed, the price allocates it among those prepared to pay the most for it. If the supply can be increased or reduced, it will adjust itself – after a time – to consumer demand, although the efficiency with which it does so will depend on the structure of the supplying industry.

The distinction between a command economy and a market economy is not the same as that between state ownership and public ownership. Because of the impossibility of deciding every detail of economic life in the planning office, even socialist[5] economies have to make some use of the price system. In the 1930s, some economists devised models for a socialist market economy in which managers would not be given quantitative directives, but would merely be given general rules for pricing and production policy; these were designed so that, if they were followed, consumers would obtain the choice of goods they preferred, given their incomes and the prevailing costs of production.[6]

But the growing number of studies of the attempts in Eastern Europe to introduce market mechanisms suggest that an effective market is impossible without the creation of property rights of some kind (e.g. the profit-sharing rights of workers in Yugoslav firms). These studies (so far confined mainly to manufacturing) also suggest that, although a Yugoslav type of system is much superior to Stalinism – from a 'liberal' point of view – its lack of a capital market creates serious problems. Perhaps a more promising means of reconciling 'market' and 'social' virtues is a system in which a substantial proportion of the market is composed of autonomous public or non-profit bodies, in competition with each other, and with private firms. An example of an urban development system of this type is provided by West Germany. Non-profit enterprises, both large national organisations like *Neue Heimat* (the largest building firm in the country) and small local co-operatives, are a major force in the housing industry. There are also public bodies (homestead companies) which organise development for any type of client, and supervise urban renewal.[7] At the same time, local authorities have become large owners of developable land, without having a monopoly. A market system of this type is as different from a market system of the type prevailing in late 19th century housing as it is from a 'command economy' such as British council housing.

PRICE CONTROL

Since the market system operates through prices – land and house prices, rents, mortgage rates – prices must, on occasion, be able to change, up or down. In a period of inflation, prices will have to rise with the general price level to remain constant in real terms. Prices may also have to rise or fall in real terms, to balance demand and supply. Prices can be prevented from falling by monopolistic restrictions on supply. The most serious monopolistic practices today tend to be those enforced by the state. Governmental restrictions on land use are a form of monopoly, which can restrict supply and raise the price – justifiably or otherwise.

The opposite policy is to hold prices down below the equilibrium level, as is down when governments control rents or mortgage rates. Government price controls are, in the long run, more harmful than monopolistic practices because they can cause a complete breakdown of the market system. If the price is consistently held below the level needed to give a return comparable to that in other fields, the commodity will eventually cease to be produced. Potential consumers will either have to switch to some less desired substitute (e.g. buying instead of renting) or the state will have to supply the commodity on subsidised terms (e.g. public housing). Even in the case of land which – in some senses – is in fixed supply, price control is incompatible with a market system. A temporary 'freeze' is possible; a prolonged one involves either a black market or a 'first come, first served' system of allocation, or some form of rationing.

These points are even less generally understood in connection with real property than in other fields because of the longer time-lag involved. If (as has happened) the government of a country which imports all its condensed milk sets a maximum price below the prevailing world market price, there will be an immediate shortage of condensed milk. But restrictions on the rents of houses, offices, or farms take several years to produce shortages. The construction of new homes or offices for letting will soon cease and, when leases come to an end, premises will tend to be sold rather than re-let, but it will normally take several years for the existing stock of rented property to be substantially reduced. In the meantime, the tenants will benefit, and so be inclined to support rent control, unless they take an unusually long-term view.

Controls on *rents* cause a switch to owner-occupation. If controls were also imposed on *sale prices* the effect on new buildings would be to reduce the supply (or the quality). The result for existing buildings would be that there would normally be many potential buyers at the controlled price: either 'under the table' payments would emerge (as happens in Eastern Europe with controlled prices for the lease of flats), or it would be necessary for the authorities to decide who is to be allowed to buy the house, office or shop in question.

In fact, controls have generally been imposed on rents rather than sale prices, for obvious reasons. When a house (or other building) is offered for sale, there will normally be several potential purchasers. Only if the purchaser were selected before the price was fixed (by a raffle, or by a decision of the local council, or in some other way) would he have an interest in the price being held down. Thus, price control of existing houses – a proposal made in the 1972–3 boom – would be impossible to enforce without eliminating all freedom of choice in buying and selling, and the pressures tending to undermine such a system would be extremely strong.

EXTERNALITIES

There is a familiar qualification to the efficiency of a market system, of particular importance in the urban field. If the 'private' costs, incurred by the supplier, diverge significantly from the 'social' costs, reflecting the costs to the community as a whole, the market system will not necessarily satisfy consumers' preference. The difference between 'social' and 'private' costs, known as an 'externality', can be either positive – if social costs are less than private – or negative. Negative externalities – the more problematical case – are those costs of producing a good which do not enter into the profit and loss calculations of the firm or individual producing it. The 'classic' case quoted by Pigou was a smokey factory chimney, which causes a divergence between 'private' costs – the costs incurred by the firm – and the 'social' costs, which include a figure for the extra laundry bills, general unpleasantness, etc., caused by the smoke.[8] The fact that consumers are prepared to pay the 'private' costs does not necessarily mean that the good should be produced, or produced in the way it is.

There is thus a strong case for controls on serious pollution (especially when the results have long-term consequences) or for the use of taxes and/or subsidies. However, as Professor Coase has pointed out, even Pigou's simple and 'classic' case is by no means as clear-cut as has usually been assumed.[9] The fundamental point made by Professor Coase is that when governments intervene to deal with externalities, 'the *total* effect of these arrangements in all spheres of life should be taken into account', since such corrective measures are inevitably associated with other changes in the system, which may do more harm than the original deficiency.

This often overlooked point is of particular importance in urban policy. There are some clear-cut negative externalities – releasing poisonous wastes into rivers or building a petrol station in the middle of the Royal Crescent in Bath – which virtually everyone would accept as justifying control. Many writers make a far wider jump – from the existence of externalities to the justification of an almost unlimited system of development control, or of monopoly in urban development by state bodies. This involves implicit assumptions which are examined and questioned by the American 'public goods' school.[10] It assumes that every development has clear negative (or positive) externalities, which can be accurately assessed by the planners. But many developments have external effects which are *both* negative and positive, when one considers the likely alternatives. If major developments are stopped (rather than modified or shifted) the frustrated demand usually emerges in other ways, often unforeseen and insidious ones. If supermarkets are prevented from expanding on new sites, retailing firms will be forced to redevelop the High Streets, destroying them in the process: if urban motorways are turned down, existing roads will become more congested, with eventual pressure for them to be widened (which can be environmentally far worse than well-planned urban motorways). Thus if a planning authority is considering allowing or prohibiting a particular development, it should ideally weigh up the external consequences of both giving *and refusing* assent.

One of the difficulties in assessing externalities is that the important developments are *new* ones (at least for the country in question), on the consequences of which different opinions are possible. British planners, for example, have argued against suburban shopping centres on the grounds, among others, that they reduce the 'urbanity' of town centres, penalise people without cars, and waste agricultural land. As a result, such developments have for the most part been stopped, and super-markets have been forced to locate in crowded High Streets. Looking back, and comparing what has happened in Britain with what has happened in the USA and Canada, and even in West Germany or Scandinavia, it is far from clear that this was a wise decision, or even one based on correct forecasts. In the 1950s this policy – like some others – was based on an underestimate of population growth and car ownership and the growth of shop floor space. It is also arguable that it has been based on a misunderstanding of the nature of the modern city and that the more recent type of suburban centre (which has by no means killed off city centre shops) provides a better environment than congested High Streets. Moreover, in cities which, up until the 1950s had large numbers of old buildings in the city centre, this policy has meant the loss of an irreplaceable heritage, for the sake of a layout inferior by modern standards.[11]

This is not to maintain that an unplanned expansion of suburban shopping centres, as took place at first in the USA, would have been ideal. (I use the term 'suburban' rather than 'out of town', which is a mistranslation of the American expression 'out town' – the converse of 'down town'.) The early American shopping centres were crude, ugly and wasteful – even if convenient. An alternative would have been to guide market forces rather than oppose them – by, for example, making a shopping centre the basis for a multi-functional community centre so as to make better use of parking facilities and provide variety in the townscape. This is what is happening in the more recent shopping centres in North America and continental Western Europe. Granted that some planning is necessary to cope with 'externalities', it is far from clear that in this (and other) respects the British type of planning, with its theoretically unlimited powers and generally 'anti-market' philosophy, has correctly diagnosed these externalities. It is not frivolous to suggest that, in this case, a contributory factor may have been that most planners are not of the shopping sex. If they had had the experience of shopping for themselves in Britain and in North America, the outcome might have been very different. Thus it does not follow that externalities can be taken care of if only the town planning authorities are given sufficient power.

Other ways of dealing with the problem have been suggested. One suggestion is to extend the law of property so that individuals have an 'amenity right' and can sue airlines, local authorities, etc. for infringement. This approach is based on the idea put forward by Professor Coase (*op. cit.*) that bargaining between gainers and losers would produce an optimal allocation of resources – given perfect information, perfect organisation, and a dispute-solving system operating at zero cost. But these conditions are frequently not found. The 'civil law' approach is possible in some cases, and has been used. It is certainly undesirable to exempt public bodies from the normal provisions of the civil law unless an overwhelming case is made for doing so; in these cases, generous compensation arrangements should be provided.[12] But this approach has obvious limitations; in a densely populated and rapidly changing urban society, it is impossible to lay down clear-cut definitions of personal 'amenity', or to quantify infringements.

Another method is to 'internalise the externality' by extending the operations of the 'firm'. For example, it is often argued that the improvement of old urban areas is inhibited because it would not pay any individual owner to improve his property unless everyone else does the same. This question will be discussed below (Chap. 11).

Many externalities could be removed if consumers were charged the full social cost of the resources they use, e.g. if motoring in town centres were subject to a system of road pricing. In this way, the 'private' costs to the motorist could be raised to the 'social cost'. This approach is attractive, but depends on a pricing system being (a) technically feasible, (b) administratively practicable, (c) sufficiently cheap in operation to justify its use. It is clear, for example, that road pricing is technically feasible,[13] but whether it would work in practice may be questioned. Thus although the use of the pricing system for dealing with serious urban externalities needs to be examined, it is not always practicable. In these cases, some form of intervention may be unavoidable – assuming that the externality is sufficiently serious to justify it.

Public intervention can take the form of either administrative controls or taxes and subsidies. It may be considered desirable to restrict certain types of development in certain areas if, because of externalities or the absence of a road pricing system, problems of congestion arise. But administrative controls suffer from the disadvantages – in practice – of being arbitrary, erratic and conducive to lobbying, not to say palm-greasing. They also give a windfall gain to existing owners. A 'congestion tax' on specified types of development in certain areas (as has been adopted in Paris) does not suffer to the same extent from these disadvantages, and thus has much to be said for it, if applied in time. In practice, government action often lags so far behind events that, by the time a congestion tax is being seriously considered, rapid dispersal is taking place as the result of market forces: e.g. London and Rotterdam in the early 1970s.

We will provisionally conclude that there are substantial externalities in urban development, but that they are seldom clear-cut, solely positive or negative, or foreseeable. Therefore the idea (stemming from Pigou's chimney) that the problem can be solved simply by giving the state unlimited powers of development control is questionable. We shall return later to the kind of town planning we need.

PUBLIC GOODS AND MARKET FAILURE

The problem of 'public goods' overlaps with that of externalities. 'Public goods' take two forms. There are those urban facilities which can clearly only be provided by the state, e.g. roads. One reason for this was given by Adam Smith when he included among the 'duties of the sovereign' the provision of,

> these public institutions and these public works, which though they may be in the highest degree advantageous to a great society, are, however, of such a nature that the profit could never repay the expense to any individual or small number of individuals, and which it therefore cannot be expected that any individual or small number of individuals should erect or maintain.[14]

This argument depends on the impossibility of selling the product, and confining its use to the purchasers – as in the case of roads. But even if this difficulty can be overcome – for example, by the use of toll roads – there is a further problem. Roads have such an impact on so many people and arouse such controversies (e.g. on the siting of urban motorways or whether they should be built at all), that decisions can be taken only by the government.

The term 'public good' can also be applied to those aspects of urban 'amenity' which can only be achieved by imposing controls on individuals, e.g. banning traffic in certain streets, imposing 'clean air' regulations, controlling development in 'green belts', preserving areas of historical interest, etc. These are cases in which the market may not work, and in which control by administrative decree may be the only way of achieving results generally agreed to be desirable. However, the case for government intervention to cope with 'market failure' is, in practice, by no means as clear-cut as has often been argued. In the first place, some problems of negative externality are, in time, coped with by the market mechanism. For example, congestion in town centres may not immediately affect the profits of shops located there. In the longer run, however, there will be a tendency for some shops to move to the suburbs, where there is space for car-parking. When problems of congestion, pollution, etc. are realised, firms often engage in energetic quests to solve them.

In the second place, state intervention is *also* subject to grave defects. Some of these – slowness and top-heaviness – could probably be reduced by improvements in administrative organisation, but some may well be inherent in politically controlled bureaucracies possessing statutory monopoly. J. S. Mill pointed out over a century ago the corrupting effect on a society in which advancement depends on gaining the favour of the government machine.[15] Other defects of state intervention have been analysed by Professor F. A. Hayek[16] and – perhaps more convincingly – by Mr Samuel Brittan.[17] Governments are more susceptible to the influence of particular industries or organisations, whose political pressure is concentrated, than to the interests of consumers and tax payers, whose political influence is diffused and weak. They have recently given massive subsidies for projects which were not only unprofitable in the private but also in the social sense, i.e. with few positive externalities or even negative externalities – Concorde is the classic case. 'Consumerism' provides a salutary counterweight – although one sometimes wonders how far the views of 'consumer spokesmen' reflect those of the man in the street. The next form of countervailing power to emerge may well be that of taxpayers, as California casts its shadow ahead.

The defects of monopolistic state control are particularly great when the problem is one of coping with *new* demands, new products and new techniques.[18] Under a competitive market system – which does not preclude the participation of nationalised or non-profit bodies – different firms will seek to cater for new demands by offering a variety of products. Some will prove successful and will sell well, others will be unsuccessful and will be withdrawn. But when a state organisation has a statutory monopoly, it tends to settle for the product which it believes to be 'in the public interest' and to continue producing this product, even in the face of evidence that it is not what the public wants, and is prepared to pay for. For example, there are various ways of providing for the needs of shoppers – central department stores, suburban shopping centres with easy parking, big stores with cheap prices and no service, small shops with the personal touch, etc. But when the state either runs shops, or exercises close planning control over private firms, there is a tendency to decide on a particular form and stick to it. At the same time, state bureaucracies tend to suppress facts which do not accord with the accepted doctrine. (There is a similar tendency within private bureauc- racies, but competition, if allowed, tends to render it ineffective).

Another defect of the extension of the state sector into 'optional' areas is the effect it often appears to have in lowering the quality of administration in those areas where state action is unavoidable. When the state is regarded as responsible for everything, including matters which it probably cannot control, there is less pressure for well- considered and decisive action in those fields which it can control. This phenomenon is very marked in British urban and regional policy. The siting of roads, airports and ports is – virtually everyone would agree – something that must be decided by local or central government, and these decisions have a crucial effect on urban development. But when the state is also responsible for providing most rented housing, deciding whether Mr. Jones can build a porch over his front door, whether a certain factory should be given an investment grant, and a thousand other things where it is highly doubtful whether state action is necessary, civil servants and politicians simply do not have the time to think deeply about the issues which they alone can decide.

THE ECONOMICS OF POLITICS

Thus the mere existence of negative externalities does not provide a clear-cut justification for state intervention. An existing market econ- omy, with many imperfections (some due to state action) should not be compared with an ideal command economy operated by saints possess- ing the omniscience usually attributed only to God – any more than an existing command economy should be compared with a theoretically ideal market economy. The issue is sometimes confused by a theory of state action too closely modelled on the 'theory of consumer behaviour'. The author of a recent, and in many ways excellent, theoretical study outlines the imperfect workings of market processes in land use which form the basis for government intervention. Turning to the planning authority, Mr Harrison writes:

> Just as the individual is presumed to maximise his utility, we shall assume that the authority aims to maximise social welfare and that it does so . . .[19]

He concedes that the 'maximising of social welfare' raises difficulties. 'How is welfare to be defined and measured? How is the welfare of citizen X to be compared with the welfare of citizen Y?' However,

> We simply assume that there is some means available to the planning authority, be it political judgement or analytic technique, of combining the welfare of all those living in the city or affected by what goes on within it, just as it was assumed in Chapter 2 that we did not have to enter into an analysis of relationships *within* the household.[20]

This is surely pushing the analogy too far. A family deciding whether to buy a new house and a planning authority deciding whether to give permission for a housing development are not comparable. Admittedly, household decision-making raises intriguing questions which economists rarely investigate. As Professor Stigler puts it – with a wit and wisdom not always found in expositions of demand theory:

> The family may consist of several persons with a single thought and purse or, what is more common and interesting, an intricate structure of his, hers and their friends and somewhat less than unanimity of desires. We shall, nevertheless, take the family as a unit and treat its decisions as those of a single, rather feminine, person.[21]

There is no justification for making a similar assumption about a planning authority, which involves more parties and *takes decisions for other people.* Anyone with any experience of local government must wonder whether the assumption that it 'maximises social welfare' is not too simplified to be useful, or even positively misleading. The phrase is derived from welfare economics but, as economic theorists – not to mention the astonished students of public administration – have pointed out, the concept of a 'social welfare function' is questionable even on a theoretical level.[22] The danger in this approach – more obvious in expositions lacking Mr. Harrison's careful qualifications – lies in the implicit assumptions that it is possible, by an impartial examination of the evidence, to decide on one optimal plan for any aspect of the built environment; that the planning authority wishes, and is able, to implement this plan; and that it does not suffer from any of the imperfections of market processes. This view of town planning is questionable on several grounds. It may be possible to say, for example, that, of six possible routes for a new road, one would be preferable from all points of view. More usually, there are *pros* and *cons* for several different routes; which is 'best' depends on the weighting given to the interests of different groups or different considerations. Moreover, administrators or politicians are influenced by empire-building needs, prejudices, and political pressures of all kinds. To assume that the planning authority necessarily operates 'in the public interest' can easily be turned from an unhelpful tautology into a conclusion that 'the public interest' can therefore be assured only by all-embracing state ownership and control.

A different analysis leads to different policy conclusions. In particular, a very different type of 'maximising' analysis has been developed by American political economists of two related schools – 'the economics of politics',[23] and the somewhat broader 'economics of property rights'.[24] These approaches seek to extend the neoclassical theory of production and exchange so as to explain the behaviour of a wide range of organisations. The unit of analysis is the individual decision-maker rather than the firm, and his objectives are widened so as to include nonpecuniary as well as pecuniary elements. The theory recognises that there are institutional constraints limiting the decision-maker, and that obtaining information and undertaking change involves costs.

This approach has been used to explain the behaviour of organisations as varied as multi-national corporations, Jugoslav co-operatives, and the Soviet State; there would seem to be scope for some fascinating applications to town planning procedures. It concentrates on the factors influencing decision-makers within the organisation rather than on the organisation's announced objectives (i.e. 'what is in it for them?' or 'cui bono?'). Politicians may be assumed, for example, to seek to maximise their term of office, and administrators their status and influence. Although this approach is one of the most important advances in economic thinking since the War, the basic idea is not new; it underlies Machiavelli's *The Prince*. The followers of Machiavelli have reasserted an old truth about the imperfections of political processes – even democratic ones – which has recently tended to be overlooked. Nevertheless, some of the proponents of 'the economics of politics' have attributed to politicians and administrators a ruthless egoism which is as unrealistic as the assumption that they are selflessly devoted to the public good. Politicians and administrators are not *purely* self-seeking, so that no 'maximising' theory can be wholly realistic. To be at all realistic, any approach must recognise that human beings are impelled by a variety of motives. It would be an advance on current theory to adopt Adam Smith's classification of 'self-love, sympathy, a desire to be free, a sense of propriety, a habit of labour, and a propensity to trade', but to these must be added economic and social attitudes and beliefs. In Britain, for example, some local councillors and planning officials are opposed in principle to private development, and believe that the development control machinery should be used to stop developers making profits. This is merely one of a wide range of motivations which influence politicians and administrators. No approach which ignores these motivations, and merely puts forward the public (and un-exceptionable) objectives of development control can be regarded as a remotely realistic basis for explaining what actually happens.

All this does not necessarily deny the need for *some kind* of town planning. But there is a wide spectrum of types of planning, and of combinations of a market and a command economy: there is the choice between 'comprehensive redevelopment' and 'cellular renewal' (Chaps. 10 and 11); between a British-style local authority near-monopoly of rented housing and diversified ownership on West German lines; between detailed discretionary development control and broad 'zoning'; between more local autonomy and more national planning. The type of market system, the type of planning system, and the mix of the two, should – from the point of view we have suggested – be based on an assessment of the defects and possible improvements of both. Neverthe-less, a case can be made for treating the market process, diversified ownership and local action as the norm, from which any departure must be justified, on the grounds that 'A fool is wiser in his own house than a wise man in another's'. All this, of course, is merely a prologue to a discussion of urban development policy: some might describe it as mere common sense. Indeed, but it is an approach quite contrary to much recent theory and practice.

THE MARKET AND THE STATE

Whatever the difference of opinion on the scope and nature of state action, most people accept that there are activities which can only be undertaken by the state and activities which can be left to the market, and that there is a need for some measure of town planning. The system of administrative control and the market system, react on each other, and many problems in urban land economics centre around this relationship.

It is sometimes argued that all these problems would be avoided if all land, buildings and businesses were state-owned. This is doubtful. Since managers in a socialist system (at least of the Soviet type) are judged by their plan-fulfilment, they have no more incentive than managers in capitalist countries to take negative externalities into account. Indeed, since there is no independent agency acting on behalf of the public, they are likely to have less. In the UK government departments and nationalised industries are exempt (under 'Schedule 90') from local planning control, and there are many monuments to their indifference to negative externalities. Similarly, the high-rise flats favoured by British local authorities in the 1960s could only have been produced under a command economy, since they were both unattractive to tenants and extremely costly to build. The main economic argument for a collectivist system is that the rulers could impose controls which would not be possible under a liberal regime, but which might be to the long-run advantage of the population; e.g. restricting car ownership. This is Plato's argument that 'Guardians' should give the public what is good for it. The principle is questionable, and the practical applications have never been quite as edifying as Plato envisaged.

At the other extreme, some extreme liberals maintain that no state intervention is needed in the urban field, and some disillusioned students of British town planning seem to have come to the conclusion that it does more harm than good. This is a view which deserves serious consideration. However – to anticipate the conclusions of Part II – it is not a view which the author is able to accept. Granted the case for some measure of state intervention, it is an intellectual problem – and a complex and difficult one – to devise forms of state intervention which are efficient in coping with 'market failure' and do not hamper – or hamper as little as possible – the efficient operation of the market mechanism where it works well. Whatever the 'mix' of planning and market mechanism, the problems of resource allocation in the urban field have to be solved. To pretend that public ownership would avoid them is merely wishful thinking (as is now to some extent recognised in industrial economics), while to advocate methods of state control which while purporting to regulate, in fact undermine the market system (as has happened with private rented housing in the UK) is intellectually dishonest.

EFFICIENCY

The market system will respond only to effective demand, i.e. what consumers are prepared to pay; it therefore adapts supply to the prevailing distribution of income. If some consumers are very poor – in relation to the general level of income in a community – it may be felt that they should be enabled to buy more of certain commodities, such as housing, and this can be done in various ways. But it is important to distinguish between these considerations of *equity*, and considerations of *efficiency* in resource allocation. A market economy is efficient if it gives consumers what they are prepared to pay for, taking social costs into account. If, therefore, one group in the community has very low incomes and lives in slums, while another group has high incomes and lives in mansions, this does not (necessarily) indicate any inefficiency in the system. The differences in housing standards may simply reflect differences in income, and if these offend the community's sense of equity, they can be reduced by increasing the poor group's purchasing power.

The conditions for efficiency in the allocation of 'private' goods – simplifying the pure theory somewhat – can be expressed as follows. *All consumers must be free to buy all goods at prices equal to the long-term marginal costs of producing them.*[25] However, this is taking a static view of the economic optimum. In a dynamic economy, the precise optimum conditions will rarely be achieved at any one time because, when real incomes and technology are changing, the optima will themselves be changing. In so far, therefore, as at any one moment the optimum is not achieved – e.g. if a shortage of a particular good leads to the price being above its long-term marginal cost – the economy must be so organised that it moves towards the optimum as quickly as possible.

Let us apply these conditions to housing. The 'goods' are dwellings of varying size and quality, in various locations, for sale or renting. Under 'efficient' conditions, construction costs will vary according to the size and quality of dwelling, while land costs will vary according to the pressure of demand. If dwellings are available for sale at various sale prices, corresponding to costs (including 'normal' profit and land costs), and available to rent at rents based on current rates of interest, the consumer can make a choice on the basis of relative cost and scarcity. The housing market will either be in equilibrium in the strict sense that there is neither a 'surplus' nor a 'shortage'[26]; if it is not in equilibrium, landlords, developers and builders will quickly respond by increasing or reducing the supply. A reasonably prompt adjustment to a moving equilibrium is usually the 'efficient situation' – even though, with the flattening-off of population growth and the end of the acute (overall) housing shortage, the extent of disequilibrium in the foreseeable future is likely to be lower than in the recent past.

A system is inefficient if consumers' demands, which could be economically supplied at the prices they were prepared to pay, are in fact not met. For example, if housing of a certain quality could profitably be supplied at a rent of £x per week, and potential tenants would willingly pay this amount, but rented accommodation were not available at this price, the system would be in some way inefficient. This inefficiency could be the result of institutional weaknesses – e.g. a lack of organisations geared to supplying rented housing – or of government policy, such as rent control at well below £x.

These formal principles for economic efficiency may seem rather abstract. However, in conjunction with a few other basic principles, they provide pointers to rational decision-making. When governments intervene, on grounds of equity, to improve conditions for 'under-privileged' groups, we need to examine (a) the objectives of the intervention; (b) the administrative consequences; (c) the way in which the market economy will react to the new conditions; (d) the advantages and disadvantages of possible alternative policies. Good intentions are not enough. Unless the consequences of a particular policy are thought out, it may fail in its objectives, give rise to new problems or at least be less efficient than alternative policies.

For example, given the problems of low-income families seeking rented accommodation, three policies have been adopted in different countries: controlling rents, subsidising the rents of certain houses and selecting tenants for them, or giving housing allowances for which all tenants are eligible. The first policy makes it unprofitable to build houses to let and, if no similar restriction is imposed on sale prices, it will become more profitable to sell than to continue letting. Thus the supply of rented housing will decline. Although controlling rents may benefit existing tenants, it will harm young people seeking rented housing. The policy may be a rational (although disingenuous) one if a decision has been taken, on political grounds, to eliminate private tenancy; it will not be rational if it is embarked on for reasons of short-term expediency, without understanding the longer-term consequences. The provision of subsidised housing is free from these defects, but it means that the benefit is confined to a particular group of tenants, who may not be the most in need, or may cease to be so. The third system, housing allowances to any tenant whose income falls below specified levels, deals equitably with all tenants, but is administratively complex. (A fourth policy is simply to alleviate poverty by cash payments and leave people to choose the type of housing they prefer). Perhaps the main value of the economic approach is that it clarifies the nature of the problem, isolates the advantages and disadvantages of alternative policies, and tries to

ensure that decisions are taken with a full understanding of the
consequences.

EQUITY AND COMPENSATION

Equity is more subjective than efficiency, but also susceptible to some
useful analysis. Almost any change means that there are both gainers
and losers. A new motorway may benefit those who use it, but harm
householders who live near it. 'Urban renewal' may benefit some people
but it can mean that small businessmen lose their livelihood and other
people their homes. Even if the number of losers is small in relation to
the number of gainers, there is still a problem. Can economics give any
guidance? Since questions of gainers and losers have been discussed in
'welfare economics' (or rather the school known in the 1950s as 'the new
welfare economics'), it seems worth summarising this somewhat recon-
dite branch of economics to see whether it can provide any conclusions
for practical policy.

 The basic question was 'Can any general principles be laid down on
whether a policy is desirable, since nearly every policy benefits some
people and harms others?'. The starting point of most economists has
been that the question whether an individual is better or worse off can
only be decided by the individual himself. Accepting this 'liberal
utilitarian' approach, it is fairly obvious that, if a certain change makes
some people better off and no one worse off, it is a desirable change. It is
therefore desirable to make changes of this kind until any further change
would make some people worse off (a 'Pareto optimum'). The problem
arises when a policy benefits some people and harms others. How can
one compare the gain to some with the loss to others? A number of
economists sought to get round this difficulty by postulating that the
gainers should compensate the losers, in money. If the gainers pay the
losers enough to leave the losers no worse off, while the gainers still
remain better off, one is back in the first situation, and the change is
desirable. This abstract principle can be applied in problems such as
road building, although in a less direct way. It is rarely possible for the
gainers (e.g. the road users) to compensate the losers (e.g. the
dispossessed householders) directly. However, if £x is needed to
'compensate' the householders (in the sense defined above), and if the
local authority thinks that the gain to road users is substantially more
than £x, then it would seem desirable to pay the householders £x, and
build the road.

But what if all the losers are *not* fully compensated? What if some householders feel themselves worse off? Can one say that because the gain is more than *would* be needed to compensate the losers, the change is desirable. There is no way of demonstrating this; but it is often the attitude taken when the gainers appear to far outweigh the losers (and the basis of cost-benefit analysis). If a relief road is going to be of enormous benefit to many travellers, but will involve a loss to a few householders, we do tend to take the view that the interests of the majority should prevail. But there is no way of showing that those who take the opposite view are wrong.

The above is a brief but probably fair summary of the modest conclusions of fierce controversies between welfare economists in the 1950s. At about this point, most economists decided that 'the new welfare economics' was not really getting them very far, and turned to other fields. Nevertheless, some of the concepts of welfare economics have, in an indirect way, reappeared in more practical applications, such as cost-benefit analysis. Cost-benefit analysis, as recently practised, is justifiably out of fashion. But if practised in a simple, common sense way it does have the virtue of pinpointing gainers and losers.[27] And there is no need simply to adopt the scheme giving the highest benefit/cost ratio (or whatever). The avoidance of suffering can be given high priority, in two ways. New developments can be planned so as to minimise disruption and hardship, usually at the price of higher expenditure. The first British urban motorways were built with little regard for their disturbing effect on neighbouring areas. Subsequent studies recommended greater use of screening, cuttings, etc., which would increase the cost substantially.[28] Similarly, urban renewal can be carried out in a sensitive way which finds out what local people want, and seeks to ensure that, if possible, no one suffers or is driven out of the district: the recent West German schemes are based on this principle. But if someone has to suffer a loss of some kind he can be *generously* compensated, either in kind (land or housing) or in money. A few extra thousand pounds may or may not make him 'as well off' in the rather unoperational welfare economics sense, but it will in most cases soothe the hurt considerably. This approach can be defended on the grounds not only that it is equitable to compensate the victims of change but also that it reduces the opposition to it. There is likely to be far less opposition to a motorway if people near it know that they will be generously compensated.

The whole idea of compensation as a political ideal indeed is something which, one suspects, creeps into political life from economics. The idea that it is often better to buy somebody off than to knock him down is a thoroughly economic idea. It does not appeal much to men of principle, moralists and revolutionaries, but it very probably adds to human happiness and diminishes human misery. This is not a bad accomplishment.[29]

The 'compensation' approach has often been rejected both by advocates of the collectivist philosophy which underlies a certain type of town planning, and by local authority Treasurers. Collectivist planners argue that private interests should not be treated with kid gloves, while local Treasurers argue that they do not have the money. The economist would reply that, in a fundamental sense, the state can afford to be generous, because if the gain from the project (expressed in terms of the monetary value to all who benefit from it) does not substantially exceed the cost of compensating the losers, there is no case for undertaking the project anyway. It is true that, although the benefits to the public greatly exceed the cost of adequate compensation, the financial resources available to a *local authority* may be limited. But this is a problem of the distribution of resources between the various tiers of government. It may also be desirable to seek means of recovering some part of the benefit directly from the users, e.g. infra-structure charges, or giving local authorities a share in the taxation of development value. But the poverty of a local authority under a particular financial system is no ground for a general principle of miserly compensation (See Chap. 9). The issue was well summed up by the late Miss Honor Croome:

> What is needed is an approach aimed, on the one hand, at reducing the discontinuities and uprootings induced in dynamic change, and so making it more acceptable, and on the other, at compensating, in greater measure than at present, those on whom such discontinuities and uprootings nevertheless arbitrarily fall.[30]

SUMMARY

The problems of producing and allocating real property can be tackled by a *market economy* (which is not synonymous with private ownership) or a *command economy*, or some combination of the two. Both have virtues and defects, which should be examined in any attempt to devise the most appropriate 'mix' of policies. A market economy can to some extent operate within a 'command economy' framework: e.g. town planning. But certain policies – notably price controls (rent control) and marginal tax rates above a certain level – are ultimately destructive of a market economy. A market economy in which there is *participation* by 'non-profit' bodies is likely to be the most satisfactory and durable.

The existence of 'externalities', both positive and negative, may justify physical controls, or taxes or subsidies. But the assumption is some economic theorising that state intervention necessarily improves the situation is one-sided; the *total* consequences of any policy must be considered. 'Welfare economics' has at least brought out the point that *equity* as well as *efficiency* should be considered in policy decisions: it suggests (arguably) that urban policy should be framed so as to minimise suffering and loss, as well as minimising the excess of gains over losses. Since non-pecuniary losses to some people are unavoidable, they should receive generous monetary compensation.

REFERENCES

1. P. A. Samuelson, *Economics: An Introductory Analysis*, Chap. 1.
2. Many books critical of private ownership and market forces lay considerable stress on the communal landownership of nomadic peoples (e.g. R. W. G. Bryant, *Land: Private Property, Public Control*, Montreal, 1972). The same nostalgia for a communal Golden Age is found in poets since Virgil. But this system is possible only in a situation which pre-dates not only urban settlement but even settled agriculture, and in a society dominated by totem and taboo. Thus it is hard to see much direct relevance to modern societies in primitive land tenure systems (although much can be learned from some 'primitive' peoples in their general attitude to life). It is the life of present-day Russians or East Germans that should be studied as the alternative to a market economy, not that of 18th century American Indians.
3. For a typical example see *After the Planners* by Robert Goodman, Penguin Books, 1972, particularly the introduction by John Palmer. The philosophy is an amalgam of ideas from Marcuse, Sartre etc., and Professor Galbraith. Galbraith's term 'technostructure' is used to designate the crypto-fascist alliance of property developers and government officials which has imposed town planning on the people.
   Professor Galbraith, who can be forgiven much for the wit which –

in his earlier works – he brought to economics, has suggested in *The New Industrial State* that 'conventional economics' treats externalities as a minor blemish on a well functioning market mechanism, whereas the truth is that the 'technostructure' has interests contrary to those of the public. If only it were so simple! Technocrats can certainly develop toys which benefit few apart from themselves or a small *elite*, if they are given the public funds to do so. But once a project has then started, workers also acquire vested interests, which are then reflected in the political process: witness Anglo-French jingoism over Concorde. It is vital to initiate a frank and informed debate *before* large public investment projects are started. However, in most cases technology, which can be so destructive in many directions, is catering for genuine public wants. People *want* to own cars.

4. A. Lindbeck, *The Political Economy of the New Left*, Macmillan 1975, Chaps. 1–3.

5. 'Socialism' is used here to mean – in the words of the Labour Party constitution: 'the public ownership of the means of production, distribution and exchange'; in the present case the public ownership of land, houses and other buildings. It has, of course, been given other definitions, some of which – e.g. that given by the late Mr. Anthony Crosland in *The Future of Socialism*, (London, 1956, p. 103ff) (concern for the underdog, a desire for harmonious relations in society, etc.) can inspire anti-socialists as much as socialists. 'Persuasive definitions', which flit between some unexceptionable moral objective and a specific system of economic organisation, obscure the question whether the one is best calculated to achieve the other.

6. A brief account of the 'Lerner-Lange' model is given in *Scarcity Challenged*, Heinz Kohler, New York, 1968, Chap. 20.

7. Graham Hallett, *Housing and Land Policies in West Germany & Britain* 1977 Pt 2.

8. A. C. Pigou, *The Economics of Welfare*, (4th edn., 1932), p. 183.

9. Ronald Coase, 'The Problem of Social Cost', *Journal of Law and Economics*, October 1960. Reprinted in W. Breit & H. M. Hochman, *Readings in Microeconomics*, Holt, Rinehart & Winston, 1968, p. 423. Professor Coase points out that although economists have assumed that the owner of the chimney should be taxed by an amount equal to the pollution caused, it is far from clear that this is what Pigou implied. In any event, there are three possible courses of action: a tax, a subsidy for smoke-abating equipment, and a right of

the adversely affected parties to compensation: the results are not necessarily the same.

10. See *The Theory of Public Choice*, by J. M. Buchanan and R. D. Tollison, Michigan U.P., 1972.

11. In the early 1950s, the centre of Gloucester was an area of considerable historic interest and charm, with a variety of old timber-framed buildings. In the 1960s the council adopted a policy of expanding shopping and council housing in the town centre. This involved massive demolition – in twenty years, 60 per cent of the timber-framed houses listed by the Ministry of Housing were demolished. By 1972, the centre of Gloucester consisted of an isolated cathedral surrounded by supermarkets and car parks, which destroyed the charm of the city without preventing serious traffic congestion. At the centre of this devastation was a small undistinguished pedestrian square, which could have been in any American suburban shopping centre: opening it, Mr. Peter Walker, Minister of the Environment, stated that the redevelopment of the centre of Gloucester was 'an example to the country'. If it had been Lord Butler, one might have suspected irony.

12. In 1971, some people living near Orly Airport, Paris, successfully sued an airline for disturbance. In the USA, some airports are engaged in million-dollar lawsuits, and have had to buy up large areas of nearby land. This legal pressure, together with widespread protest against noise, has wonderfully concentrated the minds of airlines and manufacturers on the need to develop quieter planes, and striking progress has been achieved, although it will take a decade for the fleet to be changed. In the UK the right to take legal action was abolished by the Civil Aviation Act, 1949 (passed when Parliament had no inkling of the noise nuisance which would develop).

13. Ministry of Transport, *Road Pricing: The Economic and Technical Possibilities*, HMSO, 1964.

14. *Wealth of Nations*, Everyman Ed., Vol. 2, p. 211.

15. J. S. Mill, *Principles of Political Economy*, Bk. V, Chap. XI, Para. 6.

16. F. A. Hayek, *The Constitution of Liberty*, London, 1960.

17. Samuel Brittan, *Capitalism and the Permissive Society*, Macmillan, 1973.

18. F. A. Hayek, 'The Use of Knowledge in Society', *American Economic Review*, September 1945, pp. 519–530. See also S. C. Littlechild *The Fallacy of the Mixed Economy*, Hobart Paper 80, I.E.A. 1978.

19. A. J. Harrison, *Economics and Land Use Planning*, Croom Helm, London, 1977, p. 35.

20. *Ibid.*, p. 87.

21. G. Stigler, *The Theory of Price*, rev. ed., 1952, p. 43.

22. The theoretical difficulties are pointed out in I. M. D. Little, *A Critique of Welfare Economics*, 1950, and Charles K. Rowley and Alan T. Peacock, *Welfare Economics: A Liberal Restatement*, 1975. More readable and forthright is P. Self, *op. cit.*

23. Anthony Downs, *An Economic Theory of Democracy*, Harper & Row, 1957. William A. Niskanen, *Bureaucracy: Servant or Master?*, Hobart Paperback 5, Institute of Economic Affairs, 1973.

24. E. G. Furubotn & S. Pejovich, *The Economics of Property Rights*, Cambridge, Mass., 1974.

25. This is not formally as correct as the rules given in e.g. I. M. D. Little, *A Critique of Welfare Economics*, Ch. VIII. But the formal rules are very abstract, and hard to apply directly to the urban market. Little's rule (II)G will be met if prices equal the lowest possible construction costs for any type of dwelling, plus land costs (on the assumption that land is freely interchangeable between uses, or that any planning controls correctly take account of externalities). To assume that people make choices in line with their preferences is, in practice, the only possible assumption, since consumers' preferences can only be deduced from what they actually do.

26. Like an elephant, a 'shortage', 'surplus' or an equilibrium in housing is difficult to define but easy to recognise. However, some attempts at definition can be made. If population, and the demand for housing, were constant, definition would be easy; the condition for equilibrium would be the usual one, that there would be no economic incentive to increase or reduce the supply of housing.

But if population, or the demand per head, is rising, the equilibrium will be a moving one, with the supply curve moving to the right at the same speed as the demand curve. Additions to the housing stock will earn only a 'normal' profit. A shortage can be indicated by various signs: an acceleration in the rate of rise in prices; vacant houses being snapped up very quickly; evidence of families being forced to share houses, etc. A surplus is indicated by a flattening-off of prices, difficulty in selling houses, etc.

27. This is the virtue of Professor Nathaniel Lichfield's 'planning balance sheet', especially, perhaps, in the simple form in which he

originally put it forward in *The Economics of Planned Development*, 1966.

28. See *New Roads in Towns*. Report of the Urban Motorways Committee, HMSO., July 1972.

29. K.E. Boulding, *Economics as a Science*, McGraw-Hill, 1970, p. 91.

30. Honor Croome, 'Progress Without Tears', *Lloyds Bank Review*, July 1959. It can be argued (Little *op. cit.*, Chap VI, VII) that compensation cannot be divorced from equity i.e. perhaps those who suffer from expropriation *should* suffer. There may be rough justice in this approach when the issue is a major dispersal of property ownership e.g. land reform in South America. But when real property is more widely distributed, the arguments are stronger for treating seperately the questions of compensation and policy on the distribution of ownership.

3 The Property Market

A social psychologist once chided an economist:

> You say that prices are determined by supply and demand, but I know
> they are determined by people.[1]

This argument has regularly been applied to the property market.
Professor Boulding's reply could hardly be bettered:

> It is quite true that prices, like every other aspect of economic and
> social life, are the result of decisions by people, and economists would
> do well never to forget this. Nevertheless, in analysing problems such
> as the determinants of the price system, the behaviour of people must
> be expressed in a simplified form and especially in a form capable of
> aggregation. In these terms, the economist can make a strong defense
> of his demand and supply curves as singling out the significant aspects
> of the behaviour of people from the point of view of that aspect of the
> system in which he is interested.

In this spirit, let us examine the demand and supply curves for land
and buildings. Although the general principles are the same as in any
other field, the 'goods' involved have some peculiarities. Land is, in some
senses, limited; buildings have a relatively long life; both are un-
homogeneous. No piece of land or building is exactly the same as
another, if only because it is in a different place. In some cases, there may
be a large number of buildings (especially houses) fairly similar in
structure and location; in other cases the nearest equivalent may be very
different. This makes valuation more difficult; there is a need for
professional valuers who can draw on a knowledge of broadly similar
properties. But there will always be a margin of error in valuation.
  Although each piece of real property is unique, real property can be
divided into broad categories such as undeveloped land, houses, shops,
offices, factories etc. Within these categories, we can use the familiar
concepts of price, demand and supply. The available data is usually very

limited, but a little theory helps to provide a framework for what is available.

DEMAND AND SUPPLY FOR REAL PROPERTY

The price of the various categories of real property, and hence (eventually) land use is determined – on the familiar diagram – by the intersection of demand and supply curves, but the main interest of this analysis lies in the examination of the factors *behind* demand and supply. These can be divided into

(a) Factors originating outside the property market.
(b) Factors directly concerned with the property market.

The influences under (a) relate to general economic trends and government policy on the management of aggregate demand, the money supply and the availability of credit. A rising level of real income tends to increase the demand for real property – both directly, as in the demand for housing, and indirectly in the demand for commercial and industrial premises. A sharp rise in demand may raise prices. The normal sequence is at first, greater intensity of use (e.g. a fall in vacancy rates), followed by a rise in prices (or rents) which will produce an increase in supply and reduce prices to a cost-covering level. But fluctuations in growth rates are sometimes increased by 'waves of optimism and pessimism'. The euphoria of 1972–3 was followed by a couple of years of slightly exaggerated gloom, as indicated by the movements in property yields, the price of property company shares, and house prices (Table 4, and Chap. 5).

General economic conditions also affect supply. Changes in wages, interest rates, tax rates etc. affect costs of construction or operation; unless these cost changes are immediately reflected in output prices, they can affect profitability, and hence supply. Monetary conditions are particularly important. The availability, and cost, of credit affects the demand for owner-occupied buildings. It also affects supply, since builders and developers rely heavily on credit. Easy credit thus boosts both demand and supply, whereas tight credit dampens them. Real property has historically shown greater sensitivity to changes in monetary policy than other types of investment.

The factors more directly concerned with the property market can be divided into the influence of the Government and of non-government institutions.

GOVERNMENT INFLUENCE

Government influence operates through a range of policies – notably housing policy, regional policy, town planning, and land taxation. Two basic points need to be stressed (which might seem obvious if they had not regularly been ignored). In a market economy:

(a) Anything which reduces supply tends to *increase* prices.
(b) Anything which holds down prices tends to *reduce* supply.

(1) HOUSING POLICY

Government policies can have marked effects on the total stock of various categories of housing: in Britain they have caused a reduction in private tenancy and an increase in council housing and owner-occupancy. Controls on rents under the Rent Acts have caused older tenanted housing to deteriorate and in some cases become derelict: in other cases it has been transferred to owner-occupancy or council ownership. The present situation is one in which there is a rough balance in the total housing stock, combined with a shortage of accommodation for people who cannot afford to buy a dwelling and do not obtain a council tenancy.[2] In Britain, the market mechanisms can thus be considered as applying only to owner-occupied housing, but there is a functioning market in rented housing in many countries.[3]

(2) REGIONAL POLICY

Regional policy – in the usual, if somewhat narrow, definition – refers to government policies which seek to reduce economic activity in some regions and increase it in others. In the UK since the War, the general policy has been to restrict activity in the South East and the West Midlands, and increase it in the 'development areas' (although attention is turning to problems, such as that of 'inner city areas' *within* regions; see Chaps. 6 and 10). Two main methods have been used in 'regional policy'.

(i) Grants for industrial investment in the 'development areas'.

  (ii) Restrictions on the construction of offices and factories in non-development areas, through Office Development Permits and Industrial Development Certificates, or on housing development, through the town planning system.

Since method (i) causes a shift of employment from, say the South-East to the North of England, it might be expected to reduce land values in the South-East and increase them in the North. Method (ii), on the other hand, has the effect of raising the prices of buildings and of potential building land. A particularly striking case was the 'Brown ban' on all office development in Greater London in 1965. This caused losses to property companies which has acquired sites, but had not yet begun construction. On the other hand, it increased the rents, and capital values, of existing offices.

(3) TOWN PLANNING

The theory of town planning is that it takes account of 'social' considerations and leads to a better pattern of development than would have prevailed in its absence. The *general level* of land and property prices will be affected only if the *amount of development* is restricted in a particular city.

(4) TAXATION

If they reduce the profitability of developing, or selling, to such an extent as to reduce supply, then taxation arrangements affecting property will raise similar issues (Chap. 9).

THE INFLUENCE OF NON-GOVERNMENTAL ORGANISATIONS

'Institutional' investors – building societies, banks, property development companies, etc. – are affected by general economic trends. As to whether they can themselves affect prices and land-use, opinion is divided. It ranges from the neo-Marxist-Galbraithian view that they decide everything to the view that they follow, rather than lead, the market. The aftermath of the property boom certainly casts doubt on the idea that they dominate the market. But it seems reasonable to conclude (as in the long debate on industrial economics) that the structure of the industry and the attitudes of its participants can have *some* influence, especially in the short run.

The building societies also have some power to affect the property market. They have to match the demand for mortgage funds with the supply through various methods:

(a) *Changes in interest rates*
Higher deposit rates – in relation to the general level of interest rates – increase the supply of funds and limit the demand for them. To a large extent, the building societies have to keep in line with the general level of interest rates, but they possess some margin of discretion. For example, the extremely sharp fall in interest rates in 1977 led to a fall in building society rates, but the societies were able to maintain rates slightly more favourable than those of the banks and hence attract more funds. The societies were in fact under strong political pressure to keep rates down as an anti-inflationary measure.

(b) *The size of reserves*
Building societies have, by law, to maintain minimum liquid reserves ($7\frac{1}{2}$ percent). Above this level, they can vary reserves, thus *temporarily* breaking the direct link between receipts and expenditure.

(c) *Requirements for borrowers*
The societies have a 'normal' amount that they are prepared to lend, depending on their valuation of the property and the income of the applicant. They do not normally lend more than 90 per cent of their (conservative) valuation of the property and $2\frac{1}{2}$ – 3 times the borrower's gross income. But both these requirements can be adjusted and/or mortgage 'rationing' imposed. When funds are in short supply, strict policies are adopted, which tend to be relaxed when funds are plentiful.

The boom of 1973 focused attention on the alleged ability of the building societies to affect house prices by altering the supply of mortgage funds. They may possess some power of this type in the short run, although general monetary conditions (largely the responsibility of the Government) are almost certainly more important (Chap. 5).

In addition to the large institutional investors, there are a whole range of individuals and organisations concerned with building and managing buildings – landowners, houseowners, developers, local authorities, housing associations, etc. Although discussions of land use are often couched in aggregate ('macro-economic') terms – so many thousand acres of agricultural land used for housing, so many hundred thousand old houses being modernised, etc. – it needs to be remembered that the practical decisions are taken by large numbers of people concerned with relatively small areas of land. If aggregate developments are to be understood and influenced, the conditions under which these 'microeconomic' units operate, and the factors which influence their decision-making, also need to be understood. Many of the failures of urban development policy have been due to a failure to consider reactions at the 'micro' level.[4]

THE SUPPLY CHARACTERISTICS OF BUILDINGS

The supply of land and buildings has special characteristics. Owing to the long life of buildings (60–80 years, and often much longer), the annual supply is a small proportion of the total stock; for housing, this proportion is nearly always under three per cent and in Britain in recent years has been under one per cent. This means that it can take some years to overcome a shortage. But once the market is saturated, demand is apt to fall sharply for several years until the obsolescence of older buildings, or an increase in demand, necessitates an increase in supply. Hence the 'boom or bust' cycles which have always characterised the construction industry.

The construction industry operates, for the most part, under conditions of constant long-run costs, and hence infinitely elastic supply. A 'cost-covering' price is needed to make construction worthwhile; if this price cannot be obtained, the buildings will not be constructed. But in the short run, prices can be above or below this level. If they are above it, excess profits will produce an increase in output, which then depresses prices and eliminates the excess profits. At the other extreme, a sharp fall in demand for new construction can depress prices below the 'normal' level, and builders may for a time accept below-normal margins – the position in several countries after 1973. But this situation cannot last indefinitely, and a normal level of profitability will tend to be restored as some firms leave the industry.

Buildings are not only built and demolished, they can also be transferred from one use to another. Cinemas can be turned into bingo halls, or chapels into squash courts. Similarly, if there is a shift in demand from tenanted to owner-occupied housing, owners will eventually seek to sell rather than to let. The same result will occur if controls are imposed which hold rents below the level (the 'supply price') needed to maintain supply. But whereas in the first case the change reflects consumer demand, in the second case it does not. Changes of this type may be slowed down by legal restrictions, but not stopped for long.

THE PROPERTY MARKET

The relationships in the market for buildings are illustrated in Fig. 1. The basic relationship, which asserts itself through short-term fluctuations, is that between 'Demand' and 'Stock'. Demand can be direct – notably for housing (the largest category of buildings) – or indirect. The demand for housing appears to be closely related to income and price (in

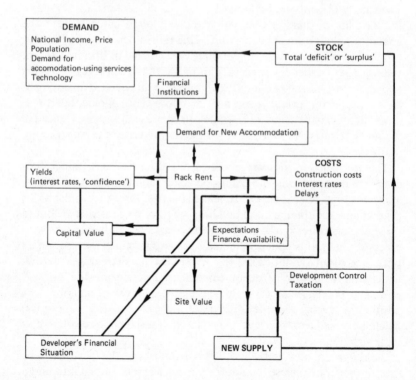

FIG. 1. The Property Market

real terms): historically, there has been an upward trend in the average amount of housing *per capita*. The (indirect) demand for shops, offices, etc. can be affected not only by consumer demand for the goods and services they are used to produce, but also by changes in technology – e.g. the decline in the demand for port warehousing. On the other hand, the big expansion in office space since the War has reflected changes both in consumer demand and also in technology which have resulted in relatively fewer 'blue collar' and relatively more 'white collar' workers.

The total demand for 'property services' (i.e. square footage per year) reacts with the existing stock of property to determine the demand for 'new' accommodation – including renovated buildings. However, demand is also to some extent dependent on price – in this case 'rack rent' or sale prices – in a way better illustrated by the familiar demand and supply diagram. For rented property, consumer demand operates directly on rack rent, which in turn determines capital value *via* yields. For owner-occupied property, consumer demand operates directly on capital value. In this case, however, purchasers usually require loans, so that lending institutions – such as building societies – play a role. The efficiency of the institutions, their attitudes, and possible government pressure, can affect the supply of finance and hence effective demand.

Rents and prices thus depend in the first instance on the demand/supply situation. If there is a glut, rents and prices will be low: if there is a shortage they will be high. But they tend to adjust themselves to costs, through the effect of costs on supply. Costs consist primarily of construction costs and interest charges (land costs are to some extent a residual, to some extent a 'cost', as explained later in this chapter). Capital values, on the other hand, are derived from actual, and expected future, rack rents. 'Yields' (i.e. rack rent ÷ capital value) depend to some extent on general economic conditions, e.g. interest rates and the supply of finance. But they have in recent years been more stable than share yields, and far more stable than bank rate or gilt-edged yields. They are, however, influenced by expectations; there is a history of booms in which investors sought to make money quickly (or protect their savings from inflation) and so bid values up, and yields down, to unsustainable levels. In such a situation, which is usually preceded by a sharp expansion of the money supply, there is also a surge of construction, which is 'speculative' in the sense that it is based on euphoric expectations, and financed by over-generous credit. But when these new buildings come on the market and cannot be let for the expected rents, the boom collapses, capital values fall and yields rise again.

THE SUPPLY OF LAND

Whereas the supply of buildings (in the long run) is nearly infinitely elastic, the supply of land is, in some senses, fixed; the total land area of a country (or the world), and the area of a particular site, cannot be changed significantly. However, the fact that the total land area is fixed is rarely of much relevance in urban economics. The area devoted to any one use is *not* fixed. The total *urban* area, or the area of any particular *urban use* can be increased. Moreover, by building more densely, it is possible to substitute other inputs for land.

The area of *a particular site* is obviously fixed, which means that the price will depend solely on the demand for it ('economic rent', of which more will be said shortly). But here again, this is not so important if other land can be substituted for the site in question. In fact, the main characteristic of the modern city is the extent to which mass transportation has increased the range of potential sites, reduced the importance of central location, and lowered (real) prices of sites in 'inner areas'. Except in the very short run, therefore, the supply of urban land is – or can be – far more elastic than many presentations of the theory of economic rent would suggest.

ECONOMIC THEORIES OF LAND USE

Economic theories of urban land use are concerned with explaining the pattern of land use, using this term in the widest sense to include the physical category of use (residential, commercial, etc.), the density of development and, in the case of residential areas, the economic and social characteristics of the residents; they do this by constructing a simplified model. The theories we shall first examine assume an economy in which the allocation of resources is basically decided by costs, prices and profits. It is assumed that individuals and firms have preferences for settling in particular locations, and that these preferences are reflected in the amount they are prepared to pay for the use of land. It is also assumed that the owners of land and buildings will let or sell them to the highest bidder. In this way, a pattern of land use and of land and building prices will be established by which land and buildings are used for those purposes giving the highest return. (Although no economist of any standing has ever denied that the participants in the market process, being human beings and not computers, will be influenced by convention, fashion, conscience, personal contacts and all the other factors that influence human behaviour).

Before examining urban land use, it may be helpful to examine the theories developed by 19th century economists to explain agricultural land use and land prices: these have since been applied to urban land, and a discussion of the simpler agricultural case brings out the essential issues.

ECONOMIC RENT

David Ricardo – writing at a time when food prices and farm rents were historically high in relation to incomes – analysed the factors determining farm rents.[5] He began by making a crucial distinction. In ordinary language, rent means the annual money payment for the use of a farm (or a house or office): we will call this 'contract rent' or 'rack rent'. (The latter term, in its technical use, has no connotations of being exorbitant: it simply means a rent paid for the use of a building, as distinct from a 'ground rent'). Part of the contract rent is a payment for the use and upkeep of buildings, and this element is similar in character to payments for any other goods or service, which (in the long run) are determined by the cost of providing them. But when this element is deducted – easier in theory than in practice – there remains that part of the rent which is paid for the use of the land as such, which has nothing to do with costs but is determined solely by scarcity. It was with this type of 'rent' that Ricardo's analysis was concerned, and it was unfortunate that he used a common word in a special sense. Subsequent writers used the term 'economic rent' to make the distinction clear. (But this again can be confusing; in ordinary language an 'economic rent' is often used to mean a level of contract rent sufficient to yield a normal return on capital).

The level of 'economic rent' depends on the profitability of farming. The difference between (normal) costs (including 'normal profit') and receipts represents the amount the farmer can afford to pay as 'economic rent'. And if the landlord is anxious to obtain the maximum rent, this will be the rent actually charged (for the land). Thus if corn prices are high, rents will be high: if corn prices are low, rents will be low. High rents do not cause high corn prices, as some of Ricardo's contemporaries argued, any more than high land prices cause high house prices, as some of our contemporaries argue. This general principle is not invalidated if farms (or houses) are owner-occupied. The 'economic rent' will then be earned by the farmer, in his capacity as landowner, and its level will determine the sale price of the farm.

Economic rent is thus a residual payment after paying the costs of production. In general terms, it is the difference between the market price of a resource and the price needed to maintain supply in the long run. As applied to development land, this means the surplus of expected receipts over expected construction costs. This can be expressed in annual terms or capitalised as a lump sum. In either case, it has to be estimated *ex ante*. A developer considering building an office block, or shops or houses, has to estimate how much he can sell the buildings for (which, if they are tenanted, will depend on the rack rents obtainable) and what they will cost (including interest costs, and a normal profit) to build. The difference is the amount he can afford to pay for the land. A typical example, from a report by an official British advisory body, is given in Table 1. It shows that between 1970 and 1974 the costs of office development rose more than rents, so that, for office development in provincial cities, the residual land value actually became *negative* in 1974. This means that, given the cost/price relationships prevailing in 1974, it would not have paid to build an office block in a provincial city even if the land cost nothing. This did not mean that the land was worth

TABLE 1. Comparative Appraisal, 1970 & 1975, showing Effect on Site Value

Central London Office Development

	1970 £	1975 £
Capital value	13750000	22000000
less Development costs	4101250	14527500
Balance	9648750	7472500
less cost of delay to full letting (at 8%, ×0.764)	(at 15%.	×0.534)
Present value of site	7371645	3990315
Site as a percentage of total cost	53½%	18%

Major Provincial City Office Development

Capital value	1050000	2100000
less Development costs	729600	2422500
Balance	320400	322500
less cost of delay to full letting (at 8½%, ×0.825)	(at 15%)	
Present value of site	264330	MINUS
Site as a percentage of total cost	25%	MINUS

Source: *Commercial Property Development*, Dept of the Environment, HMSO., 1975, p. 67.

nothing, since it would have possessed a value for an alternative use. This example does, however, bring out three points:

(a) Land prices (i.e. capitalised 'economic rent') are a residual, depending on the market value and the construction costs of buildings.
(b) They can thus vary considerably according to the state of demand.
(c) Property investment can be more, *or less*, profitable than envisaged.

Let us return to Ricardo. Having explained the residual basis of the pricing of a particular piece of land, Ricardo introduced the concept of a range of fertility. As land became less fertile, the economic rent fell to a point where it was zero. This represented the 'extensive margin' beyond which (in the long run) cultivation would not take place.[6] But changes in the price of agricultural produce (in relation to costs) will shift the extensive margin, and alter the total value of economic rent.

The Ricardian model as such – as distinct from the basic concept of economic rent – has only a limited applicability to urban land. Building on marshy ground or steep slopes is more expensive than on well-drained level ground – so that marshy or sloping ground is worth less. In general, however, the *location* of sites is more important than their physical characteristics: the basis of most economic models has therefore been the effect of distance (or transport cost) on land use and price. For industrial development, the nearness to raw materials, markets, communications and labour supply, are important. For shops, location in relation to customers is all-important. For housing, location in relation to employment is still important, although location in relation to leisure activities, schools, etc. is probably even more important. Urban models based on the influence of transport costs are essentially an application to the city of an agricultural model put forward by the 19th century German landowner, Heinrich von Thünen.

VON THÜNEN'S RINGS

In his book *The Isolated State*, von Thünen begins by assuming that there is flat plain of uniform fertility, thus excluding from his model the differences in fertility emphasised by Ricardo. He also assumes that all farm produce is marketed and consumed in the central town, and that transport costs are proportional to distance. Under these conditions, the economic rent earned in the production of any particular crop will be at a maximum on the outskirts of the town, where transport costs zero. As one moves away from the town, transport costs rise progressively, so that economic rent falls. But the rate of rise in transport costs – and hence the rate of fall in economic rent – differs between different crops,

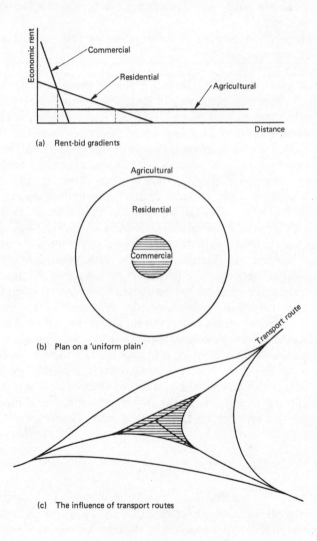

(a) Rent-bid gradients

(b) Plan on a 'uniform plain'

(c) The influence of transport routes

Fɪɢ. 2. von Thünen's rings

according to the extent to which they can 'bear' transport charges. The economic rent that can be produced by different crops can thus be represented in a series of lines sloping downwards from the centre, comparable to Fig 2(a). Producers will choose the product giving the highest economic rent, and the outcome will be a series of concentric rings of cultivation around the town.

To apply von Thünen's model to urban land use, let us assume that there are two land uses in a town – residential and commercial – and that both users prefer to be near the centre of the town. (Until the 1930s, this was a fairly realistic assumption, although it is now less so). Around the town, the land is in agricultural use. Let us assume that commercial users can outbid residential users near the centre, but that the land rent they are prepared to offer falls sharply with distance from the centre. The rent offered by residential users also falls with distance from the centre, although less sharply, whereas the agricultural rent is constant (see the 'rent-bid gradients' in Fig 2a). On a 'uniform plain', in which transport costs are the same in all directions, the outcome of the rent-bid gradients will be the concentric circles illustrated in 2b. If there are equivalents to von Thünen's 'navigable river' which reduce transport costs (or time) in certain directions – e.g. railway lines or trunk roads – the concentric pattern will become star-shaped (Fig. 2(c)).

RENT AND CAPITAL VALUE

Our analysis of 'economic rent' has concentrated on the annual value. This annual value will then determine the capital value at which the site can be bought and sold. The relation between the annual and capital values is a simple relation using the rate of interest. If £x per annum is expected to be earned in perpetuity, the capital value will be $\frac{x}{\text{rate of interest}}$ where the rate of interest is expressed as a decimal. If the annual value is £1000 and the rate of interest 5%, or 0.05, the capital value will be $\frac{1000}{0.05} = £20,000$. Thus the capital value will vary positively with the annual rate and inversely with the rate of interest; if, with the annual value unaltered, the rate goes up to 10%, the capital value will fall to £10,000. If the annual value is expected to change over time, it is necessary to use discounted cash flow tables.

When there is an active market for both sale and letting, there is likely to be a fairly close relationship between sale prices and rents, at a 'normal' rate of interest. The 'yields' for commercial property in Britain have been fairly constant since the 1920s at five to seven per cent (Table 4). If there is a switch in consumers' preferences in favour of one system or the other, this relationship may be temporarily disturbed, but will be re-established as the composition of the stock of property changes.

VON THÜNEN GOES TO TOWN

The ideas developed by von Thünen for agricultural land have in recent years been taken up by urban economists, and their models are open to serious criticism as an 'operational' explanation of the pattern of land use in cities (Chap. 6). But, as a first approximation, the simple rent-bid model is still useful. There is, however, one important qualification even at this level. The intersecting lines in Fig. 2(a) may suggest that land will be transferred from one use to another immediately the value in one use exceeds its value in another. But because of the risks and costs of making a change – not to mention inertia, delays and non-financial objections to change – there usually has to be a significant difference between the value of the old and the new use ('development value') before the change will occur. This is particularly marked at the edge of the urban area, where agricultural land is developed. Even when there have been no planning restrictions on development, the price of land sold for building has always been several times its price for agricultural purposes. There is no difficulty in explaining that house-buyers would be *prepared to pay* this sort of price, which is often a small proportion of the total costs of the house (the average price of 'raw' suburban land, without services, has in most countries generally been below 10 per cent of total costs). But the fact that farmers are *not prepared to sell* for agricultural value implies either that they do not consider agricultural value an adequate recompense for selling and/or that they possess some monopoly power. A farm can represent a life's work: its market value may not be sufficient to buy a farm which the farmer would regard as equivalent, and there is also the social disruption involved in moving. Thus the assumption which has underlain post-War legislation in Britain that 'existing use value' is the only proper basis for compensation is one that can be challenged, especially as regards agricultural land. In addition, there may be an element of monopoly in the ownership of peripheral sites, since these may be most convenient. The owners will thus be in a strong bargaining position, although a limit will be set if developers can 'by-pass' them and build further out. Thus the change from the agricultural to the housing rent-bid curve in Fig. 2(a) would be better represented by a 'cliff-edge'.

When there are controls which allow development in some areas and prohibit it in others, the bargaining position of sellers tends to be strengthened, and the height of the 'cliff-edge' increased. This effect will be at a minimum if large areas are zoned for potential development: it will be at a maximum when land is zoned for development only grudgingly and after irresistable pressure has built up. Under these conditions, prices will be raised inside the urban area. The same applies to restrictions on a particular land use within the urban area. If the total area zoned for commercial use is restricted, office rents – and hence the value of office blocks and potential office sites – will be raised.

The effect of a reduction in transport costs (in real terms) will be to flatten the curves – especially that for housing. This could be expected to lead to a lower level of land prices in housing areas and a more dispersed, lower density pattern. This is very much what has happened to West European and North American cities in the 20th century.

THE DEMAND CURVE FOR LAND AND HOUSING

The rent-bid curves represented in Fig. 2(a) are based on a given aggregate demand and supply situation for the various categories of urban land. The aggregate demand curve for urban land has in recent decades been shifted to the right by economic and technical changes: population growth; rising incomes; the advantages of single-storey layout for modern manufacturing; the voracious demand of the motor car. At the same time, the demand for land clearly has some elasticity with regard to price. If land becomes dearer, there will be a tendency to build more densely. One courageous econometrician has calculated the price elasticity of demand for housing land in the USA as 0.75.[7] This means that if the price of land rose by 1.0 per cent *in real terms*, the amount demanded would fall by 0.75 per cent *other things being equal*. (One might *a priori* expect a lower figure for Europe, where suburban densities are about double those in the USA).

Other things do not, in practice, remain equal; for example, income. The largest category of urban land use, accounting for some three-quarters of the area of both American and European cities is housing, and estimates of the income elasticity of demand for housing in recent years are around +1: in other words a one per cent rise in real income will lead to an increased demand for housing of one per cent.[8] Housing is also elastic with regard to price (including mortgage rates). Empirical estimates vary wildly but generally agree that the elasticity is unity or more.

The 'price' of housing must take account not only of the capital value, but also – since most owner-occupiers have mortgages – of the interest rate. The sharp rise in mortgage rates in Britain in 1973, combined with mortgage rationing, had a marked effect on demand. It also induced some builders to produce housing in a range of sizes – one and two-bedroom units as well as three and four-bedroom houses. This was adapting supply to demand in a way that had always been standard practice on the European continent, and is in line with changes in household size (half of all households now consists of one or two persons).

ADJUSTMENT FOR INFLATION

One of the difficulties of measuring the effects of changes in price and income on the demand for housing is the taking into account of inflation. To give figures in real terms, any time series of incomes and house prices must be deflated by appropriate price indices. The fact that the average price of new houses sold in the UK rose sixfold between 1956 and 1976 can be misleading unless put alongside the fact that over this period average earnings rose more than fivefold and retail prices threefold. Inflation raises even greater problems in connection with the rate of interest. Since most owner-occupied housing is bought on a mortgage, its 'price' consists of two elements: capital cost and the rate of interest. Should the rate of interest also be deflated by the current rate of inflation? On this basis, the rate of interest in most developed countries since the War has ranged between +3 per cent and well below zero. But this treatment of the interest rate can be misleading. A rise in the inflation rate, accompanied by a rise in the interest rate, may mean that the 'real' interest rate is currently negative. But these changes still mean that anyone buying a house has to pay a higher proportion of his income than in the earlier years. Whether he will benefit from a negative rate of interest in the end depends on the long-term course of inflation, which is impossible to predict. Recent experience suggests that a rise in the inflation rate and the interest rate does reduce the demand for housing. Moreover, it redistributes income from first-time buyers to existing house owners. This is one of the many arbitrary and inequitable re-distributions of income caused by inflation.

TABLE 2. Mortgage Rates and Inflation, UK.

	1956 to 1970	1971	1972	1973	1974	1975	1976
Mortgage rate (gross)	5.5 −8.5	8.0	8.5	11.0	11.0	11.0	
Annual increase in retail prices	3.5	9.4	7.1	9.2	16.1	24.2	16.6
„ „ „ new house prices	6.0	15.3	31.5	36.2	6.1	9.4	10.0
„ „ „ average earnings	5.5	11.3	13.0	13.4	17.5	26.7	15.5

Source: Building Societies Association. *Facts and Figures*. July, 1976. p. 16.

The effects of inflation can, in theory, be countered by 'indexing' contractual agreements. This is most easily done with rents – and to some extent has been done in the case of commercial property. Before 1939, land and buildings in the UK were generally let on long leases at fixed rents, in the expectation that the value of money would remain more or less unaltered. But with an annual average rate of price increase of three to four per cent since the Second World War (accelerating to over 10 per cent, and for a time even 20 per cent in the early 1970s) it has become obvious that long term contracts need to take account of inflation. New leases now being created always contain provision for ground rents to be revised at periodic intervals, such as seven years: there is often an automatic formula which relates the ground rent to the 'rack rent', i.e. the total rent of the building.

It is the same story with rack rents. The traditional British system was for a shop or office to be leased for a term of years at a fixed rent. At the end of the lease, under the Landlord and Tenant Acts – which give reasonable security to tenants without destroying the whole system, as the Rent Acts have done for residential property – the sitting tenant had to be offered the new lease, but at an open market rent, determined, if need be, by arbitration. Here again, current rates of inflation have led to more frequent adjustments. For shops, there is an alternative approach, common in the USA and continental Europe, whereby rents are linked to turnover.

TABLE 3. Inflation and Mortgage Repayments, UK.

	Average New House-price £	Average Initial Repayment £ p.a.	Average Earnings £ p.a.	Average Initial Repayments as a % Average Earnings		House-price/ Earnings Ratio
				(a)current %	(b)in 1976	
1963	3156	198	1007	21.2	7.4	3.1
1970	5082	398	1543	25.8	12.7	3.3
1976	13300	1264	3727	33.9	33.9	3.6

Source: Building Societies Association, *Facts and Figures*, July 1976.

PROPERTY YIELDS

When there is reasonable long-term price stability – as in the century before 1939 – yields will reflect the degree of risk involved in an investment. In the inter-War period in Britain, yields were three to four per cent on government securities and five to eight per cent on rented property. But inflation has produced the 'reverse yield'; the yield on property (or industrial shares) is *less* than on debentures, because the former are believed to offer some degree of protection against inflation. Whereas the rate on debentures, and mortgages and bank loans, has to some extent risen with inflation, the yield on commercial property has on the whole remained remarkably constant, at very much the inter-War level (Table 4). Yields in other countries are similar to those in Britain for shops, offices and factories. When there is an active market in rented

TABLE 4. Property Yields, UK.
(per cent)

	1929	1938	1951	1961	1971	1973	1975	1977
Multiple shops	6	6–6½	5	5½	6½–7	5–5½	6–6½	4½–5
Prime offices	7	7–7½	6½	7	6½–7	4–5	6–6½	5½–6
Flats	8	9	7½	8	6	7	10	8
Industrial				10	8½	7½	9	7–8
Consols	4½	3½	4	6	9	14	14.8	12.7
Bank rate	3–4	2	2½	6–7	4½–7	8½–13	10½	14.5–7
Building society mortgage rate	4–5	5	4	6½	8½	9–12	11–12	9–10

Source: Alsopp & Co., London

housing, yields are among the lowest. Typical yields in West Germany in 1977 were 5.5 per cent to 6.5 per cent for flats, 5.5 per cent to 6.25 per cent for shops and offices, and 8 per cent to 8.25 per cent for the best industrial property.

Yields are $\dfrac{\text{rack rent}}{\text{market value}} \times 100$, and in the short-term the rack rent is fixed. In other words, the yield is based on the capital value that investors are prepared to offer for property producing a certain rent. Thus a fall in yields indicates *increased* confidence about the future and a rise indicates *reduced* confidence. The fall and rise in 1973–5 reflected the inflationary expectations of the 'Barber boom' and the slump that followed. More stable conditions (in spite of continuing inflation) have since returned. Yields do not indicate whether new building would be profitable; this will depend on whether the market value of the property is above or below the replacement cost. But yields indicate the return needed to attract new investment.

Property yields are generally confined to a 'property column' read only by practitioners. They do, however, provide an important general lesson for urban development policy in an inflationary era. Provided that investors have reasonable confidence that rents can be reviewed to take account of inflation, they are still prepared to lend money at the traditional 'real' rate of five to seven per cent, even if fixed interest rates are much higher. This applies not only to shops and offices, etc., but also to housing, as the West German 'housing miracle' and the growth of private rented apartment blocks in Canada and the USA indicates. If rents *cannot* be adjusted for inflation, the return required by investors will be much higher, and the cost of financing correspondingly greater. This is one of the problems faced by public or non-profit housing, especially if the authority lacks a stock of older housing with which the costs of more recent housing can be pooled.

Whereas rents can be 'indexed' to take reasonable account of inflation, the treatment of owner-occupied property is more problematical. Fixed-rate mortgages used to be common in Britain, and are still usual in the USA and West Germany. But they tend to be undermined by high rates of inflation. In a high-inflation country, the building societies' practice of varying interest rates during the period of a mortgage provides a partial adjustment for inflation, although it does not alter the inflationary bias against 'first time' buyers.[9]

SPECULATION

(1) DEFINITION

'Speculation' and 'speculative' are used in various ways in connection with real property – frequently in an emotive way which means little more than an expression of disapproval. We thus need to define 'speculation' before we can analyse its consequences. In a very broad sense, it can mean 'any business involving risk of loss' (*Concise Oxford English Dictionary*). A 'speculative' builder is one who builds houses in the hope of selling them, rather than one who builds to order. In a narrower and more usual sense, 'speculation' refers to mere buying and selling rather than to speculative buying or selling in conjunction with building. Let us first examine the term in this sense. The definition usually used in general economic discussion (particularly in connection with commodity trading) is 'buying at a low price in the hope of selling at a higher one'.[10] Speculation in this sense involves both the hope of gain and the possibility of loss. If there is to be a gain, the rise in the price between purchase and sale has to rise by more than the cost of holding the land. If there is no yield, this loss will be the compound interest on the sale price, using either the rate at which the speculator can borrow, or the rate of return he could obtain elsewhere on his capital. If the property yields a below-average return on the purchase price – as is usual with agricultural land – the ultimate gain will have to be sufficient to compensate for the low return during the time the property is held.

Speculation, as defined above, is not necessarily harmful. If speculation in, say, wheat is well-judged it will cause wheat to be carried over from a glut to a scarcity, thus smoothing out supplies and prices. The case of land is less clear.

It has been well observed that a speculator who, without manipulating prices by false intelligence or otherwise, anticipates the future correctly. . . . generally renders a public service. . . . but that a speculator in land in an old country can render no such public service, because the stock of land is fixed. At the best he can prevent a site with great possibilities from being devoted to inferior uses in consequence of the haste, ignorance or impecuniosity of those in control of it.[11]

But speculation of this kind, whether it is well-judged or ill-judged, and whether it performs a public service or not, will merely raise prices when the speculators buy, and lower them when they sell. This will not influence the general level of prices, although it can – and often has – raised prices in a boom and lowered them in the subsequent slump (Chap. 5)

This destabilising effect does not affect the level of prices over a longer period. Speculation will only raise the long-run level of land prices if land is permanently held off the market in the belief that prices will always rise so fast as to more than offset the costs of withholding land from sale. There must, in other words be a *continual* restriction on the supply of land for development.[12] Moreover, this type of 'speculation' can be undertaken by owners who have not *bought* the property with speculative intentions, e.g. farmers. To affect land prices significantly, this behaviour has to be widespread. It has often been asserted that this happens, but evidence is singularly lacking.

Speculative land hoarding was generally blamed for the sharp rise in land and house prices in Britain in 1972, and this view was accepted by the Conservative Government, which proposed a penal Land Hoarding Tax if development did not take place within three to four years after the granting of outline planning permission. It immediately became clear that the largest 'land hoarders' were *bona fide* house-building firms who, in order to maintain land availability under current British planning procedures, needed 'land banks' equivalent to about five years' production. These land banks are 'speculative', but they are associated with what most people would consider a socially desirable form of production. As an illuminating study of land supply points out, profits on house-building have generally been low, and only the profits on the land banks have enabled some firms to continue in business.[13] Finally, the boom of 1972–3 turned into a slump in 1973–4, which casts even more doubt on the argument that speculative land hoarding is a major and permanent factor in raising land prices.

A different type of 'land hoarding' or 'land withholding' is that practised by public authorities. There have been many examples of public authorities – notably British Rail, port authorities and the military – retaining land years after they had ceased to have any use for it (Chap. 10). This is an example of the harm that can be caused by the *absence* of a profit motive in land use. These public authorities generally obtained no benefit from selling surplus land, so that there was no counter-weight to administrative inertia. But even this 'hoarding' pales into insignificance by comparison with the influence on land supply exercised by British local authorities through their powers of development control. Whatever view one takes on the British development control system, no serious student of the question denies that, when land is withheld from development, it is predominantly through the exercise of local authority planning powers.

There is, however, anecdotal evidence of private 'land-withholding' in three types of case. The first is where the tax rate on the proceeds is so penal as to make the sale not worthwhile. Under the 1947 'development charge' there was a tax of 100 per cent on 'development value', which inhibited sales. Since 1973, development value has been taxed under the Development Gains Tax and subsequently Development Land Tax at rates which can be as high as 80 per cent or even 98 per cent and this has in some cases discouraged owners from selling. If any financial incentive to sell land is removed, a system of compulsory state acquisition must be substituted: whether this is likely to be an adequate alternative will be discussed below.

A second type of 'withholding' is when an owner of a strategically-placed small piece of land can block a large development until he is bought off for a high price. Although this type of action is unlikely to affect the *total* land cost significantly, there is a case in such circumstances for giving the developer the power to buy out a small landowner at the normal market price.[14]

A third type of 'withholding' is when the owner of, for example, a farm or a house with a large garden or 18th century park says 'I am not going to sell out however much you pay me. I have lived here and intend to die here'. At the time, this type of behaviour has often been dismissed as 'resistance to progress'. Subsequently, however, these 'islands' in a sea of one period's development have provided either valuable recreational areas, or elbow room for facilities which developed only in later generations. Thus it is far from obvious that this type of 'withholding' is always undesirable, or justifies 'steamroller' legal powers. The 'passing over' of land has, in fact, been more common in the USA than in European countries since the War. It has been criticised by several land economists, and usually attributed to speculation. But it is not clear that this explanation is correct; if the land is not developed within a few years, any speculation is *ipso facto* unprofitable, and the complaint is that some pieces of by-passed land are *never* developed. They have often been deprived of access by surrounding development, sometimes suffer from some kind of industrial blight and – at least when there seemed to be unlimited supplies of suburban land – have been unattractive to developers.

There is, in general, a sound case for imposing some kind of tax on undeveloped land in urban areas (*cf.* site value taxation, Chap. 9). But taxes of this sort cannot be relied on to eliminate vacant land (or vacant buildings), since there are so many other factors involved.

Speculation tends to be concentrated in the 'zone in transition' and in the urban fringe. Unless it takes the form of continual land withholding (for which, as explained above, there is little evidence) it will not affect the price ultimately paid on development: it will merely change the recipients. But if a speculator buys, the previous owner has to sell; if the buyer is well informed of the likely future value of his land, the price at which he is prepared to sell will be raised correspondingly. There may be occasions where the speculative buyer has the advantage of being better informed. And in countries where legal titles are obscure, peasants illiterate and officials bribable, small landowners can be tricked or bullied into selling at a low price to speculative buyers. But on the urban fringe in Britain or the USA, the smooth City man is more likely to be gulled by the rustics than *vice versa*.

Finally, the term 'speculation' has been used in connection with the attempts of owners to sell rent-controlled or rent-regulated housing with vacant possession. Under the successive British Rent Acts, rents have been held down to a level which gave little or no return on capital, and at times have fallen well below the cost of the maintenance needed to keep the housing in sound condition. The Rent Acts, however, have given tenants a hereditary right of occupation. When the dwelling became vacant, therefore, most owners chose to sell rather than re-let. Some owners who did not wish to wait so long tried to get tenants to leave, either by bribes or by harassment (which has been a legal offence since 1965). In both the legal and the illegal case, the owner who sells with vacant possession is trying to get a higher return than the capitalised equivalent of the controlled rent. But this does not fall within our definitions of 'speculation'. In other cases, the owners sold out to persons who hoped to be able to eventually make a profit by selling to the tenants, or with vacant possession. For example, after the 1965 Rent Act applied unremunerative 'fair rents' to the higher-rated flats which had previously been uncontrolled, most owners eventually decided to sell out. Some were able to sell all their flats to sitting tenants, but in other cases only a proportion of tenants were prepared to buy. Rather than retaining ownership of a proportion of flats and gradually selling them off over the years, some companies sold out to 'break-up specialists', at a price below vacant possession value. The buyers were prepared to sell the flats one by one and, in effect, speculated that they would be able to sell them soon enough, and at prices high enough, to yield them a profit. The type of poorer housing which had been rent-controlled since 1939 sometimes attracted a cruder type of speculator, who sought to get the tenants out by harassment or threats.

The term 'Rachmanism' was coined, after a shadowy underworld character who operated in this way in the early 1950s. These *methods*, although not the desire of owners to sell, were largely eliminated after they had been publicised. None of these types of speculation *caused* the decline in the stock of privately tenanted dwellings, although they may in some areas have accelerated the process. The basic cause was rent control, at levels below the price needed to maintain the supply of rented housing.

The tendency to use 'speculation' as a purely pejorative term usually causes it to be used too broadly, but sometimes causes it to be used too narrowly. Mr (now Sir) Harold Wilson once argued that:

> . . . if you buy land on which there is a slag heap 120 feet high and it costs £100,000 to remove, this is not land speculation in the sense we condemn it. It is land reclamation.[15]

It is undoubtedly true that reclaiming a slag heap is a socially beneficial activity, even if it is also profitable. But to buy the slag heap, in the hope that the value of the materials sold, together with the value of the reclaimed land, will yield a profit over the purchase price and the cost of reclamation, is a highly speculative operation.

(2) POLICY

What then are the economic consequences of speculation in real property, and what, if anything, should be done about it? Contrary to popular belief, speculation (on any objective definition) is sometimes socially beneficial. Speculative house-building and the maintenance of 'land banks' by builders are necessary if houses are to be built cheaply. In other cases, speculation is less important than is commonly imagined: there is no evidence that speculation in land has had any *permanent* effect on land prices. Speculation in buildings – whether connected with the sale of rent-controlled housing or the conversion of old buildings to new offices, etc. – is merely a symptom of more fundamental causes. And, in spite of Centre Point, there is no evidence that it has ever paid to hold offices empty – except perhaps during a couple of months at the height of the 1973 boom, when rents were rising daily. Having said that, there are three provisions which can be made to ensure that speculative motives do not produce a significant divergence between private and public interests. The tax system should not encourage possible 'hoarding' by levying little or no tax on vacant land or empty buildings. On the other hand, very high taxes of this type – often based on mistaken ideas about the extent of 'hoarding' – can cause inequities or discourage development. The Land Hoarding Tax proposed by the Heath Government would have harmed house-building, and the imposition, after 1974, of penal rates on empty buildings (known curiously as 'void rates') caused inequities and discouraged development. As in other fields of taxation, the need is to establish the likely results of different arrangements and to strike a balance between differing objectives – a banal conclusion, perhaps, if it had not so often been ignored.

The second requirement is that potential buyers and sellers should be placed on an equal footing by clear legal titles and as 'transparent' a land market as possible. Market transparency is assisted by a public Land Register (which, except in Scotland, Britain still lacks) and by the kind of local price information provided under the German Building Act. The third is the avoidance of excessive booms and slumps, such as that of the early 1970s. This requires, on the one hand, avoiding excessive use of the brake and the accelerator in general economic policy; on the other hand, avoiding the creation of artifical shortages for any type of real property by an ill-judged development control policy.

We have so far dealt with 'speculation' in a 'trading' and 'hoarding' sense. But someone who builds houses or offices in the expectation of being able to sell or let them profitably – rather than building to order – is known as a 'spec builder', and this is often used as a pejorative term by those who dislike the aesthetics of British suburban housing. But it is worth pointing out that this system is employed in the production of cars, clothes or shoes (apart from a handful of expensive 'custom' producers) and that, except in conditions of shortage, speculative building (and speculative land banking) is necessary to ensure a reasonable steady flow of work and thus keep down costs and house prices. Moreover, whatever the detailed shortcomings of owner-occupied suburban housing in the USA and Britain, it is a type of housing which the majority of the population has shown that it wants, and to which continental Europe is now turning. For some years, several American intellectuals have challenged the view that the suburbs necessarily represented a debased form of life.

More violent criticism than that of 'spec' housebuilders has been aroused by speculative office building since the War, and in general by the activities of property development companies within built-up areas.

There are three main criticisms: that speculative building encourages poor design; that it encourages excess supply; that it undermines good planning. It is arguable that a developer who builds offices speculatively will be inclined to produce a standardised undistinguished product, whereas a firm which plans to use the building will have more interest in aesthetic and environmental standards. There may be such a tendency, although it is not universal. Some buildings custom-built for public bodies (including Universities) are deplorable, whereas Centre Point is visually one of the more interesting office buildings.

The second criticism (also mainly confined to office building) is that speculative building can result in excess capacity, if developers are too optimistic. This is quite different from the unconvincing argument advanced in connection with Centre Point that it *pays* to build offices to stand empty. If offices are not let within the expected time, the developer loses heavily. But during the boom of 1971–3 office developers in several cities in Europe did become too exuberant, and did overbuild (just as residential construction firms in West Germany built too many flats to let). The excess supply was slow to be taken up in the recession, but the summer of 1977 saw clear signs of movement, and in a year or two normal vacancy rates are likely to prevail in most cities. The overbuilding was a mis-use of resources, but one that should not be exaggerated. Some spare capacity is normal and necessary in any economic activity, and it is easier to judge the precisely optimal level of output after the event than before it. But the property boom-and-slump certainly has lessons for both developers, financial institutions, and Governments; developers and financial institutions, at least, have learned them.

A third criticism is that speculative organisations are not suitable for exercising a major role in large-scale urban planning. Property companies are favourite bogeymen of our time. Criticism of them is often part of an argument for state socialism which displays little interest in how this system works in practice. But there is a more limited criticism which can be shared even by those who see great virtues in dispersed ownership and a market economy.

Urban history suggests that, for *large-scale* urban development (as distinct from the continued renewal of small pieces of the urban mosaic) a purely commercial approach, by purely commercial operators, does not produce very distinguished results. What are generally regarded as the finest examples of urban design had their main outlines planned by men whose vision was more than purely commercial. But even in these cases, the construction and management of individual buildings was carried out commercially. Mr. Lewis Mumford, whom no one could accuse of extreme economic liberalism, remarks after his eulogy of the 'Plan of the Three Canals' in 17th century Amsterdam:

> But note: the carrying out of the plan was the task of private enterprise, undertaken by individuals and small groups for profit. . . .[16]

(a system very similar to that used three and a half centuries later in West Germany for the 'new towns' and for urban renewal; see Chap. 11). From this point of view, there may have been some justice in criticisms of 'speculation'.

Criticisms of 'speculation' generally arise in periods of rapid urban change, and in the districts particularly affected – the urban fringe, the edge of the CBD, old housing areas being redeveloped. In these districts, losses to some people may be accompanied by windfall gains to others, familiar landmarks may be destroyed, and a demand can easily arise for the state to 'stop speculation'. However, the issues are rarely clear-cut. Since speculative building normally reflects some kind of consumer demand, there may be clashes of interest involved. The replacement of 19th century houses by blocks of private rented flats in some North American cities is understandably opposed by local residents, and yet it does meet a demand from a more transient population. (A visiting British University teacher of moderately conservationist inclinations was in a good position to appreciate both points of view). Moreover, some remedies for 'speculation' can be as bad as the disease. It is reasonable to insist that changes in 'conservation areas' should be in keeping with the scale and character of the existing buildings, but to stop *all* change can in the long run kill an area. And a state monopoly in the development and ownership of buildings – as exemplified in British council housing – does not seem to many people who have made international comparisons to possess the virtues claimed for it. What is needed is a combination of commercial acumen with development planning based on more than merely commercial considerations.

SUMMARY

The market for real property is subject to essentially the same principles of price formation as other markets. It is, however, complicated by the long life of the product. Annual output is usually less than two per cent of the existing stock. This means that prices depend on the relation of *demand* and *stock*. Prices depend on *costs* only indirectly. If there is a 'shortage' and prices are high in relation to costs, output will tend to increase (if allowed to do so). When shortage changes to surplus (which can happen very quickly), prices fall below costs and output will fall sharply until a realignment of prices and costs. Thus prices tend to fluctuate around costs, while output tends to fluctuate more than in industries producing short-lived goods.

The price of an individual site is a 'residual', viz. the difference between the value of the building and the cost of producing it. This is an example of 'economic rent', i.e. the price depends solely on demand, since the supply is fixed. But the supply of building land *in total* is not fixed, and the price offered for land does affect the supply.

The spatial pattern of land values depends on the strength of demand for different types of buildings in different districts. *In the aggregate*, land values depend on building values and not *vice versa*. In the 19th century, von Thünen developed a model to illustrate how the price of agricultural land, and its use, would vary according to the distance from a market town: the general principles of this model can be applied to urban land.

In the case of tenanted property, (rack) rent is related to capital value according to the appropriate rate of interest. Property yields are affected by other rates of interest but have, in recent years, been affected by inflation. For commercial property, periodic rent reviews are now normal. This provides some 'hedge' against inflation, so that investors have been prepared to accept lower yields than on fixed-interest investments: yields have on the whole remained constant since the 1930s.

'Speculation' is not necessarily harmful, and in some respects (e.g. builders' land banks) is desirable. It can be de-stabilising when it exaggerates general economic fluctuations, but probably has only a very short-run influence on land prices.

SELECT BIBLIOGRAPHY

D. Richmond, *Introduction to Valuation*, Macmillan, 1975.
I. H. Seeley, *Building Economics*, Macmillan, 1972.
P. A. Stone, *Building Economy*, Pergammon, 2nd ed. 1976.

REFERENCES

1. K. G. Boulding, *Economics as a Science*, McGraw Hill, 1970. p. 73.
2. A valuable statistical compilation, and a possibly complacent analysis, is given in *Housing Policy; a Consultative Document* H.M.S.O. Cmnd 6851, 1977. For a more critical view, see *Housing, rents, cost and subsidies*, A. Grey *et al*, Chartered Institute of Public Finance & Accountancy, 1978.
3. Graham Hallett, *Housing and Land Policies in West Germany and Britain*, Macmillan, 1977, Pt.I.
4. This appears to be what Professor Denman means by his concept of 'proprietary land use analysis'. (D. R. Denman and S. Prodano, *Land Use: An Introduction to Proprietary Land Use Analysis*. Allen & Unwin, 1972).
5. *The Principles of Political Economy and Taxation*, Chap. 2.
6. Ricardo's emphasis on 'differential' rent illustrates an important point, but can be misleading. Economic rent is, more generally, based on scarcity, and can arise even when there is no 'differential': e.g. an island of uniform fertility, once all the land is cultivated (Stonier & Hague, *A Textbook of Economic Theory*, p. 276 ff).This is more than an academic quibble. I have heard a surveyor of great experience argue that the traditional theory of land pricing did not apply in a heavily populated island like Britain because there was no land left which earned no rent.
7. R. F. Muth, 'Urban Residential Land & Housing Markets' in *Issues in Urban Economics*, H. S. Perloff & L. Wingo Jr. (eds), Johns Hopkins Press, 1968, p. 286 ff.
8. Margaret Reid, *Housing & Income*, University of Chicago Press, 1962.
9. Ideas have often been put forward for 'low start' mortgages, in which both payments by borrowers and interest to depositors would rise over time, in line with house prices. Indeed an enterprising British finance house introduced a scheme of this type in 1972. It failed because, although many people wanted to lend on these terms, no one was anxious to borrow. It is also worth pointing out that the normal repayment mortagage, combined with tax relief on mortgage, is in fact a 'low start' mortgage since the proportion of interest payment (attracting tax relief) starts high and falls over the period of the mortgage.
10. *Everyman's Dictionary of Economics*, A. Seldon & F. G. Pennance (eds), London, 1965.

11. A. Marshall, *Principles of Economics*, 8th edn., p. 432.
12. One study *defines* speculation in the sense of 'witholding'. This brings out the point, although it is not normal usage. (Dr. W. K. Risse, *Grundzüge einer Theorie des Baubodenmarktes*, Domus Verlag, Bonn, 1974, p. 76 ff.
13. *Housing Land Availability in the South-East.* The Economist Intelligence Unit and the Housing Research Foundation. HMSO 1975.
14. The British Property Federation, which criticises the Community Land Act for its curtailment of the owner's right of objection, proposes powers for over-riding an owner who has no more than 10 % of a development, in the way that the Companies Act gives powers to buy out minority shareholders. *Policy for Land*, 1966, 2:6.
15. *Parliamentary Debates (Commons) 1973/4.* 4 April, Col. 1441.
16. Lewis Mumford, *The City in History*, Penguin, 1966, p. 504.

4 Redevelopment and Modernisation

> Thus all value in city land undergoes a continuous evolution from a state of non-existence through a cycle of changes, to a final dissolution, or to a new birth, when the process is repeated on the same land
>
> Richard M. Hurd, *Principles of City Land Values*, 1903, p. 17.

A city is an elaborate mosaic, in which pieces are continually wearing out and being replaced. Whether redevelopment occurs, the form it takes, and the districts where it occurs, involves complex factors including the social conditions of the district, local resistance to redevelopment, town planning policy, investment in new transport routes. For this reason, it is impossible to consider an individual site completely in isolation from its surroundings, and there is no clear-cut relation between a building's age or condition and redevelopment. Replacement occurs only when there is strong demand for a site, and when the existing building becomes inadequate. But the simple theory based on building value and site value is a useful framework for analysis, provided it is used with an appreciation of the many 'external' factors which impinge on these values.

BUILDING VALUE AND SITE VALUE

To examine the factors affecting building value, let us take any building which yields a money income, e.g. an office block, a shop or a block of flats. The net income of the building will be the gross rent it can command, less all necessary outgoings. Assume that an office block is let to various tenants and brings in £20,000 per annum. Outgoings are rates and maintenance averaging £2000 per annum so that the net rent is £18,000 per annum. The value of the building in its existing use is then based on the capitalisation of the net rent. If we assume that the building has an expected life of more than, say, 30 years, the capital value of the income stream can be regarded as the net rent of £18,000 multiplied by

$\dfrac{1}{\text{rate of interest}}$ or the number of 'years' purchase'. If the rate of interest

is 5 per cent (20 years' purchase), the capital value will be £18,000 × 20 = £360,000: if the rate of interest is 10 per cent, the capital value will be £180,000. If a shorter period is taken – either because of a lease or because of the building's likely physical life – the capitalised value can be looked up in valuation tables.

The calculation is basically similar – but less quantifiable – with an owner-occupied building. The 'rent' is the value the owner derives from occupying the building. This value is the 'opportunity cost' of alternative buildings; i.e. what it would cost to rent or buy comparable accommodation, *plus* or *minus* any changes in other 'costs', such as transport costs or working conditions.

The value of the site on which the building stands is based on the 'residual' principle, but is inevitably somewhat conjectural. If a new building were erected, what would be its value, and what would be the total cost of development? The difference gives the *estimated* site value but this has to be decided *ex ante* on the basis of *expected* costs and prices, which may turn out to be mistaken. Assume that there is a vacant site on which a developer proposes to build an office block. On the basis of calculations discussed below, the developer decides to erect a building of 10,000 sq. ft. of floor space. He believes that he can let this space at an average price of £1 a sq. ft. per annum, giving a total income of £10,000 per annum. At an interest rate of eight per cent, this means that the building has a capital value of £125,000. The total costs of construction, including profit margins, come to £100,000. Thus the amount that the developer can afford to pay for the land is £20,000. But many of these estimates are inevitably conjectural, and may, in the event, prove wrong. Costs may be higher or lower than expected, and rental earnings may also be higher or lower. This uncertainty means that land prices are subject to a considerable rate of indeterminacy, and the prices actually paid reflect both the prevailing state of business confidence and the degree of competition.

In the calculation above, we have implicitly assumed that the land is bought freehold, and that payment is made as a lump sum. If it is bought on a leasehold basis, as is still common for commercial developments in Great Britain, the payment for the lease consists of an initial lump sum, called (somewhat misleadingly) a 'premium', and annual 'ground rent'.

A ground rent and a premium are substitutable, a premium being equivalent to the value of a ground rent capitalised at the appropriate rate of interest for the length of the lease.

To recapitulate, the current use value of a building is the capitalised value of the total rack rent it can command (or its capital value to an owner-occupier). The value of the site for redevelopment is the value of the proposed new building *minus* construction costs. Only when the site value exceeds the current use value (plus the costs of demolition) does redevelopment become profitable.

The conditions for profitable redevelopment can be expressed as follows:

If Ve = capital value of existing building
D = cost of demolition
S = site value
Then the requirement for profitable redevelopment is:
$$Ve + D - S < O$$
The site value $(S) = Vp - Cp$
Where Vp = capital value of proposed building
Cp = cost of proposed building
The requirement for profitable redevelopment can be written as:
$$Ve + D + Cp < Vp$$
i.e. the value of the existing building *plus* demolition costs *plus* the cost of the new building must be less than the value of the proposed building.

Whether the redevelopment is carried out by the freehold owner of the building, or whether the land is sold to a separate developer, makes no theoretical difference; both will have to make the same calculations. But if the site is actually sold, the previous owner obtains an objective value; thus at least one variable in the equation (or rather the inequality) is definite. If no sale takes place, site value is somewhat hypothetical, and merely a matter of internal book-keeping.

Modification is sometimes an alternative to complete redevelopment; old houses can be modernised, or converted into offices or hotels; obsolete stables can be turned into desirable mews residences. In this case, the condition for profitable conversion is that the value of the existing building, plus the cost of conversion, is less than the value of the converted or renovated building.

THE LIFE-CYCLE OF A BUILDING

Over time, the value of a building will normally fall (in relation to the general price level). Repair costs rise sharply when a building reaches a certain age, and the design often becomes obsolete. However, substantial stone or brick buildings, if kept in good repair, will last almost indefinitely. Thus many 18th or 19th century houses still provide very satisfactory accommodation and maintain high prices (partly for their 'antique' value). But for most buildings, value eventually declines. It may eventually fall to zero, when the receipts only cover the costs of upkeep; in recent years the value of redundant churches, cinemas or music halls has fallen to virtually zero, except where they have found new uses. We can therefore illustrate the value of a building as a line sloping downward to the right. (BV in Fig. 3)

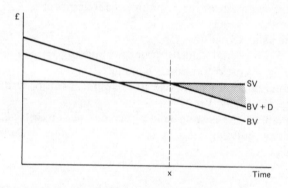

FIG. 3. Building and site value

At the beginning of a building's life, the site value will normally be well below the total value of the building. Indeed, if the developer's calculations are realised, the difference will be the total cost of putting up the building. As time passes, the site value may rise or fall. It will rise if there is an increased demand for land in the area, or if economic changes make possible a more profitable form of development. A legal prohibition on more profitable forms of development (such as a prohibition of office development in a residential area) will hold down site values but, if this prohibition is relaxed they will rise sharply. On the other hand, site values in unattractive old urban areas can drop sharply, as some East Coast American cities demonstrate.

In Fig. 3 the site value (SV) is shown as horizontal. If the cost of demolition is added to the building value, we obtain the line BV + D; the point at which SV crosses BV + D indicates the time (X) when it becomes profitable to redevelop. This diagram is purely expository, and the slopes of the curves are not meant to be realistic. It is quite possible, for example, for building value to remain constant (i.e. BV is horizontal or even rising) while SV rises and crosses it. But whatever the slope of the curves, when SV exceeds BV + D, redevelopment becomes profitable.

Moreover, these curves are better thought of as bands: thus there is not one precise point in time when redevelopment becomes profitable, but rather a period of time. Redevelopment may be delayed because of planning decisions or – more important in Britain – uncertainties about planning decisions. The social character of a neighbourhood is also important. As Professor Bourne's study of Toronto indicates, re-sidential redevelopment, or office development, will rarely take place in the middle of a depressed, low income area, if more attractive opportunities are available.[1] On the other hand, some higher income areas may organise effective resistance to redevelopment. The con-struction of underground railways and motorways has a marked effect. Thus areas can be thought of as having differing 'potentials' for redevelopment. A few areas will attract redevelopment, which seems to have a 'snowball' effect; only when the potential of one area has been exhausted will attention turn to other areas. Changes in land require-ments also play a role. Apartments require less land than houses, and will be built in central areas if the conditions are right. But warehousing and large-scale manufacturing needs more land than previously, and has tended to move out to the suburbs. One aspect of this Toronto study which strikes anyone writing with British cities in mind is that extensive housing redevelopment has been undertaken privately. Professor Bourne advocates some renewal by public bodies but assumes that most renewal will be private. 'The real choice for cities is not between public renewal and that generated by the private market but between scattered, uncoordinated replacement of buildings and planned, programmed renewal.' This implies a very different situation from that prevailing in British 'central cities' and brings out the point that the British situation is the outcome of the policies that have been pursued, not a law of nature.

REDEVELOPMENT OR RENOVATION

Subsidy systems can have a marked effect on the type of redevelopment or modernisation that occurs. In recent years British local authorities have redeveloped a great deal of old housing when the renovation of old houses would have been more economic. They did this mainly because the subsidy system (and the valuation rules under compulsory purchase) favoured redevelopment as compared with renovation. There has recently been a swing (in all countries) in favour of renovation as against redevelopment. Even in 1978, however, it was doubtful whether the bias of the British subsidy system in favour of redevelopment had been ended.

The life of a modernised building may well be less than that of a new one, but even a delay of ten or fifteen years can be of considerable economic benefit. If the modernised building has a life of *n* years, modernisation will be more profitable than rebuilding if the cost of modernisation (m) *plus* the present value (pv) of the cost of rebuilding in *n* years times is less than the present cost of rebuilding (r). Assume that the interest rate in eight per cent, and that the modernised building will have to be rebuilt in 15 years. The present value of £1 in 15 years at eight per cent can be looked up in the tables; it is 0.315242. Thus the condition for profitable modernisation is:

$$m + 0.32r = r$$
$$\text{i.e. } m = 0.68r$$

Modernisation will thus be more profitable than rebuilding if the cost is less than sixty eight per cent of the cost of rebuilding. We have, however, ignored inflation by assuming that the cost of rebuilding in the future will be the same as now. If the cost of building rises, this will reduce the advantages of modernisation; this can be taken into account by reducing the rate of interest. If we assume that building costs rise at three per cent, this has the effect of reducing the effective interest rate from eight per cent to five per cent. Or if building costs rise by ten per cent, but the nominal interest rate is thirteen per cent, this would give an effective rate of three per cent. Even at five per cent or three per cent, the 'permissible' cost of modernisation can still be surprisingly high, as can be seen from Table 5.

This calculation assumes that there is no limit on the amount of money the developer can borrow; a 'capital constraint' favours modernisation still more.

TABLE 5. *The Maximum Permissible Cost of Modernisation*
(as a Percentage of the Cost of Rebuilding)

$(1 - \text{Present Value of } 1) \times 100$

Life of the modernised	Rate of interest		
building in years	3%	5%	8%
10	26%	46%	54%
15	36%	58%	68%
20	45%	67%	79%
25	52%	74%	85%

Except where it is part of a subsidised 'urban renewal' scheme, the redevelopment of old housing areas is often profitable only for commercial uses or high-income housing. The more common choice for older, but still structurally sound, housing is between various grades of renovation, and doing nothing. The condition for profitable renovation is that the difference between the capital value of the building in its unrenovated and renovated form exceeds the cost of renovation. This difference is again the 'development value' which provides the financial justification for the investment. If the building is let, the 'unrenovated' and 'renovated' values will depend on the rents obtainable in either case.

When no kind of renovation is profitable (or considered to be profitable), the building will steadily decline in value and may eventually become derelict: there are plenty of examples of this in rent-controlled property in Britain or in the 'ghettos' of the older American cities where tenants are unable, or unwilling, to pay for anything other than the poorest accommodation. But there are also examples in both countries of older districts which, after a period of decline have attracted renovation (usually by owner-occupiers) and have 'come up' as residential areas. This process has often taken place without any public intervention: it can, however, be accelerated by subsidies. The introduction of improvement grants in Britain in 1972 soon led to a sharp increase in renovation by professional contractors, and this 'production' of houses of a modern standard for a time exceeded the production of new houses. This process of private renovation can play a crucial role in the revitalisation of old areas, but it sometimes arouses opposition. In the British case, this opposition was based on the criticism that people were making money out of renovation, which does not necessarily mean that it was socially harmful. In response to these criticisms, limitations were imposed on the period within which a grant-aided dwelling could be sold. There is, however, a more basic criticism, which applies just as much to owner-occupiers. This is that a process of renovation tends to price out the original low-income inhabitants of a district. This criticism raises the questions of 'the usefulness of the slum' discussed below.

DEVELOPMENT VALUE

When the value of the building, plus the cost of demolition, falls below site value, the difference constitutes 'development value'. This means that the building will command a higher price if sold in order to be pulled down than if sold to be kept in its existing state.

Development value has in the past arisen when there was no state control of development. It is not the product of planning permission, which merely *allows* a development value to be realised. However, when development requires permission, this has implications for development value. A property with potential development value will be sold either with planning permission to re-develop, or without it; in the former case, the buyer will value the property on the basis of the site value; in the latter case, he will value it on the basis of its existing use (plus perhaps some 'hope value' based on the expectation of possible eventual development value). But a market price is not divided up into two sums, one for the existing building and one for development value. Whether it contains an element of development value, and if so how much, is uncertain, and the smaller the probable amount of development value, the larger the margin of error. If a multiple store pays £30,000 for a dilapidated Victorian house in a shopping street, which elsewhere would fetch perhaps £10,000, it is obvious that the price must contain a large proportion of development value. But if a large house with grounds in a 'green belt' area sells for £30,000, it is virtually impossible to say whether this contains a thousand or two of 'hope value' regarding some eventual future development. In practice, therefore, development value – being a difference between two other figures, one of which is hypothetical – is subject to considerable haziness.

'Development value' is partly economic rent. It is the difference between the capitalised value of earnings in two alternative uses. But a proportion of development value is not economic rent; it is the necessary reward for the risk and trouble of undertaking development. A developer has to invest a considerable sum of money, with no certainty that he will get the money back (except in abnormal conditions of scarcity such as prevailed after the War). He often has to engage in long-drawn-out legal wrangles in land acquisition, which may involve the acquisition of tens or even hundreds of separate interests. Thus a part of development value is often the reward for vision, taking risks and perseverance, rather than a windfall gain. In other cases, it can be a payment for inconvenience; a householder may be prepared to sell land at the bottom of his garden for building only if he obtains a sum sufficient to compensate him for the loss of his view.

THE ECONOMICS OF DENSITY

In addition to deciding on the type of use, a developer has to decide on the density, i.e. the amount of investment applied to a given site. There are two influences acting on a developer; (a) economic calculations, and (b) density controls by local authorities. Les us consider both.

The density chosen by a developer depends partly on life-styles (the 'urban' and quite high-density terraces of Georgian London were laid out in open fields). But it also depends on the scarcity, and price, of land and on the changes in construction cost as density increases. Increased density means, after a certain point, building higher; with increasing height, costs rise sharply because higher buildings require stronger construction and foundations. As more and more capital is applied to a fixed area of land, the marginal return (which can be thought of as the return on the top storey) declines. If we draw a diagram with percentage rate of return on the vertical axis, the average rate of return AR (total receipts *minus* total expenditure, divided by the number of storeys) will slope downwards to the right, while the marginal return MR (i.e. the return on the cost of the top storey) will drop more steeply (Fig. 4). Given the interest rate at which the developer can obtain capital (x), the intersection with the MR curve will determine the most profitable number of storeys (y).

The *average* return, however, will be higher than the marginal return. The difference (assuming that a 'normal' developer's profit has been included in the costs) will be excess profit or 'economic rent'. Assuming that there is competition between developers, the developer will have to offer this amount in rent to the ground landlord (the shaded area). But the curves are based on a given technology and a given level of costs and rack rents; they will shift if there are changes in these conditions.

We have so far assumed that greater density means building higher. This has in fact been the tendency in European cities since the Second World War, because steelframe construction has made it possible to

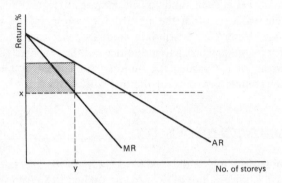

Fɪɢ. 4. Returns with Increasing Height

build higher. But – as is apparent from aerial views of tower blocks – they have an enormous amount of space between them. The preference for tall, narrow blocks has been largely an architectural fashion; the costs of building are high, and the well-being of flat dwellers and office workers has, until recently, received little consideration. It is possible to build housing at moderate densisties without putting everyone in 'sky flats'. It is also possible to build offices, hospitals, etc. of a deep and low, rather than tall and narrow, variety. This may mean reducing the amount of daylight and relying more on artificial lighting and ventilation. But this does not necessarily mean that this approach provides a bad environment. If not pushed to extremes, it may well provide a better environment than the typical tower block of the 1960s with its glare, temperature variation, draughts and noise.[2]

We have so far discussed the return on capital as it is applied to a fixed area of land. A different way of looking at the problem is to consider the change in costs (per sq. ft. of floor space) as the height of the building rises, assuming that the developer is not confined to a given area of land. In this case, the price of land can be taken as given; it becomes a cost like other inputs, and the developer has to decide how much of it to use.

If we think in terms of costs per dwelling at various densities, we can draw curves like those shown in a simplified form in Fig. 5. (In practice, constructions costs do not rise steadily, but in 'steps'). As density rises land costs per dwelling fall; on the other hand, construction costs rise. Total average costs will be the sum of the two. Thus the curve of total cost per dwelling will be 'U' shaped. If we assume that the price at which the builder can sell or let the dwellings is fixed by competition, the builder will normally maximise his profits by producing dwellings at the lowest total cost per unit (x). But if consumers are prepared to pay more for this type of housing, it may be profitable to build at a lower density.

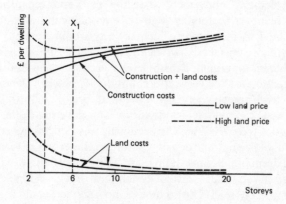

FIG. 5. Land and Construction Costs per Dwelling

When land prices are low, the point of lowest average costs will be at a lower density than when they are high. In this sense, land prices influence the density of building. More fundamentally, however, it is the demand for buildings that determines rents (or sale prices), and hence both the intensity of building and land values. The developer who is faced with high land values, and therefore builds high, will do so only if he believes that he can obtain rents that will cover the costs both of construction and land.

These points are illustrated in a study using data for 1966–7.[3] Land prices per acre varied from £42,685 for land used for low-rise flats in London to a mere £2296 for houses in Wales. Density varied in a broadly similar way; London had 91 persons per acre in low-rise flats and 76 in houses, giving average land costs per person of £363 and £470. In other parts of the country the density in houses ranged from 47 to 60. Land costs, as a proportion of total costs, ranged from around 10 per cent in the cheaper areas to 25 per cent in London. (This ratio rose sharply in 1973, but by 1977 it had fallen back to the 1966 level.)

DENSITY CONTROLS

There is a notable lack of criteria for the residential density limits imposed by local authorities, and the present situation can only be explained historically. The idea of setting *maximum* densities arose as a reaction to the high densities of the Victorian city; it was argued by the early 'garden-city' movement that the market mechanism led to densities being unacceptably high on environmental grounds. Their ideas pointed to the way in which the city would develop, but they tended to ignore the fact that *given the prevailing technology and the level of urbanisation* quite high densities were necessary and desirable.

The situation looked very different in the 1930s when the motor car, together with unprecedentedly low land prices, led to suburban development at extremely low densities. This gave rise to the criticism that densities were *too low*. The argument was now the reverse of the previous one. The optimal density for the developer was allegedly below the social optimum, because it involved a disproportionate expenditure on roads, sewers, etc., wasted agricultural land, and made public transport uneconomic. (The argument about services could presumably be met by a more commercial pricing policy). However, 'American' densities (three to four houses per acre) were confined to the early 1930s. As land prices rose (and life-styles changed e.g. fewer paid gardeners) private development settled down to slightly higher densities (around 10 houses per acre).

Prevailing planning attitudes have varied considerably, both over time and from one local authority to another. In the 1950s 'garden city' densities were in fashion, enforced by *maximum* densities; even in the 1960s new moderate-density layouts – terraces, Raeburn and similar traffic-free layouts, a mix of flats and houses etc. – were often stopped by local authorities on density grounds. On the other hand, the 1960s also saw a fashion for high-rise and high-density. In Britain, this international fashion had little influence in the private market but it was widely implemented in council housing. There has since been a reaction against this type of construction.

There has recently been a tendency to set *minimum* as well as maximum levels. The Greater London Development Plan laid down a range of 70 to 140 habitable rooms per acre.[4] The Layfield Committee sought to discover the *rationale* of this range; as with many other figures in the plan, the GLC witnesses were unable to give any.[5] The Committee itself recommended a range of 70 to 100 but pointed out that higher or lower densities could be justified in special cases; e.g. higher around a transport 'node' or lower to preserve a wooded area. Other information is of a more anecdotal kind. There is, however, evidence that some local planning authorities have opposed 'mixed' development, with 'studio' and 'one bedroom' flats as well as three- or four-bedroom houses. It is clear from the changing composition of household sizes and market reports that more 'small dwellings' are needed. The arguments put forward for opposing this trend are that this type of development will become the 'slums of the future', or that the slightly higher densities allow developers to make more money.[6] On the first point, experience in other countries gives no support to the view that a range of sizes encourages slum formation – rather the reverse. On the second point, it needs to be stressed that adjusting output to a more profitable mix, because of changing demand, is socially *desirable*.

What conclusions, if any, can be drawn regarding policy on density controls? It seems clear that prevailing limits usually lack an objective economic rationale; they may or may not be reasonable. But it is possible to say that certain policies are inconsistent – e.g. a restrictive policy on zoning for development is inconsistent with maximum density controls, or attempts to hold land prices *down*. If there are 'external' reasons for trying to bring about higher densities, land prices should be *raised*.

Since there have been cycles of land prices, and hence density, a theoretical case can be made for planning authorities undertaking long-term 'smoothing', e.g. holding densities down before 1914, holding them up in the 1930s. However, this assumes that the planning authority is better placed than the developer or his client to judge the future course of personal preferences and land prices. The post-war swings in planning views on density hardly encourage this assumption. It is, in any case, extremely difficult to make predictions of this sort. Are current densities too high or too low, in the light of likely changes over the next, say, 50 years? The author, at least, is unable to discover any objective basis for such a judgement.

Even more questionable than general limits are discretionary decisions on density and design, which sometimes – e.g. on layouts with a substantial proportion of 'small dwellings' – appear to be based on design prejudices or anti-developer feeling. Various policies would encourage a more satisfactory type of planning. Local authorities could be given less scope for discretionary decisions. Efforts could be made to give planning officials a better understanding of the housing market – by more dialogue between planners and developers, and perhaps changes in planning education. There could be encouragement for 'non-profit' development agencies. Moves in this direction would bring Britain more into line with most other countries.

THE BAD ECONOMICS OF TOWER BLOCKS

The analysis represented in Fig. 4 can be used to answer the (recently) topical question: are residential blocks of 20 and 30 storeys economic? Are they, as has often been asserted, the result of high land prices? The number of storeys which gives the lowest average total cost is that at which the increase in the average construction cost per dwelling is numerically equal to the fall in average land costs. It is thus possible to calculate the land price which would be necessary to justify a certain height of building.

TABLE 6. The cost of land saved by building high

	1964
	£ per acre
4 storeys instead of 2	21500
10 storeys instead of 4	44400
15 storeys instead of 10	46700

Note: 4 bed space dwellings, England and Wales excluding London
Source: P. A. Stone, *Urban Development in Britain*, p. 157.

A comparison of the extra construction costs of building high with the consequent saving of land has been made by Dr P. A. Stone, by expressing the extra costs in terms of pounds per acre of land saved. If this figure is well above the current prevailing land price, there is a *prima facie* case for saying that the higher building is uneconomic, in 'private' terms. Using 1964 data, the value of land saved by building at four storeys instead of two was £21,000 per acre; building at ten storeys instead of four gave a figure of £44,000 per acre. Land prices of over £20,000 per acre were unknown at the time except in central business districts. Thus the very high blocks of flats built by local authorities were not justified by market prices at that time (not to mention the much lower agricultural value of land). Updated British estimates substantiate this conclusion. Figures from other countries, although indicating a higher minimum point on the 'U curve', point in the same direction: German figures indicate that the minimum cost point in 1975 was six to eight storeys. The evidence clearly supports Dr. Stone's conclusion that 'building high is an extravagent way of saving land'.

However, this 'cost' approach needs to be modified by 'market' considerations, i.e. what consumers are in fact prepared to pay. On the one hand, families with children are prepared to pay more for houses as opposed to flats. On the other hand, experience in countries such as the USA and Canada where there are well equipped blocks of private flats (often with swimming pools and other facilities) indicates that the childless families who choose this type of housing often prefer the *higher* storeys to the lower ones.

We can therefore conclude that, given the construction costs and land prices prevailing since the 1950s in Western Europe and North America, a combination of houses and medium-rise flats has been the optimal 'market' output in all but exceptional cases. The high-rise blocks built by British councils were uneconomic from the point of view of minimising construction and land costs and unsatisfactory from an environmental point of view. High densities have been justified on the ground that a compact layout reduces transport costs, or makes a public transport system feasible. This is a factor on the other side, although whether it justifies very high densities is questionable. Perhaps the main lesson of this episode is the hazards of a system from which the market has been eliminated.

SUMMARY

Buildings wear out, or become obsolete with the passing of time, and redevelopment or extensive renovation become necessary. When the value of a building falls below the value of the site, it pays to redevelop. *Development value* is the profit from development.

Whether development or renovation occurs depends to a large extent on factors external to the site. Sometimes redevelopment occurs readily, in other cases an area experiences a cumulative process of decline in which redevelopment is unlikely to take place unless it is subsidised. In the case of housing, renovation (as distinct from redevelopment) often has economic, as well as environmental advantages. Whether housing is redeveloped or renovated depends to a large extent on subsidy sytems. The subsidy system in Britain since the War has strongly favoured council redevelopment as against renovation. Housing renovation has been shown to be very responsive to subsidisation.

Land values are related to density but, in the aggregate, it is the price of buildings – reflecting demand – which determines land values, and not *vice versa*. Very high residential buildings are expensive to construct, and are economic only in exceptional cases. Residential building densities are subject to controls by local authorities but their economic *rationale* is far from clear.

SELECT BIBLIOGRAPHY

P. A. Stone, *Urban Development in Britain*, Cambridge University Press, 1970.

REFERENCES

1. L. S. Bourne, *Private Redevelopment of the Central City*, University of Chicago Press, 1967.
2. The defects of British post-War buildings are beginning to be appreciated by hard-headed developers since post-War offices have been extremely costly to heat and maintain. Clients are beginning to lay more emphasis on the future costs of maintenance, so as to minimise long-run, rather than merely initial, costs. For public buildings, the need is for 'negative feedback'.
3. National Building Agency, *Land Costs and Housing Development*, 1968.
4. Density can be measured in various ways e.g. the floor area/site ratio or 'bed-spaces per acre', which is usually regarded as the best indicator of persons per acre. The Layfield Committee assumed that the number of habitable rooms and persons was roughly equal, which is surprising, since the average number of persons per room is around 0.6.
5. Greater London Development Plan, *Report of the Panel of Inquiry* (Layfield), Vol. 1, p. 2044ff.
6. CALUS, Reading University, *The Market for Small Homes in the Reading Area* 1977.

5 Booms, Slumps and Trends

But the course of land value seems to 'crook and turn upon itself in many a backward streaming curve'

F. Y. Edgeworth *Papers relating to Political Economy* Vol. II 1925
p. 197 (written in 1905)

One of the recent failings in the analysis of urban economic problems has been an excessively short-term outlook. As in all other types of economic activity, there are cyclical movements, in the supply, demand and price of urban land and buildings. Politicians and journalists, and even economists from J. S. Mill onwards, have regularly extrapolated recent cyclical movements indefinitely into the future, and based policy prescriptions on this prognosis. The few available studies of long-term movements – of land prices, rents, housing supply, etc. – have usually been undertaken by chartered surveyors and geographers, rather than economists, and have remained largely unknown. Let us summarise some of the evidence available.

TABLE 7. Persons per Room

	1911	1931	1961	1971
Great Britain	1.10	0.83	0.66	0.6
West Germany	1.00	0.90	0.83	0.66

Source: Censuses

Although it is difficult to isolate the effects of price and income on the demand for housing, or even to measure 'price' in conditions of inflation, it is clear from long-term series of housing statistics in developed countries that there has been a clear upward trend in the amount of housing available per head (Table 7). The common complaint of many writers that we are able to afford less and less housing does not tally with the long-run statistical evidence. Some houses are smaller than they were, partly because of a more egalitarian distribution of income, and there can be fluctuations around the long-term trend, but the pattern of a secular rise in *average* space per head (as well as in appliances like central heating which increase the usability of space) is universal.

LONG-TERM PRICE MOVEMENTS FOR LAND

This increase in the *per capita* consumption of housing, together with population increases (until recently) and increases in other types of urban land use, have meant that the demand curve for land has shifted to the right over time, although more rapidly at some times than others. In fairly densely populated countries like the UK, one might expect a long-term upward trend in land prices in real terms. Rather surprisingly, the

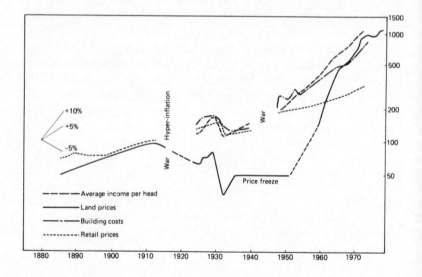

Fɪɢ. 6. Land prices, incomes, building costs and retail prices
Germany 1885–1977
(1913 = 100)

Source: City of Cologne

available figures do not indicate such a trend. Although the data is fragmentary, there are three distinct sources; checked against each other, they provide a reasonable indication of what has happened.

(a) Official or unofficial figures of average land prices, deflated by incomes, construction costs or retail prices.
(b) The proportion of site costs in the total costs of new housing.
(c) Estimates of the share of 'pure' land rent in national income.

The price figures for Germany and the UK show large fluctuations, but no clear upward trend since the turn of the century in relation to construction costs or incomes (Figs. 6, 7). In all three countries, there was a rise in the latter part of the 19th century followed by a fall, which was continued after the First World War to unprecedently low levels in the 1930s.

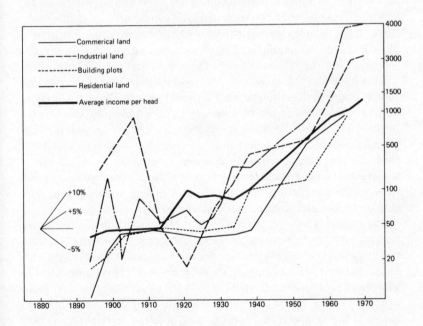

FIG. 7. Land Prices, England 1880–1969
(1910–16 = 100)

Source: Vallis *op.cit.*

TABLE 8. Price of Building Plots in Relation to
National Income Per Capita. England. 1892–1969.
(1958–69 = 100)

1892–95	1910–16	1931–35	1958–69
62	125	70	100

Source: Based on E. A. Vallis, 'Urban Land and Building
Prices', *Estate Gazette*, May–June 1972.

There has generally been a rise since the War but a decline since about
1973. In Germany, land prices are lower today than in 1914 in relation to
incomes and construction costs, although not retail prices. In England
(*sic*) the figures produced by Mr. Vallis for the 1890s to the late 1960s
suggest a somewhat similar pattern, although with differences between
different categories. Industrial land shows the largest fluctuations; the
level just after the turn of the century was higher in relation to income
than it has ever been since. Both commercial land and building plots fell
behind income between the Wars and later caught up. In the late 1960s,
however, both types were slightly lower in relation to income than in
1914. Prices of 'residential land', i.e. 'raw' building land, rose faster than
incomes after the 1930s, although the late 1960s saw a flattening-off.

This historical series ends in 1969, and excludes the sharp rise that
shortly followed. But this rise was followed by an equally sharp fall (Fig.
8). The whole episode can now be seen as an inflationary 'hiccup': the
boom of 1972–3 was not the start (or continuation) of a long-term trend,
as most commentators asserted at the time. Between 1967 and 1976,
land prices remained virtually constant in relation to house prices,
construction costs and average earnings – although they rose in relation
to retail prices. During this period, land prices, houses prices, construction costs and average earnings all trebled.

The second type of 'land price' data is the proportion of site costs in
the total cost of new housing. In the UK, since the beginning of the 20th
century, the figure appears to have fluctuated between about 15 per cent
and 25 per cent, with a norm of about 20 per cent. (This figure refers to
sites ready for building, divided up and with all services, which amount
to around half of the final cost). The data for Germany, which refers to
blocks of flats, suggest that the proportion in recent years has been lower
than before 1914. In German 'social housing' the cost of land (excluding
infrastructure) has remained fairly constant since the early 1960s, at 6 to
8 per cent of total costs.[1]

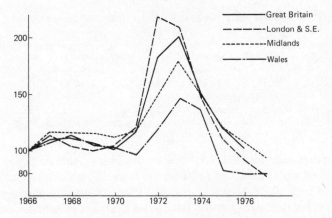

Fig. 8. Land prices in real terms 1966–77. Great Britain
House plot prices ÷ average earnings
1966–1977 (1966 = 100)

Source: Nationwide Building Society

TABLE 9. Land and house prices 1967–76
England and Wales 1967 = 100

	Land prices	House prices	Construction costs (a)	Average earnings
1967	100	100	100	100
1971	175	139	134	146
1972	287	186	162	165
1973	458	249	224	186
1974	449	262	258	220
1975	318	287	283	278
1976	315	311	301	321

(a) tender costs for local authority housing.
Source: Housing Policy: a Consultative Document, Cmnd. 6851 p. 148

The third approach is to estimate the value of 'pure' land rent in relation to national income. One study for the USA indicated that the value of non-agricultural land as a percentage of national income (i.e. a comparison of capital value with annual income) fell from 63 per cent in 1900 to 37.7 per cent in 1958.[2] A similar study for the UK suggested that the value of residential land as a percentage of national income rose from 40 per cent in 1845 to 100 in 1893, fell to 60 in 1931 and rose again to 121 in 1964.[3]

TABLE 10. Site value*as a percentage of the total cost of new houses. UK. 1901–1976.

1901–16	1931–35	1968	1971	1972	1974	1976
c.20	c.15	21.2	23.9	29.2	24.3	20.3

* With roads, sewers and all services.
Source: Vallis, *op. cit.*, and Nationwide Building Society, *Occasional Bulletins*

Another study for the USA, based on the annual 'pure' rent of all land (including agricultural), indicated a fall from 7.7 per cent of national income in 1850 to 6.4 per cent in 1956.[4] There are no current figures for the UK, but the factor income 'rent' was 4.4 per cent of national income in 1976. This is gross rent (including an imputed rent for owner-occupiers) of land *and buildings*; on this basis, the rent of the land itself can hardly be more than 2 per cent of national income, less than the annual yearly rise in real income since the War. It seems clear that there has so far been no long-term upward trend in land prices in relation to national income, and that 'pure' rent is a very small proportion of national income.

The ups-and-downs of land prices can to a large extent be explained in terms of the 'jerkiness' of demand and the lagged response of supply. If population increases in an urban area which is more or less limited, the result will be a rise in land rent and density. This was the experience during 19th century urbanisation, when most people had to walk to work. If the development of new forms of transport then enables large numbers of people, and employment, to decentralise, there will be a fall in land rent and density. As Dr. Colin Clark puts it:

It was the arrival of the electrically driven tramcar in the 1890's which began to chisel apart the compact Victorian city, reducing population densities, and at the same time reducing relative land values.[5]

This downward trend was aggravated by the depression of the 1930s, leading to exceptionally low prices, which then recovered after the War.

THE PROPERTY BOOM AND SLUMP OF 1972–4

Within these broad trends there have been smaller fluctuations, reflecting booms and slumps in the building industry and in the economy as a whole, sometimes aggravated by ill-judged speculation. A striking example occurred in the period 1972–4 which saw a world-wide boom and slump in the economy as a whole, reflected in an even more acute cycle in the property market. In spite of differences between countries, the broad trends were remarkably similar: the report by the 'five wise men' of the OECD noted that:

> It was the excessive rate of monetary expansion which accounted for the speculative features of the subsequent boom. The price of real estate, gold and other traditional havens of nervous capital in inflationary times soared. . . . . .[6]

In all countries in 1972–3, there was a sharp rise in demand, and an increase in the construction of both housing and commercial property. In countries with a functioning market in rented housing – such as West Germany, the USA and Canada – there was an increase in the construction of flats for rent as well as for sale. In Britain – where even retaining the ownership of rented housing had been made uneconomic by 'fair rents' – there was a reverse effect. Inflationary expectations and easy credit (with the Building Societies sharing in the general liquidity glut) made sitting tenants more willing to buy, so that the stock of private rented housing contracted. Thus, in Britain, the boom was confined mainly to offices and housing for sale. Figure 9(a) shows how property yields fell sharply in 1972–3 (to 4 per cent for offices) as capital values were bid up to unrealistic levels. But in the second half of 1973, bank rate rose from seven to thirteen per cent, and the boom collapsed. Figure 9(c) shows how land prices, and office rents, rose faster than national income, and then fell. Over the period 1971–6, there was little change in land prices in real terms, while office rents fell. Property companies' shares moved even more volatilely.

The boom was brought to an end primarily by self-correcting mechanisms within the property sector itself, reinforced by the general swing from boom to slump. The boom occurred at a time when shortages in most types of property were being ended; the spurt in supply, quickly followed by a fall in demand resulting from the recession, pushed the market across the narrow line which separates too little from too much. Since the boom was based on inflationary expectations, it collapsed when it became clear that investment in bricks and mortar was not an El Dorado. Thus in many countries the property boom was over by the time the Government introduced general stabilising measures, and often took measures against 'speculation'.

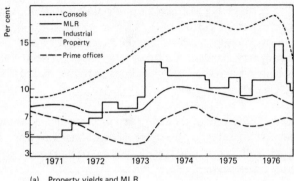

(a)   Property yields and MLR

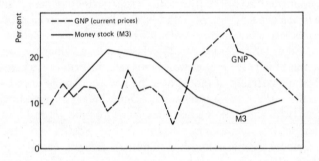

(b)   Annual changes in money stock and national income

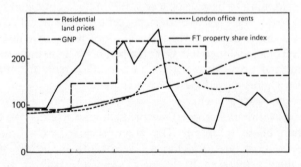

(c)   Property shares, land prices, office rent and national income (1971 = 100)

Fig. 9. The Property Boom and Slump. Great Britain

Developers found themselves squeezed, on the one hand by rents and sale prices which flattened off and sometimes fell; on the other hand by sharp rises in interest rates and construction costs. The effects were particularly marked for the British 'property companies' discussed below. But all firms in the industry suffered, and some went into liquidation. The British property companies found themselves facing not only massive falls in the capital value of their holdings, and losses on current developments, but also a series of penal taxes introduced by the Conservative Government in 1973 and a rent freeze for shops and offices. The effect was virtually to put a stop to commercial development for four years, and force some firms into bankruptcy. Many others were saved only by a 'lifeboat operation' launched by the Bank of England, and by the abandonment, by the Labour Government, of the rent freeze. Although the Labour Government might have borne the bankruptcy of the property companies with fortitude, a crash of 1929 proportions, with widespread repercussions, would have been unwelcome. There was also a shake-out among the secondary banks; many sponsors of 'mushroom' finance houses became wiser and poorer men – although they rarely went as far as the MP-financier who staged his 'drowning' on Miami Beach.

By 1977, there were signs of recovery from the slump, and a restoration of more stable conditions. The whole cycle can now be seen in better perspective. The basic cause was the heavy-footed use of accelerator and brake in general economic policy. However, the general inflationary boom triggered off a speculative boom which was bound soon to collapse; when it did, the main sufferers were the speculators themselves. In some ways, the property boom and slump was similar to property booms in the century before 1914; some knowledge of the past would have enabled public figures to have made a more realistic assessment of the situation than they actually did.

It was widely argued in 1972–3 that, in a market economy, excessive profits would always be made by property companies, and that the amount and type of property produced had nothing to do with consumer demand; it was even profitable to build offices and shops to stand empty. The argument was that, since property values steadily rose by more than the cost of borrowing money, an empty office block would be used as security for a loan to build another office, and so on *ad infinitum*. Other writers suggested that rack rents depended on capital value, not *vice versa*, so that if capital values were raised by speculation, rack rents would have to be raised correspondingly. These theories do not explain the subsequent slump, and would seem in retrospect (like the similar predictions about land prices) to have been based in part on a not unusual tendency for commentators to extrapolate the events of the last six months indefinitely into the future.

The most harmful effect of the property boom was when it produced hasty and ill-considered legislation. This applied particularly to Britain, which differs from most Western countries in that far-reaching economic legislation can be drafted and implemented in months rather than years. Few students of the question would deny that the Development Gains Tax, the Development Land Tax, the First Letting Tax, the Community Land Act, the rates surcharge on empty offices (and the proposed Land Hoarding Tax which would probably have been implemented if it had been proposed a few months earlier) were too hastily drafted, and proved in practice to be unsatisfactory (some of them were, in fact, repealed after a few years).

'STABILISING' THE BUILDING SOCIETIES

A similar objection can be made to government policy towards the building societies. During the boom the building societies were widely blamed for the rise in house prices. One influential article charted the rises in house prices and in building society advances between 1960 and 1972, and obtained an apparently good fit – especially for the upsurge of 1971–2.[7] Accepting this type of explanation, several political spokesmen (in all parties) concluded that the flow of funds through the building societies should be controlled and stabilised by the Government. Such a policy was, in a sense, adopted when the Conservative Government, after unavailingly having tried to persuade the building societies not to raise their rates in response to the general rise in interest rates in the autumn of 1973, offered the societies a large loan, on condition that interest rates were not raised any more. The Building Societies Association accepted this offer, which ushered in the era of 'cooperation' between the societies and the Government.

In the General Election of the autumn of 1974, the Conservative Opposition promised to bring down the mortgage rate from 11 to 9.5 per cent by Christmas, but was not called on to implement this promise. The 1974 Labour Government apparently accepted the policy of 'stabilisation' advocated by the late Mr. Anthony Crosland. A committee representing the Government and the building societies became well established, and the societies agreed in effect that they would follow Government directives. With signs of recovery in early 1978, the Government became alarmed at a prospective rise in house prices of perhaps 15 per cent – in a possible election year – and instructed the societies to restrict their lending in order to hold down the rise in house prices, the stated aim being to hold down the rise in 1978 to the level of the rise in retail prices.

This particular intervention was criticised by the housebuilders and (privately) by the building societies as misguided – for reasons discussed below. But both the analysis of the 1972–3 boom in house prices as the result of an increase in building society advances and the whole 'stabilisation' approach is open to question. The parallel movement of economic variables cannot *ipso facto* be taken to indicate a causal relationship: A may move in the same direction as B, but does A cause B, or B cause A, or are they both caused by C? The surge of funds into the building societies in 1972 was part of the exceptionally rapid expansion of the money supply. Moreover, it seems clear with the benefit of hindsight that the property boom of 1972 was aggravated by several other conditions – notably a fully employed building industry and a euphoric state of expectations in which buyers were prepared to pay (and lenders to lend) more than would normally have been regarded as prudent. These external factors acted to increase both available funds *and* the demand for them. This is not necessarily to deny that the building societies might well have exercised a little more old-fashioned banking caution – merely that it is taking a blinkered view to regard them as a prime cause of the boom.

Moreover, even though an abstract case can be made for stabilising the flow of advances, experience in other fields (notably agricultural price 'stabilisation') indicates that it is difficult for governments to decide on the level of prices which can be seen in retrospect to have been correct, since they are under sectional and electoral pressures to take a short-term view. These pressures have been to hold both mortgage rates and house prices *down*. But such policies can reduce supply. If house prices do not yield a 'normal profit' on new construction, few houses will be built. The recovery of prices in early 1978 was from an exceptionally depressed level – in relation to costs – which had led to widespread bankruptcies and a sharp fall in housing starts. After four years in which house prices had risen *less* than building costs, it was necessary that they should rise *more* in order to make new construction profitable (Fig. 10). In any event, a change in the financial climate in mid-1978 led to a fall in building society receipts, and the government restrictions became a dead letter. The emphasis of Government thinking changed from advances to rates. Should a rise in mortgage rates be resisted in the run-up to an election, or would it be better to get the rise out of the way well before an election? The experience of government intervention in the building societies' operational decisions between 1973 and 1978 reinforces

Fɪɢ. 10. House Prices and Construction Costs in Real Terms. Great Britain 1966–1977. Average new house prices and construction costs ÷ average earnings (1966 = 100)

Source: Housing & Construction Statistics

theoretical doubts about the practical consequences of a 'stabilisation' policy.

This does not mean that the large fluctuations in mortgage rates which took them from $12\frac{1}{4}$ per cent at the start of 1977 to $8\frac{1}{2}$ per cent a year later were desirable. But these movements reflected general movements in interest rates, and any failure in policy was by the Government. Building societies cannot remain far out of step with the general movement of interest rates. Even if it were possible to isolate mortgage rates from general movements of interest rates through a large 'stabilisation fund' (operated by governments whose 'fine tuning' of the economy has not been notably successful in the past), this would increase the fluctuations in other types of investment. The demand for housing has been the first type of investment to respond to falls in interest rates.

The leaders of the building societies have, since 1973, taken the view that it was necessary to accede to all government requests in order to forestall even more direct government control of building society affairs. Whether this approach is likely to succeed seems doubtful. The building societies have become a large, somewhat cartelised, sector of the financial community which is free of the supervision exercised over other financial institutions, and some form of supervision or control in the future seems highly probable. If there is to be control, a system of general structural supervision by the Bank of England would seem, on recent experience, preferable to discretionary, informal interventions by Ministers. The prospects of developing such a system might have been increased if the societies had shown more spirit in resisting what they believed to be ill-considered interventions of this type.

SUMMARY

The available statistics on the long-term movement of land prices do not bear out the widespread belief that 'landowners make money, as it were, in their sleep' (J.S.Mill). Figures for Britain and other countries indicate that – in real terms – there have been large fluctuations, but no clear upward trend. Land prices – in relation to retail prices, building costs and incomes – rose in the 1880s and 1890s but fell sharply after the First World War; they then recovered after the Second World War. The sharp rise in 1972–3 was followed by an equally sharp fall, and can be seen in retrospect as a 'hiccup' caused primarily by inept macroeconomic policy. The allegedly large profits made by property companies in 1973 were, as the subsequent slump showed, primarily paper profits based on over-optimistic valuations.

Any generalisations about long-term price trends are difficult to make. In addition to unsatisfactory data, there are large fluctuations, as well as differences between sub-markets. Probably the most reasonable generalisation is that since both the beginning of the century and the early 1960s, land prices have risen slightly more than retail prices, less than incomes, and at about the same rate as building costs.

Although the property boom of 1972–3 quickly turned into a slump, it produced in Britain a legacy of hastily-drafted tax legislation and a questionable analysis which subsequently influenced government policy – notably on the municipalisation of development land and the 'stabilisation' of building society advances.

SELECT BIBLIOGRAPHY

J. Parry Lewis, *Building Cycles and Britain's Growth*, Macmillan 1965.
O. Marriott, *The Property Boom*, Hamish Hamilton, 1967
Towards Full Employment and Price Stability, O.E.C.D. Paris 1977.

REFERENCES

1. *Neue Heimat Jahresbericht* 1973/4, p. 43.
2. R. Goldsmith. *The National Wealth of the United States in the Post-War Period*, Princeton University Press. 1962. p. 118.
3. Colin Clark in P. Hall (ed.) *Land Values* 1966 p. 137.
4. J. S. Keiper. *The Theory and Measurement of Rent*, New York University, 1961.
5. Clark *op. cit.* p. 139.
6. *Towards Full Employment and Price Stability* O.E.C.D. Paris, 1977. p. 13.
7. Alex Henney, 'Reasons for Today's Housing Shortage' *The Times* March 28, 1973. The striking correlation indicated by a graph in this article is reduced if the more meaningful *percentage* changes in advances are used, and breaks down completely after 1972.

6 Urban Spatial Structure

A cursory glance reveals similarities among cities, and further
investigation demonstrates that their structural movements, complex
and irregular as they are, respond to definite principles,

Richard M. Hurd, *Principles of City Land Values*, 1903, p. 13.

A great deal of urban economics is not geographical; it is concerned with
the production and allocation of urban 'goods', such as housing,
without being primarily concerned with their location. But some of the
most acute problems of cities are concentrated in particular areas or are
linked with the location of residences and workplaces. A study of urban
spatial structure is therefore a necessary background to the examination
of certain aspects of public policy. This is a field which overlaps with
urban geography, and much of the best recent work has been done by
geographers, although the founding fathers of the subject were a
sociologist and two practising land valuers.

Detailed surveys of particular cities are of no more than local value
unless they can indicate certain general relationships which to some
extent apply to all cities, or at least all cities of certain type. In fact, the
similarities between cities are as striking as the differences. Cities vary
according to age and size, the prevailing level of income, the social
characteristics of their people, the policies of planners, and the accidents
of history. Nevertheless there are some broad similarities between cities
of similar size throughout the developed world, and between cities in
developing countries.

A good case can be made that the 'Adam Smith' of urban spatial
structure was a practising valuer, Richard M. Hurd, whose *Principles of
City Land Values* was published in 1903.[1] This short book, full of
fascinating early photographs, is far more than a manual for valuers. It
illustrates a few simple theories of urban change with practical
examples, and lays stress on a 'sector' approach.

Cities originate at their most convenient point of contact with the outer world and grow in the lines of least resistance or greatest attraction, or their resultants. . . . Growth in cities consists of movement away from the point of origin in all directions, except as topographically hindered, this movement being due both to aggregation at the edges and pressure from the centre. Central growth takes place both from the heart of the city and from each subcentre of attraction, and axial growth pushes into the outlaying territory by means of railroads, turnpikes and street railroads. (p. 14).

Professor Wendt expressed the opinion in 1956 that 'no more comprehensive analysis of the dynamics of city growth has appeared since his (Hurd's) work'.[2]

THE BURGESS MODEL

Better known than Hurd's work, and often regarded as the beginning of the modern work on the concept of the urban form, is a collection of essays published in 1925 by a group of Chicago sociologists, known as 'human ecologists' because they stressed the analogy of human and plant communities. The main essay is by E. W. Burgess, *The Growth of the City: An Introduction to a Research Project*.[3] The modesty of the title indicates that the original article was not as dogmatic as some subsequent expositions of, or attacks on, the 'concentric zone theory' might suggest. Burgess suggested that the layout of Chicago could be explained in terms of concentric zones:

Zone I: The Central Business District . . . The heart of this district is the downtown retail district with its department stores, its smart shops, its office buildings, its clubs, its banks, its hotels, its theatres, its museums, and its headquarters of economic, social, civic, and political life. Encircling this area of work and play is the less well-known Wholesale Business District with its 'market', its warehouses, and storage buildings.

Zone II: The Zone in Transition, . . . areas of residential deterioration caused by the encroaching of business and industry from Zone I . . . a Zone in Transition, with a factory district for its inner belt and an outer ring of retrogressing neighborhoods, of first-settlement immigrant colonies, of rooming-house districts, of homeless-men areas, of resorts of gambling, bootlegging, sexual vice, and of breeding-places of crime . . . As families and individuals prosper, they escape from this area into Zone III beyond, leaving behind as marooned a residium of the defeated, leaderless and helpless.

Zone III: The Zone of Independent Workingmen's Homes . . . largely constituted by neighborhoods of second immigrant settlement. Its residents are those who desire to live near but not too close to their work . . . While the father works in the factory, the son and daughter typically have jobs in the . . . (CBD), attend dance halls and motion pictures in the bright-light areas, and plan upon marriage to set up homes in Zone IV.

Zone IV: The Zone of Better Residences . . . in which the great middle-class of native-born Americans live, small business men, professional people, clerks and salesmen . . . In this zone men are outnumbered by women, independence in voting is frequent, newspapers and books have wide circulation, and women are elected to the state legislature.

Zone V: The Commuters' Zone . . . a ring of encircling small cities, towns and hamlets which . . . are also, in the main, dormitory suburbs . . . Thus the mother and the wife become the center of family life . . . The communities in this Commuters' Zone are probably the most highly segregated of any in the entire metropolitan area.[4]

The 'Burgess theory' is usually represented by his simplified diagram of five concentric zones for 'all rapidly growing industrial cities'. But the diagram he used for Chicago – with its 'Black belt', ' "Two-flat" area', 'Vice' and other intriguing entries – indicates a far more complex pattern, with marked 'sectoral' aspects (Fig. 11). Burgess made it clear that his diagram was merely expository and that the zones were in practice not circular or clear-cut. He merely suggested that there were zones of broadly different types arranged in a broadly concentric manner, and that this provided a useful frame-work for the study of urban land use. There is obviously some truth in the idea. Cities have in fact grown outwards from the centre: this leads to districts built at different times, and hence some characteristics are different for this reason alone.

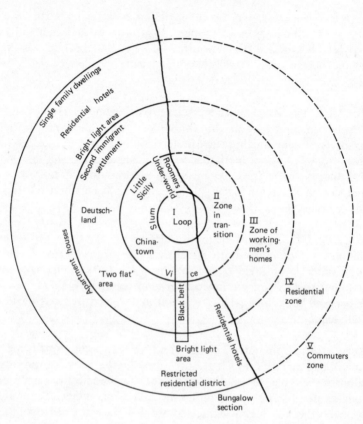

FIG. 11. The Concentric Zonal Pattern of Urban Residential Areas, as applied to Chicago

Source: Burgess, 1924.

THE HOYT MODEL

A somewhat different descriptive model was put forward by Mr. Homer Hoyt in 1939. This model was based on studies of a large number of American cities in connection with a Federal mortgage guarantee scheme[5] and his previous study of the Chicago real estate market over a hundred years.[6] In criticising the concentric zone theory, Hoyt concentrated on the way changes in transport were chiselling apart the closely-knit late 19th century city, still to some extent mirrored in the Burgess model. He pointed out that in both commercial, industrial and residential land use, the pattern bore little relation to one of circular zones. The CBD was not the only commercial centre in many large cities, and often extended in 'strips' along the main streets leading out of the centre. Heavy industry followed transport routes or waterfronts in long bands of growth. This was primarily the result of the growth of car and lorry transport, which severed the close ties between workplace and worker's residence and made suburban districts, with their more extensive and cheaper sites and easier access, more attractive locations for industry. In the case of residential use, there was no uniform change in rent or income as one moved outward from the centre. There were some high-rent, high-income apartment districts near the CBD, and

Such apartments can rise even in the midst of a poor area because the tall building itself, rising from humble surroundings like a feudal castle above the mud huts of the villeins, is a barrier against intrusion.

Similarly, in the commuters' zone,

some of these settlements are occupied by fine homes, but other towns may be middle class in character and others may consist of shacks. It is not true that one progresses from dilapidated dwellings at the center to an encircling belt of mansions on all points of the periphery of the city.

As far as 'fashionable residential districts' were concerned, Hoyt detected in most American cities a tendency for movement outward from the centre, but concentrated in one or more directions. Around the turn of the century, these districts were located near the centre but, for various historical reasons, in one particular direction from the centre. Over time these districts had tended to move outward; this sometimes led to a 'sector' looking on the diagram like a slice of a pie; in other cases the previously fashionable areas declined. Conversely there were low-income 'wedges' between the high-income ones.

Hoyt explained the outward growth of the high-rent sectors as being the direction of least resistance.

High rent or high grade residential neighbourhoods must almost necessarily move outward toward the periphery of the city. The wealthy seldom reverse their steps and move backward into the obsolete houses which they are giving up. On each side of them is usually an intermediate rental area, so they cannot move sideways. As they represent the highest income group, there are no houses above them abandoned by another group. They must build new houses on vacant land. Usually this vacant land lies available just ahead of the line of march of the area because, anticipating the trend of fashionable growth, land promoters have either restricted it to high grade use or speculators have placed a value on the land that is too high for the low rent or intermediate rental group. Hence the natural trend of the high rent area is outward, toward the periphery of the city in the very sector in which the high rent area started. The exception to this outward movement is the development of deluxe apartment areas in old residential areas.

But the precise direction of movement was influenced by the fastest transportation lines and the attraction of lakes, golf courses, open country, etc. It could, to some extent, be bent by developers. The outward movement of higher income groups was accentuated by the influx of alien groups to the city centre which 'causes a shifting, a filtering process that profoundly affects every neighbourhood in the city'. However, Hoyt believed – correctly, as it turned out – that the expansion of the central commercial uses was being checked by, on the one hand, skyscraper development and the growth of suburban business centres and, on the other hand, by the decline in wholesaling and city-centre manufacturing. He therefore believed that the zone of transition could become one of semi-permanent blight, initiated by the ageing of the buildings.

Houses with increasing age are faced with higher repair bills. This steady process of deterioration is hastened by obsolescence; a new and more modern type of structure relegates these structures to the second rank. The older residents do not fight so strenuously to keep out inharmonious forces. A lower income class succeeds the original occupants. Owner occupancy declines as the first owners sell out or move away or lose their homes by fore-closure. There is often a sudden decline in value due to a sharp transition in the character of the neighbourhood.

Although Hoyt's sector model' is often portrayed as an alternative to Burgess's 'concentric zone model', anyone who reads the originals must be struck by the fact that Hoyt's work is more a modification and elaboration of Burgess's than a contradiction. Burgess's Chicago diagram had several 'sectors', while Hoyt's diagrams clearly indicate zones *within* housing sectors. In some cities the high-rent value zone is on the periphery of the section: in others it is half-way out, so that a gradient depicting housing value (or income) from the centre to the periphery shows a 'hump'.

As a third 'classical' model of urban form it is usual to list the 'multi-nuclei' model discussed in a short article first published in 1945 by Harris and Ulmann.[7] The development of suburban commercial centres has certainly been one of the most important recent developments in the concept of the city. This process has gone furthest in American cities, but it is also noticeable in European cities – to some extent even in Britain, despite opposition by planners. In larger cities, the centre is no longer as dominant as it once was: an increasing range of commercial and cultural activities are provided in suburban centres. The large modern city is a much more loosely knit structure than the largely mono-centric city of the late 19th century, and the extent to which this trend should be resisted, welcomed or guided raises important questions for public policy. But the 'multi-nuclei' concept (which was mentioned by Hoyt) does not imply an essentially different theory – merely the application of the zone/sector theory to a number of centres instead of one.

Also embodied in Hoyt's analysis are the ideas that growth takes place along lines of communication ('axial development theory'), and that it can be blocked by physical obstacles. Both influences are still very much in evidence. The development of outer London has been clearly influenced by main roads and railways. And in central urban districts physical barriers such as railways have often acted as boundaries between social areas 'the other side of the tracks') and still do. Other barriers to movement – prisons, power stations, old warehousing areas etc. – can have the same effect, and so can urban motorways, when they have infrequent crossings (which is not inevitable). Barriers of this type often 'hem in' central business districts, causing congestion, or aggravate the decline of inner residential districts. (But the barriers can be breached, given public expenditure on a sufficient scale, in ways which not only channel development but make a positive contribution to the townscape. Examples include a park built on top of a motorway cutting in Seattle, or the pedestrian mall going under fourteen railway lines in Hanover, designed to extend the central district into what had been a 'no man's land' on the other side).

Thus the frequent distinction between the 'concentric zone', 'sector', 'axial development' and 'multiple nuclei' theories is somewhat misleading. These are all aspects of a way of looking at the urban form. It is indeed remarkable how many of the characteristics and processes which have since become so much of the stock-in-trade of urban economics –

'filtering'and the effects of district-wide ageing, the decline in the importance of the central manufacturing zone, the movement along transport routes – are found in Hoyt's 1939 report. This report, and Burgess's short article, established a way of looking at the spatial pattern of the city which is still valuable. But Burgess and Hoyt – sometimes known as the 'classical ecologists' – have suffered a fate similar to that of many 'classical economists'. Their ideas have been put forward by others in an over-simplified form which has then been criticised.

CRITICISMS OF THE 'CLASSICAL' MODELS

One criticism, from a sociological point of view, was made by Professor Firey, in connection with his studies of neighbourhoods in Boston. He denounced the idea that householders were 'economic men' operating in physical space devoid of cultural values. Sentiment and symbolism were, in his opinion, predominant in determining residential location. He explained the tightly-knit, densely populated Italian quarter of the North End as being the result of a feeling among the Italian-Americans that residence in this district was a symbol of 'social solidarity' with the Italian community and its values; the congested conditions of the North End were accepted because of these social benefits, even by those who could afford to leave.[8] At the other extreme, Beacon Hill, near the centre of the city, had remained a high-class residential area of well-maintained early 19th century houses because it had always had this reputation.

This is clearly a valid qualification to the purely deductive economic models discussed below – although less so to Burgess and Hoyt's more eclectic approach. Once established, the social character of a district can last for generations, and this is especially true of immigrant areas. On the other hand, immigrant groups have in the end been dispersed and assimilated, to a greater or lesser extent. Similarly, high-class areas can and do change. Neither Whitechapel, Limehouse nor Mayfair now have the social connotations they had in Victorian times. Moreover, closely-knit communities, where families remained for generations, tend to belong to a nostalgic past in the era of the car, the jet plane and electronic communication. There is clearly some degree of racial segregation in Britain as well as the USA, but it is too soon to say that integration will not eventually be achieved. In any case, racial segregation – arising either from choice or from social constraint – can easily be incorporated in the 'classical' model (cf. Burgess's 'Black belt').

A second criticism was that the model ignored the effects of government policy, e.g. the provision of subsidised local authority housing. Hoyt himself answered that he was concerned with a system responding to individual choice, and that he doubted the feasibility of a 'mongrel' theory incorporating both individual choice and government intervention.[9] This seems a reasonable reply, even today.

A different type of state involvement consists of town planning controls. Most countries have controls of some type, ranging from the 'zoning' system in the USA which lays down the category of permitted use – single-family housing, apartments, commercial, etc. – to the theoretically unlimited development control in Britain. It can therefore be argued that planning controls have rendered obsolete any models based on decentralised decision-making by firms and households. The planners, it is argued, can simply implement any urban pattern they, or their political masters, consider appropriate. But it is questionable whether they do, or in fact should try to, eliminate market forces. When planners diametrically oppose market forces (in other words, broadly speaking, what people want) there is a tendency for market forces to prevail in the end. British planners have generally opposed suburban shopping centres, and, as a result, have forced supermarkets into crowded High Streets. Planners in West Germany and Scandinavia have tended to oppose houses, as distinct from flats. But since a substantial number of people want to be able to shop for their groceries in comfort and live in houses, the pressure has, in an increasing number of cases, overridden the prevailing planning policies. This has led to two reactions. Some planning theorists have applied to town planning the principles of a 'corrected market economy'; that is, guiding market forces rather than opposing them. The alternative is to seek state ownership of land and housing in order to ensure the implementation of plans. These questions will be discussed below.

A third criticism was that Hoyt and Burgess merely described what had happened; they did not provide a quantifiable model which could be used to assess whether what happened was optimal. This criticism, as far as it goes, can be accepted. On the other hand, if one thing is clear from the 'new urban economics', it is that producing a quantifiable urban model which can be used to assess the optimality of urban form is no easy task. Indeed, a rigorous model which omits important influences can easily be worse than an unrigorous, unquantified, sensible, model.

A final criticism was that the 'classical' model lacked generality, and applied, at best, to cities in the USA in a particular historical period. Very different patterns were found in Europe, where the fashionable residential areas were in the centre of the city. An even more striking example is the 'Third World' cities (e.g. those of Latin America) in which the fashionable areas are near the centre and the 'suburbs' consist of 'shanty towns'. It is undoubtedly true that differences in cultural attitudes, as well as economic conditions and legal provisions, can affect the urban pattern. The Hoyt-Burgess model clearly does not apply to all the world's cities at any one time, but it is an interesting analysis when allowance is made for historical evolution.[10]

Early American cities, and some European cities in the period of the early Industrial Revolution, followed the present Latin American model, with newcomers settling in makeshift dwellings on the outskirts. The 'Third World' pattern is more striking because the spread of urban growth has been so much faster than it ever was in the already developed countries. However, the typical Latin American pattern in recent years has been partially 'sectoral', with 'proper' housing in one sector (which can be afforded by only a fraction of the city's population) and 'self-build' housing elsewhere.[11] The Burgess/Hoyt model of movement away from the centre postulated a large stock of durable housing which was being abandoned by its original inhabitants, and thus made available for immigrants. This is clearly not the current situation in Latin America, but some writers have suggested that it could develop as the present middle-income housing or the public high-rise developments begin to age. The Latin American city would then begin to display the characteristics of Chicago in the 1920s. Time will tell.

Time has probably already shown that the other comparison – that with Europe – can, to some extent, be incorporated in such an evolutionary scheme. The central areas of many British cities display all the characteristics postulated in the Burgess/Hoyt model – a development accentuated by 'New Commonwealth' immigration and rent control. In many continental European cities, the problems are far less serious; this is as a consequence of lower immigration rates, less harmful rent policies and often better-quality residential areas to begin with. Nevertheless, the 'American' trend is clearly there – as witness the extensive (and remarkably sensitive) urban renewal recently undertaken in West Germany. Inner-city decay has gone much further in the older American cities than in Continental European cities. There are several probable reasons, from intangible factors such as the American 'frontier' philosophy of abandoning the old and building anew, to the divorce of suburban and central city local government areas, combined with heavy reliance on a real estate tax. But, in a much milder form, the characteristics of the American problem can be seen even in Continental

European cities. And Britain – it is belatedly being realised – has large inner areas which can be compared to those in the USA.

RECENT DEVELOPMENTS IN CITIES

It is also clear that American cities have changed since the original Burgess and Hoyt articles; indeed these changes were well summarised by Hoyt himself.[12] He stressed the decentralisation of central manufacturing and service activity, and the development of large areas of middle-income single-family housing in what had previously been the commuter zone – all consequences of what has been termed 'the rubber city', as distinct from its predecessors 'the walking city' and 'the steel city'.[13] But Hoyt also drew attention to moves in the other direction. There has been a move back into the central city, mainly as a result of the boom in rented apartments, catering for people without children who do not want the suburban owner-occupied house-and-garden associated with the 'child-centred' life-style. There has been a noticeable expansion of this type of privately-financed construction, not only in the USA and Canada but also in countries such as Germany and Holland. (Britain differs from these countries, not because of a lack of demand but because rent regulation has made the provision of rented accommodation unprofitable).

The extent of this private unsubsidised redevelopment varies according to the level of inner-city decay. In cities like Toronto, where decay was limited, redevelopment was feasible at a number of points. (Indeed, a reaction soon emerged *against* redevelopment). In the larger, older cities of the USA, where square miles of the inner-city have become racially-segregated, depressed areas, private redevelopment is at present not in sight. This is partly a matter of externalities. Even if a site were redeveloped in a way which was attractive in itself, would anyone who could afford new housing wish to live in such an area? On the other hand, subsidised public redevelopment of whole districts, besides costing a lot of money, (which is in short supply precisely in the cities with large blighted areas) has often proved socially and environmentally unsatisfactory. On the basis of his monumental study of New York, Professor Vernon suggested that the most promising form of redevelopment for the immediate future was the construction of apartments adjacent to the Cetral Business District.[14] The CBD had retained its life and vitality in spite of its relative decline, and apartments near it

were attractive to many childless people. The main central area redevelopment in the older American cities has in fact taken place in this
area (e.g. 'Midtown' Manhattan).

A different type of renovation of old areas occurs when substantial
numbers of owner-occupiers renovate their own houses. This process is
often initiated by a move back to the central city of professional people,
such as has happened in several American cities where blight has not
gone too far (and in London). It usually occurs in what had originally
been middle-class districts, where the houses are capable of being
modernised. Being originally designed for large families, and sometimes
servants, these 19th century houses can provide ample space for smaller
modern families, together with easier access to the centre. This move
back to the central city can be explained as a response to the increase in
city size and consequent commuting problems. But there have been
other contributing factors: a reaction against modern types of building
in favour of the more solid and ornate 19th century style, the attraction
of remodelling one's own house, and in some cases the quest for a more
'urban' environment.

THE INFLUENCE OF POLITICAL ACTION

Developers' location decisions are influenced not only by 'private'
economic considerations but also by political and organisational rules
and pressures. These can be divided into

(1) Regional policy
(2) Town planning policies
(3) Local government organisation
(4) The influence of financial institutions. (*cf* Chap. 3)

Regional policy is briefly mentioned here because it can affect the
location of employment within cities. The policy practised in Britain
since the 1930s has been to divide the country into 'development' regions
which supposedly have too little employment, and 'non-development'
regions which supposedly have too much. Investment has been encouraged in the development areas by subsidies, and discouraged in
other areas by Industrial Development Certificates and Office Development Permits. It is increasingly being questioned whether this policy has
not been overtaken by events.[15] Inner areas in Birmingham or London
suffer from unemployment rates higher than in the new industrial

districts in the 'development areas'. Yet IDC's and ODP's have discouraged commercial and industrial development in these inner areas, as well as in small towns in the South East or Midlands, which did not have the 'congestion' problem of London or Birmingham.

This 'policy lag' has parallels in other countries. In the USA, Federal funds have in the past been used to channel money from the 'rich' old cities of the North-East, like New York and Boston, to the 'underdeveloped' South and West – and still do, at least according to spokesmen from the North-East. Yet today the cities of the North-East are far worse off than the 'sun-belt' cities. Similarly, in the Netherlands, public concern over the excessive growth of Rotterdam became acute just when it had ceased.

In most 'developed' countries, economic differences between large regions are smaller than differences within city-regions, and policies designed to deal with the former can be not only ineffective but even perverse in their effects on the latter. ODP's, for example, have had the curious effect of encouraging firms to stay, and even expand, in central London. Many firms were prepared to consider a move to other parts of London, or other towns in Southern England, but these moves were discouraged. There was no restriction on a move to, say, Bootle or South Shields, but this is the kind of move which firms were reluctant to undertake. Thus the ODP system has discouraged the decentralisation of office employment from central London to other parts of the conurbation, which hardly seems sensible. It seems clear that the pursuit of 'balance' between large regions (often based on the problems of a generation ago) can clash with policy aims within a city-region.

The second influence on developers is that of local town planning. The positive effects of town planning policies can range from a more orderly arrangement of land uses at the local level to the blocking of major changes which would otherwise have occurred. British town planners have in most cases stopped the development of suburban shopping centres with car parks on the American (or French) style, and forced supermarket development to take place in town centres or suburban High Streets. Whether this has achieved its purported objective of improving the quality of urban life is a subject which will be discussed below, but it has certainly had an effect.

It is also clear from the British case that extensive powers of development control and compulsory purchase do not necessarily prevent inner-city decay. The two countries with the worst inner-city conditions among the developed countries – the USA and Britain – are more or less at the opposite ends of the spectrum of planning armouries, the USA having a rather weak zoning system and Britain a system of unlimited development control. Countries such as Canada or West Germany have 'intermediate' planning systems and less inner-city decay. Any such comparisons are of course dangerous, because of the many other variables involved. But they do suggest the idea -- to which we shall return later – that certain powers are necessary for local authorities to carry out coherent and beneficial planning policies, but that unlimited discretionary powers can paradoxically lead to in-effectiveness and increased urban decay.

The organisation of local government can also affect the urban pattern. It has been argued above that the planning system (as well as the market system) is subject to inherent imperfections. Its main defect is that of any political system – that it overweights the views of adminis-trators and political activists. The hostility of British planning autho-rities to new suburban shopping centres, or of Continental planning authorities to houses (as distinct from flats) probably fall into this category, and this substitution of the interests of the rulers for those of the ruled increases with increasing size of local government areas. The recent British 'inner area studies' echo a theme familiar to American studies: that the inhabitants of these areas feel, with considerable justification, that their needs are ignored by the big city bureaucracy. This is an argument for having small local government areas – or at least devolving considerable powers to them. This is the reverse of the thinking behind the current British system of local government, which has far larger districts than any other European country.

But even if local people feel strongly about an issue, and are able to make their wishes effective through a small-scale system of local government, this can also sometimes distort the interests of citizens as a whole, as for example, when local residents oppose development which is in the interests of others. It may be in the interest of the inhabitants of a sparsely-populated suburban district to oppose new housing develop-ment, even though this housing would benefit the potential occupiers living in crowded conditions in the city. Before the 1974 reorganisation in Britain there were complaints that large cities were 'hemmed-in' by quasi-rural authorities hostile to development. Perhaps another exam-ple is the opposition of some inner-London politicians to the extension of owner-occupied housing, or 'the spreading blight of marinas, offices and luxury flats'. According to one's point of view, this can be regarded as a justified defense of local inhabitants, or as a doctrinaire reaction which helps to frustrate the regeneration of inner areas – or both, in different situations. The possibly unsatisfactory nature of even a 'community' response can be used as an argument for large units of local government. But it may be possible to get the best of both worlds through a metropolitan system of, less formally, by an association of local authorities for the purpose of strategic planning.

THE INFLUENCE OF FINANCIAL INSTITUTIONS

Finally, the geographical pattern of development may be influenced by the policies of financial institutions. The Marxist view is that 'monopoly finance capitalism' manipulates the pattern of development and land values by granting finance in some areas and refusing it in others. A diluted form of this view underlies some of the criticisms of commercial property development during the boom before 1973, and more recently of building societies. The latter criticism originated in the USA, where it was argued that savings and loan associations (the equivalent of building societies) had contributed to the run-down of central areas by refusing to give mortgages in these areas ('redlining'). Similar criticisms have recently been made in Britain. In the USA this led to the 1976 Home Mortgage Disclosure Act, under which associations were obliged to publish their total volume of lending in each postal code area.

The savings associations and the building societies deny that they are prejudiced against particular areas, and argue that they are merely concerned to ensure that money lent on a house is not going to be lost – the first loss being that by the owner-occupier himself. If an applicant is unlikely to be able to pay the interest, and if the house is unlikely to maintain its value – either because of physical deterioration or because of the 'blight' of threatened comprehensive redevelopment – then it is in everyone's interests not to grant the loan. The reluctance in Britain to lend on sub-let property is justified on the grounds that the Rent Acts can make it difficult to end a tenancy, and thus lower the sale value of the house.

Whether the building societies or their critics are right is difficult to decide, and would still be, given more facts. Information such as that called for in the American Act would not, in itself, prove whether the societies' policies were justified. British societies certainly do not rule out old buildings as such: between 1975 and 1976 the proportion of mortgages on houses built before 1919 rose from 19 to 23 per cent, which is about the same as the proportion of this type of housing in the total housing stock.[16] But this is again not conclusive. To a large extent one is forced back on qualitative and somewhat subjective assessments of the building societies and their critics.

One point on which there is increasing agreement is that it would be desirable if local authorities could clarify their plans for inner areas, thus removing the uncertainty about comprehensive development which often blights these areas, and allowing private finance to help in their regeneration.[17] The problem here is that many local authorities are either unable or unwilling to provide clear information. There are still plans in existence for the almost complete redevelopment by councils of inner areas, which are often held up more by cash shortages than by an abandonment of the principle. And the Community Land Act has greatly increased the potential area of land acquisition.

Even if one rejects the view that building societies explicitly discriminate against inner areas, and are mainly concerned with the security of their investment, it is possible that there is 'marginal range' of investment where fashion or prejudice can play a role, and where publicity and argument could tilt the balance. Thus some arm-jogging may have been justified, even if the building societies' claim is in general accepted that they serve a market situation, and do not create it. But under a system such as the British, which gives local authorities almost unlimited discretionary power to prohibit development or acquire property compulsorily, the main problem of 'redlining' would seem to lie in the political field.

The changes that have occurred in American and West European cities are therefore complex, but they are based on a few main components, which vary in importance from city to city. In all cases, there has been a spreading out of the city, accompanied by a decline in (overall) population densities. There is often a process of decay in the older areas, although this is not universal, and there has in some cases been a counter-movement back into the central city. These changes in the urban pattern are explicable in terms of a small number of social factors: mobility, family life-style and minority status, inter-acting with the effects of the ageing and obsolescence of physical structures, and sometimes influenced by political action.

THE GEOGRAPHICAL SYNTHESIS

Some geographers have recently sought to distil the case-studies of individual cities into a more modern general theory. An example by a leading American geographer is represented in Fig. 12. Families are classified into three socio-economic groups, two racial groups, and three family groups. Their locational preferences, interacting with the inertia

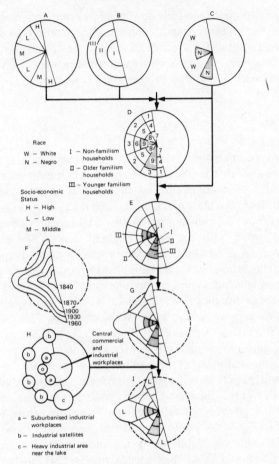

Race
W – White
N – Negro

I – Non-familism households
II – Older familism households
III – Younger familism households

Socio-economic Status
H – High
L – Low
M – Middle

Central commercial and industrial workplaces

a – Suburbanised industrial workplaces
b – Industrial satellites
c – Heavy industrial area near the lake

FIG. 12. A model of urban growth

Source: B. J. L. Berry and P. H. Rees, 'The Factorial Ecology of Calcutta' *American Journal of Sociology*, 1969, p. 445.

inherent in any settlement pattern, and various economic and social constraints, produces a zone-and-sector model which is then distorted by the irregular pattern of city growth and the development of suburban and satellite workplaces. This is a useful framework, even if one has the impression of having hacked through a jungle of 'factorial ecology', 'social topography' and all the rest only to find Burgess and Hoyt waiting on the other side! A recent study of Edinburgh also indicates the continuing relevance of the 'sector' theory.[18]

Another approach – largely developed by urban geographers because of the neglect of 'institutional' economics – is an analysis of the various groups and institutions which participate in the demand for, and supply of, real property, and the geographical consequences. A concise survey of British work is given by Professor B. T. Robson.[19]

LAND VALUE SURVEYS

Another type of empirical study is of the distribution of land values in cities. The available data varies from good to non-existent, according to the prevailing requirement for registering sales of real property. Many communities in the USA and Canada, and many continental European countries, have a Land Register in which all property sales have to be recorded, often with the price. England and Wales still have no comprehensive Land Register, and even where it exists, it is not available to the public. Studies of British land prices have therefore been 'one-off' and incomplete, but some useful results have been obtained. A study of land prices in London in 1967 showed a fairly steady fall from over £80,000 an acre within five miles of the centre to £20,000 beyond 20 miles.[20] Similarly, a survey of the whole of the UK indicated a pattern of broadly 'concentric zones' of prices for London and Birmingham, with the level markedly higher in London.[21] In the USA, however, this 'traditional' pattern has changed to one in which prices are very high in a very small Central Business District (and some sub-centres) but over most of the city do not fall regularly from the centre to near the periphery. (Fig 13) A 'contour' model of land prices shows a plateau, with differing levels in different parts, and a single towering pinnacle representing the CBD. All the evidence suggests that European cities are moving in the same direction. A detailed study of Munich, and fragmentary evidence for other cities in West Germany, indicates a *relative fall* in inner areas: prices are still higher than in the outskirts but the difference has fallen considerably. Moreover, central land prices in real terms are often below those prevailing in 1913.[22]

The change from a 'conical' to a 'plateau-and-pinnacle' land value surface can to some extent be explained by the rent-bid model. The CBD, in spite of some ups and downs, has retained its attractiveness for certain types of shops and offices, but the rent-bid curves for this type of activity fall off sharply; a few hundred yards can make a big difference. The curves for manufacturing and housing, on the other hand, are unlikely to slope uniformly downwards from the edge of the CBD: any

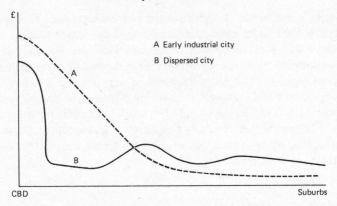

A Early industrial city
B Dispersed city

CBD   Suburbs

FIG. 13. Changing Land Value Gradients

explanation of the differing levels of the 'plateau' must bring in the physical and social structure of the neighbourhood.[23]

Another type of geographical study concerns itself with the changes in population, employment and land use in cities. One striking set of maps from the British census shows the changes in population densities between 1951 and 1961 and between 1961 and 1971. With declines in green and increases in red, all the British cities show up as large green patches surrounded by red spots.

Some geographers have undertaken detailed studies of changes in land use in cities.[24] A great deal of information has been produced for Toronto by Professor Bourne. He concludes that there was no single pattern in the redevelopment of the 1950s and 1960s but that, in so far as there was a pattern, it was sectoral rather than concentric. Apartment construction occurred in clusters in three 'upper middle' income districts: its location was the result partly of zoning but also of the presence of other apartments and nearness to the subway or to the city centre. Office development was concentrated in the centre and along the subway route. Development as a whole was at the highest level near the city centre, fell as one moved away from the centre, and then rose again on the outskirts.

The geographers who have undertaken these studies tend to stress the great complexity of the data, and the difficulties raised for traditional theories. However, geographers are perhaps not immune to the phenomenon, so marked in economics, that there are more academic rewards in making things complicated than in making them simple. The author must confess that he finds that the surveys for the most part confirm a number of straightforward and unsurprising concepts. For example, the private development of rented apartment blocks – which has been such a feature of North American cities – has not taken place in very expensive, high income districts, or in the middle of depressed low-income districts. The redevelopment of very expensive areas would rarely be profitable, as well as arousing strong local opposition. In a depressed district, the land would be cheap, but middle-income tenants would be hard to find. Similarly new development tends to 'cluster', and is influenced by new underground railways. This is nearly all to be found in Hoyt, or even Hurd.

THE RENT-BID MODEL

The urban geographers have at least assembled an invaluable body of case-studies. Most economists who have approached the question since the early 1960s have followed a different, and more questionable, route. Apart from the Marxists, whose views are discussed below, the main approach has been to develop economic models based on von Thünen's agricultural model.

The urban equivalent of this model was used by early exponents of 'the Wisconsin School' as a simple expository device to explain such obvious features as higher land values and densities in city centres.[25] Used in this way, the model can be illuminating. For example, it can help to explain the main changes between the late 19th century and the present. A reduction in the real cost of transport, by flattening the rent-bid curve for housing, would be expected to cause a relative lowering of land prices in central areas, an extension of the city and a lowering of central area densities; this is what has happened.

But the 'rent-bid' model as such is a grotesque simplification of reality. Employment is concentrated at a single point and people decide where to live solely on the basis of transport costs and land prices. But most unrealistic of all (and this cannot be modified) is the fact that such a theory gives an equilibrium pattern which would be established if the city were being built on a clean slate: it ignores the consequences of existing physical structures and social patterns.

In recent years, 'advanced' economists have sought to make the model more realistic and operational by introducing more variables, without changing the basic concept: translated into the language of mathematics, this approach ominously calls itself 'the new urban economics'.[26] Professor Alonso has introduced the effect of consumer preferences regarding space, combined with differences in income.[27] If people are prepared to pay for more space and lower density – and all historical series suggest that the income elasticity of demand for space is high – then those who can afford to do so will move to the lower-priced land on the periphery, and consume more of it. People with lower incomes will be unable to afford the commuting costs, and so would be forced to remain on expensive central land, consuming small quantities of it. This purely theoretical construction is a useful footnote to the simple rent-bid model. It does not tell us anything that was not already known, but it does show that the 'Burgess' residential zones can be explained by the rent-bid model.

The restrictive assumption that employment is found only in the centre can also be relaxed, and different types of household can be introduced. Moreover, some theoreticians have made courageous attempts to apply their theories to actual cities, with what they claim to be reasonable success.[28] Nevertheless, it is felt by all geographers and sociologists, and some economists, that these theories are inadequate because they ignore the pervasive influence of established physical structures and social patterns.

To quote a recent article by an urban geographer:

Most economic models of residential location (following Alonso, Mills & Muth) assume that population and housing stock distributions are one and the same . . . the trade-off between accessibility to work and living space is determined as if the latter were plastic, tastes were invariant and workplaces were either fixed at one location (city centre) or were ubiquitous, instead of being concentrated at several nodes within the city. The resulting patterns (of housing, population) are in fact, identical to those which would be obtained if an urban area was constructed again each year in a systematic form around the city centre. No one, of course, now believes these results.[29]

The point is not new. Mr. Turvey argued in 1957 that a city is an economic system moving towards equilibrium but never reaching it. The long life of buildings imposes a long time lag before the actual situation can be changed to the equilibrium one, while changes in income, technology and population mean that the equilibrium itself is constantly changing. For this reason

It is impossible to present a comparative statics analysis which will explain the layout of towns and the pattern of buildings: the determining background conditions are insufficiently stationary in relation to the durability of buildings.[30]

This does not mean that the rent-bid model is useless, since it can indicate the *direction* in which the city is likely to move. But, for this purpose, a simple and partial approach is adequate. It is becoming increasingly apparent that the quest for a comprehensive economic model of city form has led up a blind alley. One reaction has been agnostic: it is all very complicated, every city is different, one cannot generalise. Mr. Turvey himself goes on to argue,

In other words, each town must be examined separately and historically. The features of London, for example, can be fully understood only by investigating its past: it is as it is because it was as it was.

This is probably going too far, since the similarities between cities (of comparable sizes and ages) are as striking as their differences. The problems of central areas, for example, are not exclusively American, as Europeans once complacently assumed. The way ahead is perhaps to return to simpler and more partial models, recognising that there are various simplifications which can be applied to urban form, each of which can be useful, provided that their limitations are recognised. The basic rent-bid idea, the filtering concept, the simple models of housing ageing and redevelopment, the differing housing needs of 'the seven ages of man', the influence of transport routes, and the implications of demand and supply analysis for taxation, planning, rent control, etc. can all be useful in explaining particular aspects. If they are treated as a kit of tools, to be used when appropriate, they can at least indicate some general patterns and causal relationships, and contribute to an understanding of the urban mosaic.

SOCIAL SEGREGATION

The main 'normative' issue in the study of urban social districts is whether the differences between districts – economic, social and environmental – are in some sense excessive. This raises fundamental issues concerning income distribution, of which differences between urban districts are in part a reflection. There is a crucial, and often overlooked, distinction between the relief of poverty and egalitarianism.

The 'liberal utilitarian' – to use Mr. Samuel Brittan's term – is concerned to raise the level of income of the small proportion of the population with incomes markedly below the average. Since, moreover, he emphasises the individual's freedom of choice, he favours policies such as 'negative income tax' or 'tax credit'. The egalitarian, on the other hand, is as much, or more, concerned with pulling down the rich as pulling up the poor and, if he is also a collectivist, he will favour payments in kind, such as subsidised public housing, rather than cash payments. The prevailing philosophy in official circles in Britain favours both subsidised housing and the existing range of separate allowances, for which application must be made, and which are often separately means-tested, rather than a single payment through the tax system. However, neither the British 'inner area' studies discussed below, nor the reports of the Royal Commission on the Distribution of Income and Wealth[31] suggest that the existing system of *ad hoc* allowances is particularly effective in alleviating poverty.

Advocates of the 'tax credit' approach argue that it would alleviate poverty more effectively and, together with the elimination of harmful measures such as rent control, would remove some of the most acute urban problems. But such policies would not necessarily eliminate them. There are two basic questions on urban social areas. Are there *general* characteristics of the housing market which produce excessive social segregation? Are there *specific* problems of cumulative decline in older city districts? On the first, it has been argued that the tendency of most people to locate near people of a similar type means that a market system leads to excessive segregation, and that this indicates the need for the partial or complete elimination of the market economy in housing, and the substitution of a system of administrative allocation. Some Western observers comment favourably on the social homogeneity of cities in Communist countries. But this superficial uniformity conceals both a far greater power of Party members over other citizens and also the 'perks' that are so important to the Communist 'power *élite*' (and the British?).

'Liberal utilitarians' on the other hand, see no reason why families should not spend their money on housing if they wish to do so, and deny that more housing for some necessarily means less housing for others. Nevertheless, many 'liberal utilitarians' would accept that a situation where different socio-economic groups live in widely separated neighbourhoods may not be conducive to social harmony. This is not, however, an inevitable result of allowing consumer choice in housing. People may prefer to live next to their own kind, but this usually applies only to the immediate locality: there is often a variety of social groups in what is generally regarded as a district (say 20,000 – 30,000 people). Social (and architectural) variety is encouraged if (a) a district has been developed at different periods, and (b) a variety of sizes and types of dwelling is permitted. On the first point, one American planner has challenged current planning wisdom by arguing that scattered development allows a range of buildings, of different ages, which both avoids 'New Town blues' and in the long run avoids the blighting effect when a large district becomes obsolescent at the same time.[32] On the second point, there has been considerable criticism of American exclusionary zoning which permits only large, expensive detached houses in suburban districts. But social polarisation is also caused by the British system of council housing (combined with rent control) which leads to segregation between council tenants and owner-occupiers. This segregation is not an inevitable consequence of subsidised housing, but council housing in its present form is a major cause of social segregation in British cities, and one ignored by most critics of social segregation.

It is thus far from clear that social segregation *in general* is a serious urban problem. It is still less clear that social segregation is simply a consequence of a market economy which needs to be countered by more state control; certain types of town planning policy and public housing increase social segregation. What is not in dispute is that there is a serious problem in older central districts in some cities. These 'central cities' as they are known in the USA or 'inner city areas' as they are now known in Britain, contain, on any definition, only a small proportion of the population, but a high proportion of poverty, poor housing and social problems. In subsequent chapters we will examine the problems of these areas and the not always successful policies that have been adopted towards them.

SUMMARY

Various attempts have been made to produce theories which explain the geographical pattern of land use in cities. By developing ideas first put forward by Hurd in 1903, Burgess (1924) and Hoyt (1939) put forward the 'concentric zone' and 'sector' theories. These theories – which are not as dissimilar as is sometimes believed – suggest that land uses tend to be arranged in a pattern of broadly concentric rings, combined with wedges extending outwards from the centre. The 'concentric zone' theory can be given an economic interpretation by applying the concepts developed for agricultural land use in the 19th century by von Thünen. Provided these concepts are used as rough simplifications of aspects of urban land use, they can still be of value. They must, however, take account of the fact that the modern city tends to have a number of important suburban sub-centres.

Recent attempts – on the basis of the von Thünen approach – to produce a 'rigorous' theory of land use based on transport costs have not been successful. They ignore the pervasive influence of the stock of buildings and of the characteristics and attitudes of people in various districts. There is a tendency – to some extent international, but particularly marked in the USA and the UK – for some older inner areas to suffer from a combination of decaying housing, loss of industry, and a concentration of the poor and socially handicapped; all of which can initiate a cumulative process of decline. At the same time, some inner areas in some cities have retained their attractiveness. This varied social pattern is reflected in land values, which today tend to be at a relatively high level in a small central business district and to vary elsewhere according to the 'amenities' of the district rather than merely with distance from the centre.

The behaviour of financial institutions such as building societies can possibly affect economic conditions in a district. (On the Marxist view, this influence is predominant). But it seems likely that, for the most part, such institutions follow the market rather than create it. In Britain – where extensive 'comprehensive re-development' has been carried out by local authorities, it seems likely that uncertainty concerning local government policy is a more important factor in urban decay.

SELECT BIBLIOGRAPHY

Alex Anas and D. S. Dendrinos, 'The New Urban Economics: A Brief Survey' in G. J. Papageorgiou (ed.) *Mathematical Land Use Theory*, D. C. Heath & Co. 1976 p. 23.

Harold Carter, *The Study of Urban Geography*, Edward Arnold, 2nd ed. 1975.

T. H. Elkins, *The Urban Explosion*, Macmillan 1973.

B. T. Robson, *Urban Social Areas*, O.U.P. 1975.

REFERENCES

1. First published in 1903. 1924 edition reprinted by Arno Press, New York, 1970.
2. Paul F. Wendt, *Real Estate Appraisal*, New York, 1956, p. 107.

3. E. W. Burgess. 'The Growth of the City: An Introduction to a Research Project' in Park, R. E. et. al. *The City*, Chicago 1925.

4. E. W. Burgess 'Urban Areas' in Smith T. V. and White L. D. (eds.) 1929 *Chicago: An Experiment in Social Science Research*, Chicago.

5. Hoyt, Homer. *The Structure and Growth of Residential Neighbourhoods in American Cities*, Federal Housing Administration, Washington D.C. 1939.

6. Ibid. *One Hundred Years of Land Values in Chicago*. Chicago University Press, 1933.

7. Harris, Chauncy D. & Ullman, Edward L. 'The Nature of Cities' *Annals of the American Academy of Political and Social Service* November 1945. Reprinted in *Readings in Urban Geography* p. 277. H. M. Mayer and C. F. Kohn (eds) University of Chicago Press, 1959.

8. W. Firey. *Land use in Central Boston*. Cambridge, Mass. 1947. This explanation rather weakens the case for very high density ('over 100 dwelling units per acre') made by Jane Jacobs, largely with reference to the North End of Boston. The warmth and sociability which she found so attractive may not have been due to the very high density as such, but to the fact that it was a community of Italians – a gregarious people under any conditions – with cultural and vocational links stimulated by their immigrant status.

9. H. Hoyt. 'Residential Sectors Revisited' *The Appraisal Journal* 27, 1950.

10. Leo F. Schore, 'On the Spatial Structure of Cities in the Two Americas' in P. M. Hauser and Leo. F. Schore, *The Study of Urbanisation*, New York, 1965.

11. Homer Hoyt, 'The Residential and Retail Patterns of Leading Latin American Cities' *Land Economics* 39. 1963.
It may be added that the direction of urban growth has been influenced by the questionale housing policies often adopted by city authorities. In Guayaquil, the largest town of Ecuador, there is a huge squatter area in a marsh which is flooded every day, although large areas of dry land are undeveloped. The good land is owned by the national housing agency, which builds houses which only a small proportion of the population can afford, and wishes to know nothing about the 'self-build' sector.

12. Homer Hoyt, 'Recent Distortions of the Classical Models of Urban Structure' in *Land Economics* May 1964 reprinted in Bourne (ed.) *Internal Structure of the City*. p. 84.

13. K. H. Schaeffer and E. Sclar, *Access for All*, Penguin (USA) 1975.

14. R. Vernon and E. M. Hoover. *Anatomy of a Metropolis*, Harvard University Press. 1959.
    R. Vernon. *The Myth and Reality of Our Urban Problems* Harvard University Press, Cambridge, Mass. 1966.
15. A sympathetic history of regional policy, together with some of the second thoughts which have now begun to appear in academic papers, is given in the contributions by G. Hallett and P. Randall in *Regional Policy for Ever?* IEA Readings 11, London 1973. Perhaps because of its publisher, this booklet was not reviewed in the journals. Better known are studies such as 'Evaluating the Effects of British Regional Policy' by B. Moore and J. Rhodes, *Economic Journal*, March 1973, which estimates the effect of policy changes on employment on the basis of the improvement in the overall 'regional' situation in the 1960s, or *Capital versus the Regions*, 1976, by Stuart Holland 'an author who has been influential in formulating British Government policies' who criticises traditional policy for failing to realise that 'the regional problem is caused by capitalism'. The most comprehensive survey is *The Framework of Regional Economics in the United Kingdom*, A. J. Brown, CUP., 1972.
16. Building Societies' Association. *Facts and Figures*, quarterly.
17. Professor Neutze disagrees, maintaining that local authorities would sacrifice flexibility by disclosing their plans, and that private developers would be able to undermine them. (*op. cit.* p. 173n.)
18. H. W. Richardson *et. al.*, *Housing and urban spatial structure: a case study* Saxon House, 1975.
19. B. T. Robson, *Urban Social Areas*, Oxford University Press, 1975. Perhaps the author accepts somewhat too readily the denunciations of a market economy in most of the literature he reviews: the assertion that housing is 'a social need, not a consumer luxury' (p. 52) appears less conclusive if one substitutes 'food' for 'housing' (although this is what advocates of permanent food rationing argued in the early 1950s).
20. National Building Agency, *Land Costs and Housing Development*, 1968.
21. P. A. Stone 'The Price of Building Sites in Britain' in P. Hall (ed.) *Land Values* London 1965, p. 1ff.
22. Graham Hallett, *Housing and Land policies in West Germany and Britain*, Macmillan 1977. p. 97.
23. There has been a theoretical debate in 'NUE' on the possibility of housing rent-bid curves sloping upward from the centre outward. The reality is that, even in North America, there are cities such as

Toronto where house prices generally fall from the centre outward and others where the reverse is the case: it depends on the extent of physical and social decay in the central city. But in both cases there is no *steady* rise up or down, but rises and falls, varying in different directions.

A tendency towards a 'peak and plateau' in land values is found not only in North America. Stockholm has very different land policies from those in the USA, including draconian planning regulations and extensive municipal ownership. However, a land value 'model' (literally) produced in the Royal Institute of Technology shows a very similar pattern.

24. L. S.Bourne, *Private Redevelopment of the Central City*, University of Chicago, 1961 *ibid*. 'Urban Structure and Land Use Decisions.' *Annals of the Association of American Geographers*, Vol. 66, No. 4, 1976.

25. Richard T. Ely and George S. Wehrwein. *Land Economics*, New York, 1940. p. 133ff.

26. H. W. Richardson. *The New Urban Economics: and Alternatives*. Academic Press, London, 1977.
   Professor Richardson reaches the very fair conclusion that 'NUE' is unlikely to give much insight into the solution of urban problems but that 'progress in urban economics will be much stronger if the theorists and policymakers maintain contact, and try to learn from each other' (p. 243).

27. W. Alonso. 'A theory of the urban land market', *Papers and Proceedings of the Regional Science Association* 1960. Reprinted in W. H. Leahy *et. al. Urban Economics* New York 1970. p. 55.

28. Richard F. Muth. *Cities and Housing*, Chicago 1969; see also Alan W. Evans *The Economics of Residential Location*, London, 1973.

29. L. S. Bourne, 'Housing Supply and Housing Market Behaviour in Residential Development' in D. T. Herbert and R. J. Johnston *Social Areas in Cities*, Wiley 1976.

30. Ralph Turvey *The Economics of Real Property* London 1957. p. 47.

31. *Royal commission on the Distribution of Income and Wealth. Report No. 6. Lower Incomes* Cmnd 7175. HMSO 1978.

32. J. Lessinger, 'The Case for Scatteration' *Journal of the American Institute of Planners*. Aug. 1962.

7 Marxist Land Economics

> To take 'the revolution' seriously is acceptable at many expense account lunches. It is equally 'trendy' to discuss it semi-facetiously: the one thing that is out-and-out 'square' is to be seriously opposed to it.
>
> Samuel Brittan, *Capitalism and the Permissive Society*, p. 6.

In recent years Marxism has gained a substantial following in Western Universities, and several books on urban economics have been published which are Marxist in approach. Moreover, much of the discussion of urban problems by 'community groups' and journalists uses implicitly Marxist concepts. One must begin any examination of Marxist urban economics with Marx himself.

Marx drew heavily on Adam Smith and Ricardo. He took the 'labour theory of value' (which is far from a coherent theory in their writings) and turned it into a theory of class exploitation. Like Ricardo, he was strongly influenced by the period of high food prices and high farm rents which followed the Napoleonic Wars. The 'classical' economists – at a time of rapid population growth and high infant mortality – feared that any improvements in the prosperity of the mass of the people might simply lead to an increase in population and a return to a subsistence income. Ricardo also feared that population growth, combined with an unchanged land area, would lead to a steady rise in rents as a proportion to national income, although he supported measures such as free agricultural trade, which would, at least, slow down the onset of this trend.

Marx used these ideas to construct a very different theory. All production derives from labour, and the working classes should receive the whole produce of labour. Under capitalism, however, the workers receive only a subsistence wage – just sufficient to enable them to reproduce more labourers. The difference between this subsistence wage and the total value of production is the 'surplus value' which is expropriated by capitalists in the form of rent, interest and profit, without giving anything in return. This expropriation would lead to a situation in which, as capitalism became more and more developed, the capital-owning 'bourgeoisie' would become steadily richer, and the 'proletariat' steadily poorer, until the inevitable communist revolution ushered in an era in which there would be no more class conflict, and no surplus value.

MARX'S TREATMENT OF RENT

Rent, according to Marx, is an unwarranted income from the free gifts of nature, an exploitation of the workers based on a class monopoly of landownership. In his discussion of rent in the third volume of *Capital* Marx distinguished three forms: differential rent I, differential rent II, and absolute rent. Differential rent I is based on natural differences in the quality of land (fertility, location). Differential rent II results from man-made improvements. In his discussion of agricultural rent, Marx made some important points which were later incorporated into mainstream economics. Marx is – for him – very complimentary to Adam Smith and Ricardo for their basic concept of rent. But he points out that Ricardo's theory, being based solely on differences in fertility, can be misleading. Location is equally important. Thus it does not follow that the best land is always cultivated first; poorer land can be cultivated first if it is more accessible. These points were developed in more detail by von Thünen (whose work had not been published when Marx was writing). Thus Marx's differential rent I is similar to the blend of Ricardo and von Thünen which we have outlined above (Chap. 3).

Marx's second point – developed with agricultural examples – concerns rent as resulting from the application of successive units of capital to a given area of land. Given diminishing returns, the intramarginal units of capital will earn a rent (differential rent II). This concept, applied to urban development, is illustrated in Fig. 4. – in which the hatched area can be regarded as differential rent II. It is not a different category from location rent, as Marx seems to suggest, but a different way of looking at it. On the whole, however, Marx's analysis of differential rent – although verbose and not always very clear – is broadly in line with modern microeconomics.

Marx's more distinctive concept, and the one stressed in current Marxist analysis of urban affairs, is 'absolute' rent. This arises because of the monopoly of land by the small land-owning class. The existence of rent, in Marx's view, not only represented exploitation but also hindered the modernisation of agriculture and, through higher food prices, reduced the demand for agricultural products. Thus Marx differed from Ricardo, who argued that it was high corn prices which caused high land prices not *vice versa*.

In his discussion of agricultural rent, Marx (like Ricardo) assumed the prevailing British division between wage-labourers, tenant farmers, and landowners. He appreciated that this system was peculiar to Britain, but took it to be the most developed form of capitalist agriculture (which proved not to be the case). He also relied heavily on the prevailing English land law, under which the landowner was entitled to raise the rent even as a result of improvements made by the tenant. 'Quite aside from the movements of real ground-rent, this is one of the secrets of the increasing enrichment of landowners' (*Capital* Vol. III p. 726). This legal provision was ended by the laws concerning 'tenant right'.

Similarly, in his discussion of urban property, Marx based his general theory heavily on the prevailing English pattern of urban landownership. ' . . . the census for England and Wales in 1861 gives the total population as 20,066,224 and the number of house owners as 36,032' (p. 728). (The corresponding figures for 1971 were 47,727,130 and 7,024,650.) This concentration of ownership was being increased by the leasehold system, under which ground landlords obtained both buildings and land on reversion.

'The fact is that if this system is permitted to exert its full affects for some time longer the entire ownership of houses as well as of country real estate will be in the hands of the great landed proprietors.' (p. 728)

'This illustration of property in buildings is important. . . . it shows that the capital incorporated in the soil ultimately passes into the hands of the landlord together with the land, and that the interest in it helps to swell his rent.' (p. 729)

Marx concluded that, under capitalism, the ownership of urban land was inevitably bound to become as concentrated as that of farmland, and that the income from both was bound to rise as a proportion of national income. This prognosis depended partly on 'reversionary' legal provisions peculiar to contemporary English law, which were subsequently changed, and partly on a forecast of the movement of (real) ground rents – which proved incorrect for agricultural land after about

1860[1] and for urban land after about 1910. Nevertheless, the idea of the inevitable rise in income from land in relation to total income was shared by Marx's contemporary J. S. Mill, whose general philosophy was so different. The idea was taken up by the 'land reform' movement later in the century, and recurs down to the present day.

LAND MONOPOLY

In Marx's analysis of ground rent, a central concept – echoed up to the present day – is 'land monopoly'. But Marx alternates between two meanings of 'monopoly'. One refers to the obvious fact that every site is physically unique: its owner has, in a sense, a monopoly of its use. Marx refers to ' . . . the monopoly of the so-called owner of a piece of the globe' which enables him to levy a tribute on anyone who wishes to live or work on it. But this is to use a familiar term in a special sense: it would be only slightly more forced to say that there is a monopoly in the sale of racehorses since each racehorse is unique. Although the immobility of land means that, in the short run, substitutability between sites is limited, in the longer run considerable substitution is possible – as the problems of the inner city show only too clearly. The more usual sense of 'land monopoly' implies that urban land is in the hands of a single owner, or of a small number of owners acting in collusion. This can happen. There were elements of monopoly in the mid-19th century examples cited by Marx – the great agricultural or urban estates, and the ports.[2] But the degree of monopoly in landownership today – in Britain and other Western countries – is clearly far less. The extent of concentration in the landownership pattern of any country at any time is a matter for empirical investigation. To jump from a forced use of 'monopoly' in connection with the spatial uniqueness of each site to the implication that there is monopoly in the normal sense is a mere play on words.

'USE VALUE'

Another of Marx's concepts – which plays a central role in Professor Harvey's work – is the distinction between 'value in use' and 'value in exchange'. This distinction was taken over from Adam Smith. In a somewhat parenthetical discussion of the ultimate basis of value, Smith considered the possibility that it might lie in a good's utility, but was forced to abandon this approach because of an apparent paradox.

The word value, it is to be observed, has two different meanings, and sometimes expressed the utility of some particular object, and sometimes the power of purchasing other goods which the possession of that objects conveys. The one may be called 'value in use'; the other, 'value in exchange'. The things which have the greatest value in use have frequently little or no value in exchange; and, on the contrary, those which have the greatest value in exchange have frequently little or no value in use. Nothing is more useful than water: but it will purchase scarce anything; scarce anything can be had in exchange for it. A diamond, on the contrary, has scarce any value in use; but a very great quantity of other goods may frequently be had in exchange for it. (*Wealth of Nations* Chap. 4)

This distinction, however, plays no subsequent role in his analysis, which is based on what later economists called 'equilibrium price'. But Marx took over the distinction between 'use value' and 'exchange value' and incorporated it into his theory of 'surplus value'.

Marx's main policy conclusion was that, since 'the earth is not a product of labour and therefore has no value', rent should be abolished, through nationalising all land. Under communism, both differential rent and absolute rent would disappear. This view was developed by Lenin and became a central part of the economic theory of the USSR. In official Soviet textbooks rent is treated as a capitalist phenomenon. 'Irrationality of the monetary valuation of natural resources derives from social relations under Capitalism: it is an unavoidable consequence of the economic relations where objects are treated as a source of income.'[3]

So much for the origins of Marxist theory. Before examining urban economics as viewed by Western Marxists today let us briefly review the subsequent development of 'mainstream' economics and recent trends in communist countries.

MARGINALISM

The 'marginalist revolution' of the 1860s introduced a new approach, which sought to show that the concept of utility *at the margin* could in fact explain the 'diamonds and water' paradox. Water is cheap because, when it is in ample supply, the value of a gallon more or less is low. If water were scarce, it would command a high price, just as, if diamonds were as plentiful as pebbles, they would be as cheap. On this interpretation, there is no need to make a distinction between 'use value' and 'exchange value'. This concept, together with the 'other blade of the scissors' – the supply situation – is the basis of modern price theory. This simple theory is quite successful in explaining the broad price movements of real property (*cf.* Chap. 5).

The 'marginalist revolution' led to the development of a general theory of pricing and distribution, in which the special status of 'labour' and 'land' was abandoned. 'Economic rent', on this view, arose in the case of goods the supply of which was restricted, or when increased supply meant using poorer 'quality' (poorer locations, in the case of urban land). On this view, economic rent serves a useful function in the allocation of resources. The equity of the distribution of incomes was a separate issue. If the ownership of land was highly concentrated and highly profitable – as it was when the 'classical' economists attacked the economic position of agricultural landlords – then it might reasonably be considered that the distribution of income was inequitable; this inequity could be tackled either by bringing about a wider distribution of ownership, by means of taxation, or by nationalisation. Rent was not, however, a consequence of private ownership but of scarcity; and the scarcity could in some cases depend on institutional limitations on supply.

The implications of modern price theory for land were developed in the first two decades of the twentieth century by British economists such as Marshall and, more importantly, by Swedish and German economists; some German economists continued to publish theoretical expositions up until after the Second World War.[4] In the English-speaking world, the subject has attracted little attention from economists since the 1920s. This is unfortunate because, even though there may be little to add to the basic theory, any theory needs to be restated in the language of succeeding generations, and in the light of current conditions, if it is to remain meaningful. In particular, the theory of land pricing needs to be restated in the light of the enormous widening of land ownership, and of the rises *and falls* of (real) land prices since 1914. The neglect of land pricing by mainstream economics, together with the fact that today even university students of economics are not taught the history of economic thought, has perhaps contributed to the enthusiastic reception of 'refreshingly new' Marxist theories.

THE COMMUNIST REDISCOVERY OF PRICING

Whereas the 'liberal' theory of rent is under attack from Marxists in Western countries, a reverse process is occurring in communist countries. The original doctrine was that, after land and real property were nationalised, they would not be bought and sold but, when necessary, transferred from one user to another, without any charge being made. This 'free land' doctrine has come under criticism from several economists in the USSR and the Eastern European countries, especially with regard to agricultural land. They have argued that it leads to economic inefficiency, and sought to show that the abolition of land pricing was not what Marx and Lenin really intended. One Polish economist, in a paper entitled 'Ground Rent – a Candidate for Rehabilitation' has argued that

> To deny the need and possibility of the price of land under Socialism represents a theoretical foundation of waste and irrational utilisation of natural resources.[5]

SOCIAL JUSTICE AND THE CITY

The most extensive body of Marxist writing on urban affairs is by French writers; a book by Manuel Castells is available in an English translation. But perhaps better known in the English-speaking world is a book by a geographer of British origin, now living in the USA, David Harvey, *Social Justice and the City*. I will concentrate my analysis on this substantial theoretical treatise and on a more applied analysis by T. A. Broadbent.

Social Justice and the City was hailed by the journals as 'a penetrating analysis of contemporary urbanism, which may indeed be the signal for a change of direction if not a revolution in geographic thought'. '. . . urban geography and non-Marxist urban economics can never be quite the same again'. Much of this book's discussion is of such a high level of generality as to be difficult to criticise without writing another book. I shall therefore confine myself to comments on one theoretical point (the distinction between 'use value' and 'exchange value') and on the more practical discussion of the 'ghetto' and the central business district. We have explained how Adam Smith's rather unclear distinction between 'value in use' and 'value in exchange' was incorporated by

Marx into his theory of exploitation, but was rejected as unnecessary and misleading by the 'marginalists'. Professor Harvey maintains that the distinction is a crucially important one, which lies at the root of current urban ills. It explains, he believes, why a market economy, far from responding to consumer demand, is a device whereby the capitalist class artificially creates 'needs' and why 'society is pushed down some path (it knows not how) towards a pattern of social needs and human relationships (which are neither comprehended nor desired) by the blind forces of an evolving market economy' (p. 190). Exchange value in a capitalist society diverges seriously from 'use value', just as 'need' diverges from 'demand'. Recent geographical, sociological and town planning studies have, he suggests, dealt with 'use value' whereas 'mainstream' urban economists (Muth, Mills, Alonso, etc.) have dealt with 'exchange value'; and that the Marxist reconciliation of the two offers the prospect of bringing these two approaches together, thus revitalising urban studies.

The analogy with 'need' and 'demand' – a distinction often made in connection with housing – does at first give one pause for thought. But 'need' surely means one of two things. It may be felt that every family should be able to obtain a certain minimum quantity of housing (which varies considerably according to prevailing standards). Whether this is best achieved by cash payments or subsidised public housing, or a combination of the two, is a matter for investigation. Alternatively, 'need' may mean that families should *be obliged* to have a certain quantity of housing, even if they would not choose it themselves. 'Liberal utilitarians' question this paternalistic approach, and accept it only in the case where the persons involved are incapable of a rational choice. But whether one takes a paternalistic or a libertarian view, supports or questions public housing, is it in any way helpful to revive Adam Smith's distinction between use and exchange value? Similarly, there is much that can be criticised in urban economics and 'urban studies' as recently practised. There has been over-specialisation, and a descent into a private language which reduces the need for thought. But is it any answer to this Babel to try to resurrect what (at least according to mainstream economics) was a simple muddle by Adam Smith, taken over by Marx?

Professor Harvey quotes several practical students of urban affairs in support of the Marxist distinction between use and exchange value, and the failings of 'liberal' economics.

Realistic analyses of how urban land-use decisions are made – dating from Hurd's (1903) perceptive analysis – have consequently led Wallace Smith (1970, 40) for example, to conclude that 'the traditional concept of supply-and-demand equilibrium is not very relevant to most of the problems or issues which are associated with the housing sector of the economy' . . . we may be inclined to extend Wallace Smith's conclusions to urban land-use theory as a whole. (p. 166–7).

These references are puzzling. Hurd's analysis (developed by Hoyt, not listed in Professor Harvey's bibliography) stresses sectoral and axial growth, but it is hard to see anything even implicitly Marxist in it. Hurd stresses that the price of land and buildings is derived from the capitalisation of economic rent, which is based essentially on utility.[6]

Similarly, Professor Wallace Smith's comment (on page 49 actually) looks very different in context. In this passage he uses 'the traditional concept' to refer to a situation in which there is a single product selling at a single price, with no stocks – a concept which he later (p. 138) describes as 'Marshallian'. He then points out that there are many different types of housing, selling at different prices, which do not necessarily move in line. Moreover, prices are dominated by stocks rather than annual output. Again, the situation is frequently altered by changes in taxes and subsidies; the equilibrium position is constantly moving because of changes in tastes and technology; and the most important problems in resource allocation often lie more in removing imperfections than in increasing or reducing total output. No major economist has ever denied all this – certainly not Marshall. To define 'the traditional concept' so as to exclude these considerations is coming close to knocking down a straw man. Sub-markets, moving equilibria, time-lags, stocks, taxes and subsidies, constraints on optimisation, are part of the stock-in-trade of modern microeconomics. Professor Smith goes on to stress that:

. . . micro-economics of the housing sector is a most promising approach to housing problems which seem at first like matters of macro-economics (net new investment, etc.), pure and simple. (p. 41)

(A comment which seems as applicable to the British as to the American housing situation). This microeconomic basis of macroeconomic problems is precisely what 'liberal' economists have argued in recent years. Indeed, Professor Smith's book on housing is a blend of simple microeconomics and institutional analysis which is completely in the tradition of liberal political economy. (This is also true of his later book, *Urban Development* from which I have myself had occasion to quote).[7] It is simply not true that Hurd's or Professor Smith's books challenge the basis of modern microeconomics. This is not to deny that when Professor Harvey criticises some of the complex, but essentially static and formal, urban theories of recent years he makes some telling points, and occasionally achieves a memorable phrase, such as 'the spectacular design – mysticism of Doxiadis' (p. 303). But these criticisms have often been made in non-Marxist term.

Let us turn to Professor Harvey's observations on the 'ghetto' and the central business district. Professor Harvey indicates several reasons for the 'ghetto's' emergence. He stresses there cannot be more than one land parcel in *exactly* the same position as another. There is therefore a monopoly situation, and given a class monopoly of land ownership, rent constitutes the realisation of this monopoly. He postulates a scale of different urban locations, from the most to the least desirable. The richest groups occupy the best positions, the middle-income groups occupy the middling locations and the poor have to accept what is left. Whereas the higher income groups can build new housing, the poor have to take the poorest existing housing, which is being abandoned by other groups. The poor are therefore 'squeezed' into a limited quantity of housing and forced to pay relatively highly for it. The poor are thus exploited by the class monopoly of land and capital-owners. This takes the form not only of holding up prices in central ghettos but also of withholding mortgage finance from the ghettos in order to divert these funds to suburban districts ('redlining'). Speculative withholding of land contributes to this process. Professor Harvey quotes Professor Gaffney, who attributes 'urban sprawl' to massive 'speculative withholding' in central districts. Professor Harvey considers the state of American cities to be evidence of the universality of this exploitation 'under the capitalist mode of production'.

Some of the concepts used in this analysis are neither new nor specifically Marxist. The ideas of poor immigrants being forced into areas being abandoned by higher-income groups has a long history, from straightforward geographical descriptions to formal models. However, it does not follow that a 'handing down' system *necessarily* works to the disadvantage of the poorer group. As with secondhand cars or children's clothes, the transfer of used goods from one group to a poorer group can be of benefit to both. The price paid for the secondhand housing will depend on the readiness of the previous owners to move out and the number of newcomers trying to move in. A variety of studies – mainly concerned with racial differences, which are often more important than income differences as such – suggests that these social changes can result in increases, decreases or no change in property values.[8] Both theory and experience, however, suggest that when poor 'immigrants' are flooding into older districts, rents are likely to be high, whereas when this influx stops, they are likely to fall. The cessation of the influx of 'immigrants' is, in fact, the major recent change in both American and European cities, and one which is lowering both densities and land values.

The other aspect of the neo-Marxist analysis – 'speculation' and the withdrawal of finance in central areas – has also been discussed in several empirical studies of American central districts.[9] They conclude that – as with speculation in general – this type of activity may speed up changes resulting from more fundamental causes, but does not initiate them. The neo-Marxist analysis also assumes a uniformity and cohesiveness among present-day suppliers of capital which many people will find hard to accept. Is it really true that the British building societies (and the saving and loan associations in the USA) are part of a conspiracy to withdraw capital from inner areas in order to make greater profits in the suburbs? And is there today really a 'class monopoly' of the ownership of real property and capital? Even in the 19th century, there was not a 'class monopoly' in the sense that, in the Middle Ages, only a hereditary class could own land. However, it may be granted that, in the early British industrial cities, the ownership of real property was highly concentrated. Today, in all developed countries, there is a high proportion, often a majority, of owner-occupiers of housing, not all of whom can be regarded as belonging to the 'bourgeoisie', on any other than a circular definition. As far as rented housing is concerned, a high proportion (although higher in Europe than in the USA), is owned by a range of non-profit enterprises or public bodies. Does this not mean that the current form of urban 'capitalism' is very different from that of the 19th century, if one can even use the same term? The question whether the present mixture of owner-occupiership, private or corporate tenancy, non-profit enterprises or public bodies, is still the same 'class monopoly' which Marx denounced is a major point of difference between Marxists and liberals.

Another question-mark over the explanation of depressed inner city areas advanced by Professor Harvey concerns the differences between cities within the USA and, more strikingly, between cities in the USA, and, for example, Canada and Western European countries. Both the similarities and the differences raise doubts as to whether inner-city problems can be attributed to 'capitalism'. The decline in the size of the inner-city population is universal, but the extent to which this has been accompanied by decay, poverty and crime constituting a serious social problem, varies enormously. English-speaking Canada, for example, has a great deal in common with the USA (in spite of Canádians' protestations) and housing is mainly privately financed. On the other hand, there are stricter town planning controls, planning delays which arouse criticism from developers, and extensive public 'land banking' in some cities. Canadian cities do not have inner-city problems on anything like the scale of most of the older US cities; on the other hand, land and house prices (i.e. 'absolute rent' in the Marxist terminology) are noticeably higher. Turning to Europe, there is a striking contrast between Britain and most of the rest of North-West Europe, such as West Germany, the Netherlands and Scandinavia. Only Britain has inner-city problems comparable with those in the older American cities. West Germany and the Netherlands have problems of adaptation, but not the serious problems of decay and social ills which are found in Britain. This difference cannot be explained by a more 'capitalistic' system of housing in Britain. On the contrary, Britain has a much higher proportion of public housing than other countries, since most rented housing is owned by local authorities. It is not apparent that these international differences can be explained by the Marxist theory – or, indeed, any single economic theory. On the other hand, a variety of economic concepts can at least go a long way towards explaining them (see Chaps. 6, 10).

Professor Harvey echoes Marx's idea, popularised by Professor J. K. Galbraith, that capitalist corporations can make consumers buy anything they choose to produce.

> The capitalist market exchange economy so penetrates every aspect of social and private life that it exerts an almost tyrannical control over the life support system in which use values are embedded. A dominant mode of consumption, Marx observed, inevitably creates the conditions of consumption. (p. 190)

Applying this theory to central business districts, Professor Harvey argues that land prices do not (normally) depend on locational advantage but the other way round. Absolute and monopoly rent enter into cost, and thereby has a perverse affect on land use.

> The problem under these conditions is to discover (or generate) firms with production functions which can readily absorb these costs. It is

not surprising to find, therefore, that the highest rent areas in the city are colonized by commercial activities whose productivity cannot be measured – government offices, banks, insurance companies, stockbrokers, travel agents and various forms of entertainment, are good examples. Hence arises the paradox that some of the most unproductive activity in society is found on land which is supposedly of the greatest marginal productivity by virtue of its location. The solution to this paradox is simple. Land and property rent in central locations does not arise out of the land's marginal productivity but out of the processes which permit absolute and, even more importantly, monopoly rents to be charged. (p. 188)

This formulation appears to be based on three assumptions, (a) service industries are unproductive, (b) the owners of central sites possess not only a monopoly but a captive market, or one that can be artificially created, and (c) in the case of service industries, it is impossible to calculate the marginal productivity of a central site. All these assumptions can be questioned.

The idea that any process which does not result in a physical product is 'unproductive' has a long history. It was taken over by Adam Smith from the Physiocrats: Marx took it over from Smith and made it a central part of his theory. The principle that services were not included in national income became embodied in Soviet doctrine – and raised few difficulties during the Stalinist era. But in the more advanced East European countries, this materialist pre-occupation was one of several unsatisfactory economic aspects of Marxist-Leninism as interpreted by Stalin.[10] In Western countries, the idea of the 'unproductiveness' of services occasionally recurs in political debate, but most economists reject it. They believe that it is irrelevant whether the product takes the form of goods or services, provided it is the outcome of consumer demand (or, in the case of government services, an informed political decision).

Assumptions (b) and (c) are concerned with business behaviour and can to some extent be tested by reference to what actually happens in the property market. Is it true that, if central area office rents rise in real terms – as they did in central London in 1973–4 – tenants either have no choice but to remain and/or cannot calculate whether it pays to remain or not (i.e. cannot calculate the marginal productivity of occupying the building)? The marginal productivity of an office building on a central site (and in the long run the value of the site (Table 1)) is, for practical purposes, its value as compared with the value of a building in a cheaper 'secondary' situation, in the suburbs, or in a provincial city. Assume that the choice is between a 'prime' position (e.g. in 'the City') at, say £100,000 p.a. or a 'secondary' central position at £50,000 p.a. or a suburban situation at £20,000. The questions are then: 'Would it be possible to undertake the work – or most of it – in one of the alternative sites? If so, would there be extra costs involved (sending staff to meetings in the 'City', delay in obtaining information, etc.) and would these extra costs outweigh the savings in rent?[11]. These questions cannot be answered precisely and objectively (how many economic questions can?) but they can be answered on the basis of the best available knowledge and judgement. Indeed, these questions have had to be asked, and answered, by large numbers of firms in recent years in London, New York, and many other metropolises. Different types of firm have taken different decisions. Stockbrokers, for example, are virtually bound to stay very near the Stock Exchange. (But it is noteworthy that their members have shrunk sharply in recent years, because of more institutional ownership and the competition of a decentralised market based on electronic communication. The common description of Burgess's Zone V as 'the stockbroker belt' is now anachronistic). Other firms are more 'footloose', and many have voted with their feet.

The 'liberal' explanation of the concentration of service activities in city centres, which Professor Harvey finds so paradoxical, is that Government offices and financial institutions choose central locations (and bid up rents) in order to be near legislatures, Stock Exchanges and headquarters of organisations of all types. Theatres, concert halls or massage parlours often choose these locations because large numbers of people are there or (given the traditional 'radial' pattern of transport routes) can get there more easily than to outlying locations. But there is a decentralising tendency – and this has been combined with a growth in recent years in total office employment (the most striking growth in Britain being in government service). Thus the considerable movement of office employment out of Central London in the 1960s still left office employment there slightly higher than at the beginning of the decade. This decentralising tendency has largely been brought about by rises in rents and, even more importantly, rates (local property taxes). Official policies which limit office growth can contribute to rent rises. Thus the central business district usually retains its absolute, if not its relative, importance for office employment. For manufacturing industry, warehousing etc., on the other hand, central locations have lost the advantages which they once possessed.

This 'liberal' theory explains quite well the general pattern of land values – the maintenance of high land values in the central business district (and sub-centres) together with a fall in other inner city areas. It can also explain why, for example, office rents in central London have in recent years been high by comparison with other cities whereas New York, which has had a glut of offices, has had low rents. Professor Harvey's argument hardly seems consistent with experience in the market for office space. His denial of the possibility of rational economic calculation in connection with the location of offices must be regarded by any other than the most orthodox of Marxists as a blind-spot. He accepts the concept of marginal productivity in a physical sense, but seems prevented by the materialistic Marxist doctrine of production from applying it to locations of differing commercial quality – a concept which has underlain the theoretical and the practical discussion of urban land values for nearly a century.

One of Professor Harvey's criticisms echo those of British journalists. He states, for example, that, in London after 1966, it paid entrepreneurs to keep offices empty. This argument was to a large extent a generalisation based on Centre Point, an office block in central London, owned at the time by a company controlled by a colourful property developer, which remained unlet for many years. The argument was that office rents, and hence capital values, rose by more than the interest charges which represented 'holding' costs. It was thus profitable to build offices and keep them empty in order to be able to let them later at higher rents. Once an office block was built, even if it were unlet, it could be used as collateral for a loan to build another, and so on *ad infinitum*. Even at the time, some economists questioned the logic of this theory. For one thing, unlet office blocks are not normally the kind of collateral that bankers welcome (although it must be admitted that during the explosive monetary growth of 1972–3 some banks did strange things). Secondly, even if rents were rising, rent reviews meant that it was unlikely to be profitable to delay letting for long. The issue can now be seen in better perspective. It seems fairly clear that, if it ever paid to hold offices empty, this was only for a few months during a period of explosive inflation. Centre Point was not typical; in any case its long vacancy was probably unprofitable for the company. At a time when the reputation of more than one 'financial wizard' of the 1965–73 period has been reappraised, the long vacancy of Centre Point looks more like a blunder than the diabolical cunning it was generally believed to be at the time.

More generally, Professor Harvey echoes the familiar complaint by Marx (and Carlyle) that 'Market exchange reduces every human being to the status of a commodity' (p. 278). This objection does not apply to a Cuban system under which housing is allocated administratively, without any payment, and any transfer has to take place through a government body. Perhaps this argument can best be answered *ad hominem*. Does a system like that of British council housing, or Russian housing (or, for all I know, Cuban housing), in which allocation is in the hands of officials, really give a higher status to human beings than the system found in West Germany for rented housing, and in Britain for owner-occupied housing, where the family looks at what is available on the market and makes its choice (with a safety net for the poor or incompetent)?

At bottom, Professor Harvey's criticisms of the urban market economy are based on general economic issues. The reader can only be recommended to read Marxist expositions alongside expositions of both mainstream economics and the general 'liberal' case: the critique of Marxism by Milovan Djilas[12]; the exposition of 'mainstream' economics in a broad non-materialist way by Kenneth Boulding[13]; the 'restatement of economic liberalism' by Samuel Brittan[14]

PLANNING AND PROFIT IN THE URBAN ECONOMY

A different type of socialist analysis is given in *Planning and Profit in the Urban Economy* by T. A. Broadbent. Whereas Professor Harvey is a 'pure' Marxist who, like Marx, refuses to 'write a menu for the dinners of the future', Mr. Broadbent writes in a British context and represents a viewpoint very influential in official British circles. He is more Fabian than Marxist, but many of his theoretical arguments are essentially Marxist, as are many of the writers he cites. When he cites eminent non-Marxists like Keynes, his interpretation of their views is open to question. His book begins by developing the ideas of Mr. John Palmer (*op. cit.*) and ends with – in effect – a theoretical apologia for the Community Land Act and the nationalisation of the building trade.

The starting point of the argument is that Britain is the most advanced capitalist economy in the world; indeed, it is so advanced that it is 'overdeveloped'.[15] This proposition is documented by reference to a variety of sources: J. M. Keynes' *General Theory of Employment Interest and Money*; a distinguished economic history of (capitalist) Imperialism; a study of unemployment in Japan (p. 16). These arguments seem less than conclusive. It is not altogether clear which aspects of the *General Theory* are considered to support the peculiarly 'overdeveloped' nature of the British economy today. The authors of the Japanese study maintain that Britain is now, as it was in Marx's time, the most developed capitalist economy, because of the exceptionally low proportion of self-employed people. But is not this low proportion capable of a different interpretation – such as the British tax system? Similarly, *Industry and Empire* (1969) by Professor E. J. Hobsbawm is quoted (with some condensation) for its reference to Britain as 'the most urbanised, industrialised and proletarianised state in Europe, with a relatively simple two-class social system and an unusually important role for the industrial working class in politics'. This seems to raise more issues than it resolves. There is a small, and rapidly diminishing, difference in the level of 'urbanisation' of European countries, however defined; in fact, with the decentralisation of population, 'urbanisation' is ceasing to be a very meaningful concept. The term 'most industrialised' is also problematical. The conclusion that Britain has only two classes raises a number of questions (in which one do university teachers belong?) although, as regards 'proletarianisation', Professor Hobsbawm may have a point.

This 'overdeveloped economy' has experienced problems of low economic growth and a tendency to balance of payments deficits. It is taken for granted that more state control is the answer to both general economic and urban problems. 'At first sight (Holland 1975b) state intervention appears to be the one means of creating conditions whereby the UK economy could, through the planning of investment, break out of its difficulties' (p. 25). However, Mr. Broadbent goes on to argue that increased intervention will not be effective without a major extension of state ownership, and a contraction of the market economy.

Mr. Broadbent then reviews the neoclassical theories of land use and questions the view that households in a market economy system are consumption units which choose housing as a consumption good. They should rather be regarded as 'small factories' which produce a supply of labour for the system. The implication seem to be that any talk of 'consumer sovereignty' in the housing market is misplaced. He goes on to argue – if I understand him correctly – that the growth of state ownership and control in Britain has been exaggerated, and that the trouble with town planning is that the planners have insufficient powers. He suggests that a system of state control which relies on guiding a basically market economy is unworkable, and that the approach adopted so successfully in council housing should be extended to a wider field.

' . . . the key aim should be to *emancipate* public planning, to change the rules under which it now operates, and to use the state to achieve *directly* some of the national economic and social goals and the local urban goals. This would involve the state's building new factories, carrying out redevelopment or rehabilitation; the state could build houses, employ people who are otherwise unemployed, and use its potential purchasing power in an active and positive manner to achieve social goals directly, rather than relying first and foremost on the private sector' (p. 245/6)

This type of argument will be discussed, in connection with public landownership, in subsequent chapters.

THE RELEVANCE OF MARX

Even those who are critical of Marxism can accept that Marx introduced some illuminating concepts – especially the way in which classes acquire vested interests, which influence their general political and social attitudes. Where non-Marxists differ from Marxists is in their rejection of the view that class conflict is the *sole* explanation of economic and social movements, and that the only conflict is between the proletariat and the bourgeoisie (in Marx's sense), which ends with the introduction of a communist system. It appears to non-Marxists that civil servants, technologists, professors or politicians can also acquire class interests and that 'Marxist' countries have produced a 'New Class' even more ruthless than 19th century landlords.

Some aspects of urban life can certainly be explained in terms of class interest. The economically questionable 'urban bias' of many poor countries can in part be explained in terms of the interests of an urban *élite*.[16] In Britain, the 'municipal bulldozer' was halted only when the planners and politicians encountered a class of people who were able to organise effective political action in defence of their interests (Chap. 11). The exponents of 'the economics of property rights' (Chap. 2) can justifiably claim to be, in one respect, Marx's successors.

SUMMARY

Marxism gives an alternative explanation of urban processes to that by 'mainstream' or 'liberal' economics. Whereas 'liberal' economic analysis incorporates the 'marginalist revolution' of the 1860s, Marxist economics is based on earlier ideas. Karl Marx (1818–1880) took over certain aspects of 'classical economics' – notably the 'labour theory of value' and the distinction between 'use value' and 'exchange value' – and used them to construct a theory of class exploitation. ('Liberal' economists believe that, on these points, Adam Smith was muddled). Marx believed that urban land-ownership was, under capitalism, inevitably becoming more and more concentrated in a few hands. This land-owning monopoly used its power to extract a tribute from other classes – 'absolute' rent, which was additional to 'differential' rent. Under communism, rent would disappear.

Present-day Western Marxists use these concepts to explain how the land-owning monopoly manipulates land values and land uses so as to enrich itself at the expense of the rest of society. The central business district exists, not because of any genuine demand for its services, but because the land-owning class manipulates 'wants' so as to achieve high rents. The 'ghetto' arises because the land-owning class finds it advantageous to confine low-income families to old, decaying districts. The policy conclusion is that private property and the use of the price mechanism in real property shall be replaced by a system of administrative allocation.

While the idea of land pricing as a 'capitalist trick' has been gaining support in Western countries, a reverse process has been under way in the communist countries of Eastern Europe, where the virtues of land pricing are gradually being rediscovered.

One aspect of Marx's approach – the 'economic interpretation of history' – is considered illuminating by non-Marxists, although it can often lead to conclusions very different from those of most Marxists (*cf* the 'economics of bureaucracy'). Neo-Marxist urban analysis is a different matter, but one that should be taken seriously. Whether it is convincing must be assessed by reference to whether its assumptions and predictions are realistic.

SELECT BIBLIOGRAPHY

T. A. Broadbent, *Planning and Profit in the Urban Economy*, Methuen, 1977
Manuel Castells, *The Urban Question: A Marxist Approach*, Edward Arnold, 1977
David Harvey, *Social Justice and the City*, Edward Arnold, 1973

Karl Marx, *Capital* Vol III, (Page references are to the 1909 Chicago edition)

Karl Marx and F. Engels, *The Communist Manifesto*

A more populist type of Marxist analysis is to be found in *Profits against Houses* and *Gilding the Ghetto*, 1976, Community Development Project, The Home Office, London.

REFERENCES

1. Engels, editing Marx some years later, added a percipient comment which implicitly contradicts Marx's (and Mill's) agricultural prognosis:
   'Fortunately all prairie lands have not been taken under cultivation. There are enough of them left to ruin all the great landlords of Europe and the small ones into the bargain'. (pp. 842–3)
2. 'Nearly all the docking facilities of our port cities are in the hands of the great land leviathans in consequence of the same process of usurpation' (p. 728).
   The subsequent decline of these docks illustrates that even real property is subject to 'waves of creative destruction'.
3. V. Kirichento, *National Wealth of the USSR*, Moscow, 1964, p. 46.
4. The following contributions are available in translation: F. von Wieser. 'The Theory of Urban Ground Rent' in *Essays in European Economic Thought* ed. L. Sommer, Princeton, USA, 1960.
   G. Cassel, *The Theory of Social Economy*, London, 1932.
   H. von Stackleberg. *The Theory of the Market Economy* London, 1952.
5. quoted in Wilczynski *op. cit.* p. 544.
6. In one not very clear sentence, Hurd does admittedly talk about 'exchange value' differing from intrinsic value (p. 2). But the context makes quite clear that he is referring to the fact that properties with the same net rent *at present* may have different values because expected *future* changes justify different capitalisation rates.
   'Where a locality is advancing in value, capitalisation rates are low, where stationary they are normal, and where declining they run very high' (p. 1)
   He stresses that
   'estimated future prospects form the mastering factor of all exchange values. . . . To be reckoned with under the head of

future prospects are not only local changes of utility, but the rate of growth of the city as a whole, the prosperity or depression of the surrounding section and the success or failure of the industries directly supporting it' (p. 2).

This still relevant comment on property yields makes it clear that Hurd's passing distinction between 'intrinsic value' and 'exchange value' has no 'classical' connotations, and could be phrased quite differently.

7. Hallett (1977) p. 115–6.
8. Hugh A. Nourse *et al* in Hugh Nourse *The Effects of Public Policy on Housing Markets*, Lexington, Mass. 1973, p. 107ff.
9. Leo Grebler. *Housing Market Behaviour in a Declining Area*, New York 1953.
   Vernon and Hoover, and Frieden *op. cit.* see pp. 123, 220.
10. L. Sirc, *Economic Devolution in Eastern Europe*, London, 1969.
11. There are, in practice, many other considerations.
   'It is fairly easy to make up a composite check list to see whether relocation is really worth considering:
   1. Is there a substantial rent review on the horizon?
   2. Does the property tie up capital that could be better employed elsewhere?
   3. Is the business in an unnecessarily expensive area, looking at both rent and rates?
   4. Are the buildings really suited for business today, or has the business merely grown used to fitting into existing space?
   5. Do staff have transport problems?
   6. Can you afford, or get the right staff in the present location?
   In the phraseology of the women's magazines, if your score is high it's time to think about divorcing your building.'
   John Brennan, 'Arguments for relocation' Property IV, *Financial Times* July 3 1978.
12. *The New Class*, London, 1966.
13. *Economics as a Science*, New York, 1970.
14. *Capitalism and the Permissive Society*, Macmillan, 1973.
15. The whole concept of nations being 'underdeveloped' (or 'less developed' or 'developing'), not to mention 'overdeveloped', is problematical and even questionable, as any good text book on development economics stresses (e.g. C. P. Kindleberger and B. Herrick *Development Economics*, New York 1977 Chap. 1). Britain may well be 'overdeveloped' in the sense that, because of its 19th century history, it has developed a taste for a standard of living

which its present industrial performance cannot support. It could equally well be argued that, having adopted policies similar in some respects to those of the less successful countries of the Third World, Britain has begun to show signs of 'under-development'. It might be better to abandon 'catch-all' concepts on 'state of development' and concentrate on a comparative international analysis of specific policies and institutions.

16. M. Lipton, *Why Poor People Stay Poor*, Temple Smith 1976, p. 319ff.

II Policy

Introduction

A good starting point for an examination of urban land policy is to ask why one is needed. In recent years, it has often been implicitly assumed in the academic discussion of urban questions that any extension of state action is necessarily beneficial, while the effects of existing state action have not been critically examined. The time seems ripe for a new assessment of what J. S. Mill, in a still astonishingly relevant discussion, called, 'The grounds and limits of the laisser-faire or non-interference principle'.[1] The policies with which we are concerned can be divided into:

a) State participation in the real estate market.
b) Town planning.
c) The taxation of rises in land value.

Within each type, there are aspects on which nearly everyone accepts the need for state action, and aspects where its extent, or type, is debatable. For example, public authorities have to acquire land for purposes such as roads, so that arrangements have to be made for compensating previous owners, and for public management. The amount of this type of 'necessarily public' land has increased sharply in recent decades.[2] Beyond this generally agreed level of participation in the real estate market are 'optional' fields ranging from 'land banking', the provision of public housing, to a public monopoly in the development or allocation of real property.

Similarly, everyone accepts the need for some kind of town planning. However, 'town planning' can mean many things, and it takes on a more 'anti-market' character in Britain than in most other countries. Some proponents of British-style planning and council housing even deny the existence of town planning in a country with what many people would consider such excellently planned cities as West Germany. This paradox suggests (a) 'planning' in the sense of detailed control of development can be carried out by bodies other than the state, although only central or local government can undertake 'strategic' planning, and (b)

149

planning and development systems should be judged in the light of how they actually work. For example, to lump together, and criticise, West Germany and the USA, as being 'unplanned', as many influential British writers have done, is to ignore important differences between systems, and their respective strengths and weaknesses.

The 'optional' areas of urban land policy are those in which state action is intended to correct alleged defects in the market mechanism or – a very different approach – to replace it by a system of administrative allocation. These defects in the urban land market can be divided into: (a) inefficiencies and (b) inequities. Questions of efficiency concern market failure. This can arise from various causes – insufficient information, too short a time-horizon, a divergence between private and social costs. As Professor Foster points out, some state action is needed to provide the participants in the urban development process with the information without which they cannot efficiently organise their activities; a Land Register, to take the simplest case, can be produced only by a state body. But the extensive planning control adopted in Britain has not achieved this desirable dissemination of information. Britain has signally failed to produce a Land Register, which is available in many 'less planned' countries, while it would be bizarre to suggest that British local authorities attach high priority to publishing information. Most people would agree when Professor Foster goes on to advocate the function of the planning authority as a 'spokesman for the future'.[3] But this assumes that the planning authority is a better judge of the future than the participants in the market process. No one who has studied the swings of fashion in planning circles can make this assumption with much confidence. More familiar forms of 'market failure' concern the location of industry, city size, traffic problems and urban decay. All these cases, however, indicate that there can also be 'planning failure'. It is clear, for example, that old residential areas often do not adapt well to changing conditions, and that some kind of renewal policy can be beneficial; it is equally clear that the policy of 'comprehensive redevelopment' has often done more harm than good.

Considerations of equity have underlain most of the taxes on rises in land value which have been proposed over the last hundred, or implemented over the last seventy, years. These taxes have been responses to the sudden, large financial gains which can occur on development, especially 'greenfield' development. There is a strong case on grounds of equity for some type of tax, but experience has shown that taxes designed to skim off large 'unearned' gains – when framed with little understanding of how the land market works – can cause serious inefficiencies and inequities. The taxation of rises in land value involves all the considerations discussed by students of public finance since Adam Smith. But the 'canons of taxation', and experience in many countries, have been ignored in most post-War discussion of land value taxation, and not only in Britain. A proposed Californian property tax which was nearly passed in 1978 was, according to one expert observer, 'drafted on the back of cocktail napkins'. Britain differs from other countries only in the speed with which such drafts become law. Professor Foster, after a brief survey of the British planning system, calls for 'a thorough reappraisal of planning controls – if not a bonfire, at least an intense bright light'.

The whole question of the operation of the urban land market and the role of the state raises the same basic issues as the great 'plan v. market' controversy that has taken place during the past half-century in both Western and Communist countries. There is a large amount of theoretical discussion and practical experience on these issues – the Stalinist system, the moves towards a 'socialist market economy' in Eastern Europe, the British and French experience of industrial nationalisation, price control and central planning, the 'socially re-sponsible market economy' of West Germany – which could illuminate the general issues underlying public land policy. In the event, land policy has been discussed in almost complete isolation from this body of economic knowledge, and even from any detailed examination of the land policies in other countries. There is a large field of international experience waiting to be researched. Our subsequent discussion can merely attempt to put some current issues in British land policy into a broader perspective than that within which they have usually been discussed.

REFERENCES

1. J. S. Mill, *The Principles of Political Economy*, Bk V. Chap XI
2. In Cologne, the average amount rose from 42m^2 per head in 1922 to 103m^2 in 1973.
3. 'Planning and the Market', in *The Future of Planning* (Peter Cowan ed.) London, 1973.

8 Town Planning

The issue is therefore not whether one ought or ought not to be for town planning but whether the measures to be used are to supplement and assist the market or to suspend it and to put central direction in its place. The practical problems which policy raises here are of great complexity, and no perfect solution is to be expected.

F. A. Hayek, *The Constitution of Liberty*. 1960, p. 350.

THE BACKGROUND

Town planning in some sense is as old as towns themselves. The pendulum has, however, swung between the tight formal layout of the baroque city and the minimal planning of early 19th century boom towns or some Third World cities today. The history of cities (as reviewed in Mr. Lewis Mumford's splendid, if not unchallengeable, book)[1] suggests a need to balance some measure of control with variety and initiative. Some of the most humane urban environments – such as the medieval city – have been produced under a type of planning which, within broad rules, allowed considerable scope for different styles and uses. Too much uniformity, or an excessive segregation of uses, can destroy the 'life' of a district. Sometimes this segregation results from market forces; suburban living has led to business districts which are 'dead' after 5 p.m. But an even more pervasive influence (in some countries) has been the principle of segregated uses recommended by the 'Charter of Athens' in 1933. The virtues of mixed uses was perhaps the most telling point in Miss Jane Jacob's polemic against the planners, and one which now seems to be gaining acceptance.[2]

We are concerned with the economic implications of town planning, and especially with its implications for land policy, but some discussion of general town planning philosophy is necessary, since different approaches to town planning imply different land policies. The modern town planning movement began as a reaction to the too rapidly developed, unsanitary, cities of the Industrial Revolution. It drew its philosophical bases from other movements which reacted against 19th century urbanisation; state socialism, 'Utopian' socialism, the 'land reform' movement, the romanticisation of the Middle Ages. Together with an assertion (or re-assertion) of the need for the public control lacking in the early industrial city, it shared with these movements a Utopian, anti-libertarian and anti-economic flavour.

The evils of the Industrial Revolution were worst, and the reactions against it strongest, in Britain. This set Britain on a course very different from that in, for example, Germany and the USA. Germany benefitted from its later industrialisation and, after the chaotic urbanisation of the 1860s, quickly established local authority departments concerned with surveying, the enforcement of building codes, the administration of the extensive municipally-owned property, and the system (better developed in Germany than elsewhere) of reorganising landownership for redevelopment. This type of administration differed from present-day planning departments in that it was not much concerned with broader issues such as the location of industry. But it exerted a salutary influence on urban design, and established a tradition of the supervision of private development by a firm but knowledgeable and sympathetic local administration. When planning departments as such were set up under the Federal Republic, they had to fit into an administration with a powerful 'estate management' tradition, at a time when the prevailing economic philosophy (in marked contrast to Britain) was a 'socially responsible market economy'. Moreover, large-scale development schemes were generally supervised by non-profit agencies, which helped to defuse 'anti-developer' sentiments and often raised the quality of development. At the same time, the reassertion of liberal constitutional principles led to a greater reliance on general regulations than on discretionary decisions. One of the consequences has been better relations between planners and the development industry. Although criticisms by developers of planners and *vice versa*, are not unknown, there is not the vituperative dialogue of the deaf found in Britain.

In the USA, an attachment to individual rights and a suspicion of government power led to town planning being of a limited kind. Britain has adopted neither the somewhat 'laissez-faire' approach (at least until very recently) of the USA, nor the extensive, but not hostile, public regulation of development characteristic of Germany. Before 1914, the embryonic planning movement was largely concerned with 'slum clearance', which gave it a questionable bent that later had important consequences (Chaps. 10 and 11). Only limited planning was undertaken in the inter-War years. After 1945, town planning mushroomed from a

largely theoretical doctrine to a system with 'the most extensive
professional back-up, the most complex legislation and the most
comprehensive bureaucratic organisation of any planning system'.[3]
Moreover, town planning in Britain – unlike town planning in most
countries – developed largely outside the legal system. Government
bodies, local and central, were given virtually unlimited powers of
development control, rather than being bound by legal provisions as to
the conditions under which various types of control could be exercised.

LAW *VERSUS* DISCRETION

Town planning raises in a particularly acute form the dilemma of
administrative discretion versus the rule of law, of flexibility *versus*
certainty. There is a spectrum of systems running from a pure 'rule of
law' to purely arbitrary power.[4] Under a 'rule of law' there are clear
objective regulations, within which the citizen is free to operate. The
other end of the spectrum is represented today by the view that there is
no justification for restraints on the power of the government, provided
that it has been democratically elected, since the power of such a
government is the power of the people over itself. The power of the state
to achieve social justice should not be limited by what the late Professor
Titmuss termed 'the pathology of legalism'. The rule of law can claim the
virtues of making clear to citizens where they stand, curbing the abuse of
power, and ensuring even-handed justice; it can be criticised for rigidity.
A system of uncontrolled state power can claim to provide flexibility; it
can be criticised for uncertainty, lack of accountability and – if a right of
appeal is granted – delay. In town planning, the spectrum ranges from a
legally binding 'plan' (of whatever type) to a system of 'development
control' in which the planning authority is free to take any decision on
individual cases. There are, however, intermediate positions, such as a
plan in fairly general terms, leaving some elbow-room for decision-
making in individual cases.

Countries in which the 'rule of law' approach enjoys strong general
support – such as the USA or West Germany – have attempted to apply
it in town planning, although in different ways. The USA has, broadly
speaking, had a simple 'zoning' system in which areas are designated for
various uses: single-family residences, multi-family residences, commercial, industrial, etc. However, some states are moving towards more
detailed control. West Germany and Holland make the legally binding
document a detailed 'building plan'. But recent experience has shown

that, as plans have become more complex, it is not possible to adhere rigidly to a detailed plan for a large area.[5] Over the course of the years, views and circumstances change, and the course of development on the ground drifts more and more away from the plan. Provisions thus have to be introduced to allow for modifications to the plan, or departures from it. It does not, however, follow that there are no virtues in the German/Dutch type of system.

Between 1932 and 1939, Britain had a type of planning which laid down general rules for the type of development, densities etc. It is now assumed that this system was unsatisfactory, but there has been little examination of why this was so, and whether the defects could not have been corrected without giving planning authorities the arbitrary powers they now possess.

The intention of the framers of the 1947 Act was that planning would be clear and 'legalistic', in the sense that permissible uses would be clearly laid down in the development plan: large numbers of appeals were not envisaged. In practice, the planning authorities from the first possessed considerable discretionary powers: there were many complaints of detailed control which merely reflected the aesthetic predilections of planning officers or councillors. With the introduction of 'structure plans' under the 1968 Town and Country Planning Act, the balance was shifted even more in the direction of discretionary power, since the permitted development can be laid down in highly general terms, which impose few limitations on decision-making in individual cases. Some planning authorities have, in effect, abandoned the idea of reference to a plan, and 'decide every case on its merits'. In other cases, the plans themselves implicitly or explicitly postulate objectives alien to those for which the town planning powers were granted, e.g. the provision in the plan of one London borough that land will not normally be allocated for the use of private schools. Moreover, decisions are in many cases taken not by elected representatives but by officials. The present situation, therefore, is that local authorities have virtually unlimited powers of development control, combined with a right of appeal to the Ministry. It is the extent of this discretionary power which distinguishes the British system from that in most other countries.

British post-War town planning grew out of ideas on the need for 'a planned economy' which gained extensive support in intellectual and political circles during the 1930s and the War. These ideas lay behind several reports which influenced post-War policy, in particular, three often-praised and seldom-read reports – 'Uthwatt', 'Scott', and 'Barlow'.[6] The Uthwatt Report on Compensation and Betterment was superficial and purely abstract – even if it was more realistic than succeeding legislation, which it implicitly criticised.[7] On reading the report of the Scott Committee on rural land use (as distinct from Professor Dennison's note of dissent), one can only be astounded that influential men could have subscribed to views of country life which had long been overtaken by events, and could have displayed such bland indifference to the needs of the urban population. Only the Barlow Report on the Distribution of the Industrial Population stands up at all well. On development control – the crux of so many complaints subsequently made so often by ordinary people – no report was published at all. This period needs a study like that of Professor Ashworth's study of the origins of British town planning before 1914.[8] For the moment, we must confine ourselves to a brief examination of the philosophical basis of the town planning movement.

UTOPIANISM

One strong element in the modern town planning movement has been what can be termed 'Utopianism', although a defender of the approach is today more likely to use some such term as 'normative goal orientation'. This approach holds that there is an ideal world which can be achieved if society is directed along the correct path from above: it is characterised by a mistrust of automatic processes in society, such as the market system, and support of political control to achieve the community's goals. This approach finds particularly fertile ground in town planning. The general objections to this approach were outlined by Professor Hayek in 1944[9], and have been amplified in more modern terms by writers including Mr. Samuel Brittan[10] and Professor Charles Lindblom.[11] Two basic objections arise from the diversity of human goals and the impossibility of predicting the future. Different people have different objectives, or at least rank desirable objectives differently. If a particular set of goals is imposed by the state on society, a loss of personal choice and the variety of life results. Secondly, there is the danger of having all the eggs in one basket. If only one approach is tolerated, it may prove to be disastrously wrong, whereas if a variety of approaches is encouraged, the chances of coping more effectively with unforeseeable developments is increased.

CHANGES IN PLANNING PHILOSOPHY

Although a Utopian theme has recurred in various forms in British town planning since the War, there was a change in the conception of town planning in the 1960s. In the post-War era, it was thought of primarily in terms of organising land uses and structures. One well-known writer on town planning defined it as 'the art and science of ordering the use of land and the character and siting of buildings and communication routes so as to secure the maximum practicable degree of economy, convenience and beauty'. He went on to stress that (town) planning deals primarily with land and it is not therefore economic, social or political planning, though it may assist greatly in the realisation of the aims of these other kinds of planning, and should obviously be made to fall in step with them'.[12]

In a sense, this definition is unexceptionable. Town planning *is* concerned with land use. But land-use planning has to be based on assumptions about how people want to – or should be made to – live. Some post-War planning has been criticised for being based on incorrect social assumptions; e.g. the layout of the early New Towns in tight 'neighbourhood units'.[13]

In the sixties, it was widely argued that a purely physical approach was inadequate, and that planners must move on to comprehensive, social and economic planning – a view which became a new shibboleth, often without a clear analysis of its meaning. This idea arose from a growing realisation that physical changes did not necessarily solve social problems, and that large, unforeseen, movements in employment, settlement patterns and life-styles were making obsolete many of the post-War plans. What was less clearly understood was that terms like 'social planning' can mean at least two very different things.[14] One sense is 'social engineering', as used in a most clear-cut way in Marxist-Leninist literature, which is designed to impose a particular type of society. But there is a quite different sense. This is brought out in two books with similar titles, which might seem to be making the same point, but in fact advance fundamentally different philosophies. *In Town Planning in its Social Context*, Professor Gordon Cherry advocates a wider conception of town planning, but draws a crucial distinction:

At the heart of the matter must lie a question of attitudes: social planning is either a matter of social *evolution* or social *engineering*. Planners by tradition have seen their role as community builders and changers of society. We now argue that social planning strategy is concerned more with the promotion of satisfaction through the provision of a range of opportunity and choice so that the unhampered creativity of individuals may be fostered, (p. 116).

He goes on to argue that 'planning is not a social reform movement: it holds no lofty view as to the purposive functioning of society', (p. 167).

Professor Berry, from the USA, defends a very different view of planning. He dismisses 'incrementalism' (on which he quotes 'Charles E. Lindbloom' without indicating that Professor Lindblom defends it) as 'interest group politics', and contrasts this with the 'more rational' basis of 'normative goal-orientation' in which goals are set and plans implemented.[15] He is quite clear that this necessitates sufficient coercive power to ensure plan-fulfilment, and that there is a 'problem of pluralism'. He argues against 'ameliorative problem solving' on the ground that 'in a processual sense, then, such planning is past-orientated'. But one could reverse the argument. A system which allows new life-styles to emerge through the market mechanism, while seeking to cope with – and, if possible, anticipate – the new problems that emerge, could equally well be described as 'in a processual sense future-orientated' – if one writes like that. On the other hand, when a precise long-term goal is imposed from above, the persons imposing it – being human beings – are likely to be influenced by their (past) experience. Some of the goals still imposed by British planning authorities – e.g. maintaining the high concentration of activity in town centres and High Streets – are, in the opinion of some knowledgeable commentators, based on conditions which no longer exist.

The argument that planning should expand its horizons beyond physical layout can thus lead to diametrically opposed policies, depending on 'the question of attitudes'. The approach indicated by Professor Cherry would take account of social and economic trends in framing development plans. This could in some respects mean *less* central control. For example, under such an approach, comprehensive redevelopment of inner city areas, as carried out by many British city councils, would have been ruled out. At the same time, renewal schemes of a more limited kind would have been preceded by more investigation of what kind of people lived in the district, and what kind of changes they wanted. (cf. the 'social plan' of urban renewal schemes in West Germany, Chap. 11). On the other hand, the approach advocated by Professor Berry (and even more single-mindedly by the Marxists) would decide on 'desirable' social and economic trends and take the powers needed to implement them; this leads logically to an all-embracing system of state control.

CRITICISMS OF BRITISH PLANNING

British planning has often been held up (by planners) as the envy of the world. In recent years, the criticisms always present at the practical level have penetrated academic circles. The best comparison of policies in Britain and the USA, poses an agnostic question:

> Which country did worse – Britain with a rather elaborate system of urban planning, which has produced results different from those its sponsors intended, or the USA, where city planning never really promised much, and has never delivered much?[16]

The specific criticisms of the present British system are:

1. Plans take many years to prepare, and are overtaken by events.
2. The lack of a clear framework of principles for development control.
3. Planning authorities are ignorant of the practical problems of development, and sometimes display an ideological bias against private development; it is alleged that there are excessive delays and insufficient allocation of land for building.
4. Excessively detailed interference in matters of design (or general design guides which go into excessive detail).[17]

One criticism of British post-War planning has been that long-term plans have remained the official basis for policy, long after they have been overtaken by events. This was not how planning was envisaged by immediate post-War planners.

> The plan for an area should usually comprise a long-term plan, (in outline and covering a period of 40–75 years) and a series of five to ten year plans to illustrate the stages by which the final plan is to be realised. At the end of each stage the situation should be reviewed to make sure that the assumptions on which the plan was based are still valid. (H. Myles Wright, 'Town and Country Planning', *Chambers Encyclopaedia*, 1950).

If plans were, in fact, subject to fundamental review every five years the approach would not differ much from Professor Lindblom's 'disjointed incrementalism' – which need not exclude forecasts and investment plans by public authorities for as far ahead as time-lags make necessary. But it is clear that the elaborate town plans actually constructed have not been subject to a fundamental questioning every five years. They can take ten years to prepare, and hard-pressed officials who have finally produced a plan are in no mood to start challenging immediately its assumptions.[18] However, to criticise over-elaborate plans is not to dismiss either forecasting or planning, although it is to suggest greater humility in both. There are certain issues which in a densely populated country can only be decided collectively – the location of recreational areas or the location and type of transport networks and the general direction of development – and it is desirable that such decisions shall be made after as informed an examination as possible of the consequences of alternative policies.

One of the difficulties in discussing these somewhat philosophical aspects of planning is that words are used in different senses. The 'normative goal orientation' advocated by Professor Berry is very different from the need for 'explicit goals in urban planning' recommended by Professors Clawson and Hall, (*op. cit.*, p. 277). Clawson and Hall are merely concerned that there should be a clear definition of the specific objectives which policies or powers are designed to achieve. They point out that the objectives of the British planning system have either been considered so self-evident as not to need specification or as 'absolute moral imperatives, almost entirely unrelated to any discussion of the aspirations and needs of the mass of the people' (p. 278). This is illustrated in the Greater London Development Plan. In its review of the Plan, the Layfield Committee has a delightful list of stated objectives beginning with '. . . to give new inspiration to the onward development of London's genius', and ending with '. . . improving public transport in all possible ways'.[19]

The Committee comments,

The G.L.D.P. Written Statement is full of statements of aims which do not mean anything because they can mean anything to anyone. It is not perhaps being too cynical to believe, indeed, that such aims were inserted because they could mean anything to anyone.

DISCRETIONARY CONTROL

The British system, broadly speaking, gives planning authorities unlimited discretionary control over large or small matters, but with a right of appeal. This arrangement allegedly encourages local planners to take a negative and irresponsible attitude: if anything important will go on appeal to the Ministry anyway, why should they waste their time? The number of appeals to the Ministry – on large developments or on questions such as whether a village hall should be used for bingo or the siting of a bus stop – have in recent years been around 12,000 a year, of which about one-third are 'allowed'.

The present arrangements have often been criticised by developers for excessive, often ill-informed, interference in matters of design, leading to unnecessarily high costs.[20] The proposals usually put forward to meet these criticisms involve a move towards the type of planning found in other countries, where there is less discretionary control over matters of detail.[21] They include giving legal force for government guidelines, and the use of provisions exempting minor alterations from control (e.g. the proposed extension of the General Development Order).

But these criticisms of the planning process are not universally accepted. 'Conservation groups' defend the existing 'delays' (an unfortunately pejorative term, perhaps) on the ground that it is more important to get the right decision than a quick one. Indeed, they argue that, in the case of large structures which play a key role in the townscape, there is insufficient detailed control and publicity. This latter criticism, at least, may not be incompatible with the criticisms from developers of delay and interference. It is legitimate to require publicity for the design of large central buildings which affect people's 'image' of the city, and to exercise control, in a way that is inappropriate for run-of-the-mill development. (This was, in fact, the approach adopted in many of the most admired city developments of the past). If British planners had been less concerned with lofts and porches, they might have had more time to devote to, say, the Knightsbridge barracks. To date, however, the Government has denied the need for any change in existing planning arrangements.

ECONOMIC CONSEQUENCES

The question whether planning procedures are too restrictive is one on which opinions differ. It is, however, possible to analyse the question in broad theoretical terms, and to indicate the kind of empirical data which would answer, or at least illuminate, it. Critics of allegedly slow and restrictive planning procedures suggest that they have two economic consequences:

a) The rise in costs resulting from planning delays.
b) The general rise in land prices and the restriction in housing supply, resulting from alleged failures to allocate sufficient land for housing.

In assessing the cost of planning delays, it is invalid to take – as some complainants have done – the difference in building costs between the application for planning permission and its granting as a measure of the rise in costs. If there were constant output and a constant 'planning delay', this delay could be absorbed into the firm's internal planning without raising costs. Costs will be raised, however, if delays are unpredictable, or if they rise during periods of high demand. The very limited evidence suggests that delays have in fact increased during building booms, which may therefore have increased costs and reduced supply. The distribution of delays is also highly 'skewed', with a small proportion being much longer than the average.

On the question of land availability, there has been a running battle between planners and developers on whether sufficient land was being allocated for development, which flared up during the boom of 1972–3, subsided during the subsequent recession, and flared up again with the slight recovery of demand in 1978. Many of the arguments advanced in 1971–3 about a long-term rise in (real) land prices were, as events showed, based on too short a perspective.

The slump has stimulated a number of detailed local studies of land availability.[22] They suggest that, in the boom of 1971–3, neither side may have been completely in the right. It seems clear that the information on which planning authorities were acting in 1972–3 was incorrect: a good deal of land scheduled for development was not in fact available. On the other hand, demand was less than the planners forecast, and a surprising amount of development took place on odd patches of land not taken account of in the plans. More detailed, independent, local studies are needed on this question (as in so many other respects, a Land Register is badly needed). But it would be best of all if planners were more in touch with developers and with the practicalities of the land market (public participation in the land market could play a role here, see Chap. 12).

PLANNING AND THE MARKET

In the discussion of the economic implications of town planning, the fundamental question is the relation between 'planning' and the market (see Chaps. 2 and 3). The market also involves planning, but the planning is by purchasers and developers, responding to prices and costs. Moreover, by means of taxes and subsidies, the state can to some extent operate through the market. We are concerned with state planning in the sense of administrative decisions on what can be built, and where. This involves 'strategic' planning on the general pattern of communications and changes in land use over a large area, detailed 'development control', and public land purchase as an element in development policy.

In most of the post-War literature, a sharp distinction has been drawn between planning and the market; the predominant tone has been uncritically enthusiastic about planning and profoundly suspicious of the market. (The approach of most persons who actually undertake development, either in the private or public sector, is often different, but they tend to write less). One of the best-informed advocates of this point of view starts from the assumption that planning and the market are alternative methods of organising development, and that the aim of land policy is to prevent the market undermining the aims of planning, and to extend the public as compared with the private sector.[23]

But there is a different approach, which sees both the market and state planning as essential in urban development, recognises that there is bound to be occasional tension between them, but does not think of one as good and the other as bad. This view is often found among public officials engaged in land transactions, even in Britain, and it has been the main approach in West German planning and land policy. Let us examine the questions whether planners *can* oppose market forces (as opposed to guiding them into orderly paths) and whether they *should*.

One of the arguments for a market mechanism is that the knowledge available to one small group of planners is inevitably more limited than that of large numbers of households and firms throughout the community – in their various capacities as house-owners, tenants, shoppers, pedestrians, motorists or developers, landlords, estate agents, builders, etc. If, therefore, any changes are taking place in life-styles, a market process which depends on the judgements of large numbers of individuals is likely to be more successful than a completely centrally planned system. British planners largely failed to foresee the extent of suburbanisation, car-ownership, supermarkets, air travel, or population growth (just as they failed later to foresee the consequences of population decline). There are two responses to this situation. One is to demand an extension of state ownership and control, so that planning can play a more important role as part of a command economy. Some planners have taken this route, and proposed that all development should be undertaken by the state, although few have sought the logical conclusion of control of the movement of labour.

The second reaction is to question whether one should, as a general principle, oppose market forces. This is not to deny the case for intervention in those cases in which the market mechanism does not work well, although even here, 'planning' in the sense of development control is not always the answer. Two examples at a regional level are when an excessive concentration of population or industry in one part of a country seems to justify a major effort to shift economic activity, and when the preservation of 'amenity' districts near cities is desired. Brasilia and Magnitogorsk were built with the idea of opening-up 'undeveloped' regions. On a smaller scale, the British New Towns were intended to disperse population from London, while 'regional policy' was an attempt to direct industry to regions which had suffered from severe structural unemployment. Many people (including the author) thought at the time that these policies were justified – even if more recent experience suggests that they may have outlived their usefulness. But policies of this type operate on a different level from land-use planning. If financial incentives or other measures divert industry and population from one region to another, the land market will adjust itself to these changes. It is a very different matter if land-use policy seeks to prevent the implementation of demands from existing population and industry. The attempt, merely by restrictive land-use planning, to restrict the growth of a city results, in the first instance, in high prices for property, and often long-distance commuting. After a time, it tends to break down.

For preserving recreational areas, land-use planning *by itself* is also of limited value. The main British policy since the War has been the 'Green Belt', which was originally based on the idea that agricultural land was of amenity value for town dwellers. But recreation does not mix too well with modern agriculture. It mixes better with forestry, and few people who have seen the wooded areas near German cities have any doubt that better 'lungs' for a city are provided by publicly-owned 'amenity' forests than by drawing a 'Green Belt' on the map.

This questioning of British post-War planning suggests a somewhat different approach, an approach neither 'Utopian' in that it is not based on a precise blueprint of what the region will be like in 50 years time, nor intrinsically opposed to market forces. Its objectives are (a) rational planning of public investment and (b) seeking to guide market forces in those cases where there are reasons for thinking that they are likely to have undesirable aspects, which could be reduced by development control.

Public investment in roads, railways, airports, etc., is in all Western countries a massive programme which has over-taxed the planning resources of many governments. Britain has, at most, a middling record in this field. A case can be made that the extension of planning into optional fields has detracted from the quality of the big decisions which only the state can take. Better planning does not necessarily mean more planning, rather the reverse.

In the field of development control, the type of planning we have outlined would neither ignore, despise, nor worship market forces. It accepts that if the trend is, for example, to suburban living, or shopping for provisions by car in supermarkets, it is not the responsibility of the planner to say that he does not like these things and is going to stop them. But it is equally clear that, when there is no planning at a level about that of the site, the results can be unsatisfactory. The justification for planning major developments, on this view, is to assist a spatial coordination which may be only imperfectly achieved by the market mechanism, as well as to make provision for public facilities, and for 'disadvantaged' groups (subsidised housing, gypsy sites, etc.). What is proposed is not, therefore, *laissez-faire*: indeed it may in some cases involve more 'positive' actions, as in the public ownership and management of recreational areas. It is certainly a less God-like type of planning, but what goes on in planning offices and council chambers is not really very God-like. It is a type of planning which has long been advocated by some of the more thoughtful town planners.

This type of planning would not seek to impose aesthetic control over every detail of development, according to the tastes of individual planners. (If architects, builders, and clients have good taste, intervention by planners is unnecessary, and if they do not, the planners are unlikely to have any more. Britain has more development control than Switzerland: does it have better architecture?) Nor would it oppose development as such. Planning permission would be given unless there were clear and objective reasons for refusing. This has, in fact, been urged by Department of Environment circulars for years, but it appears to be still rejected by many local authorities. Planners would watch carefully for signs of expanding or contracting land uses, and seek to assess in good time the problems and opportunities to which these changes would be likely to give rise. Recognising that the location of activities can be influenced to a certain extent, and by positive attractions as well as by prohibitions, planners would seek to guide new uses into districts where 'external' difficulties would be minimised. Take the vexed issue of office expansion in London in the 1950s and 1960s. The first response was to try to stop it (most dramatically in 1964, when Mr. George Brown halted all office development in Greater London, with many unfortunate consequences (Chap. 5). A subsequent approach, found in the Greater London Development Plan, was to divide new office space among the boroughs on some basis, the economic logic of which has never been unearthed. Little apparent consideration was given to encouraging office development in the two locations where there was no clash with other uses – over railway stations, when they were redeveloped, and in obsolescent dock areas; both opportunities were, in the event, largely missed. In the 1960s, neither British Rail, the London port authorities nor the planning authorities showed much interest; after 1974 the uncertainties of Development Land Tax inhibited development.

TRAFFIC IN TOWNS

One field in which planning is unavoidable concerns transport routes. In the post-War period, the initial response to rising car ownership was to widen roads. This tended to be environmentally disruptive and in any case to be soon overtaken by the growth of traffic. A radical reassessment was suggested by Professor Sir Colin Buchanan in *Traffic in Towns* (1963). He argued that the motor car (in its present or future form) offered such enormous advantages in terms of door-to-door transport that it was bound to be chosen by users as their main form of transport. On the other hand, the expansion of car ownership, accompanied by piecemeal modifications of the road network, would destroy the environment of cities which had not been designed for the motor vehicle. He rejected the idea of decentralisation, maintaining – without any argument – that cities had to be maintained in broadly their present form. He therefore proposed a massive 40-year programme of building a system of roads, parking and other facilities designed to combine accessibility and environment. Urban motorways would pass *between* rather than *through* areas where people conducted their business on foot ('environmental areas'). Parking (underground or multi-storey) would be located so that it was possible to walk easily to pedestrian areas.

Professor Buchanan stressed that, although some early motorways had had a damaging environmental impact, this was by no means inevitable. It was a matter of design and – in particular – expense. Moreover, motorway construction could be undertaken in conjunction with renewal. Much of the inner city housing along prospective motorway routes was near the end of its life. The motorways could be part of a reconstruction programme, in which the area immediately adjacent to the motorway could be used as parkland, warehouses, etc. For a time, Professor Buchanan became a cult figure (perhaps a contributory factor being the novelty of a traffic engineer who was concerned with environmental consequences and who could write clear and elegant English). This over-enthusiastic reception obscured both a number of defects in the Buchanan approach and, in the aftermath, its important truths.

Criticisms of the Buchanan Report came not only from those who wished to abolish motor cars. Several economists, while paying tribute to the Report's concern for reconciling accessibility and environment, questioned its approach of relying on a comprehensive motorway network within cities of broadly their present form. A well argued case was made by Mr. D. J. Reynolds, and similar arguments were put forward by Mr. J. M. Thomson in a judicious reply to the extensive motorway network proposed in the Greater London Development Plan (see bibliography). The arguments put forward by these economists included the following:

(1) The cost of the proposed programme was so enormous that the necessary funds were unlikely to be available, or only at the cost of foregone improvements in public transport.

(2) Maintaining cities in their present form might be neither possible nor desirable. Indeed, it would be incompatible with a massive motorway network in inner areas. A further movement of activities to the suburbs would greatly ease the traffic problem in the 'central city'.[24]

(3) A relatively small expansion of the central business district – into the often decaying areas that surround it – can reduce the pressure in the centre. This would make possible more 'horizontal' segregation of cars and pedestrians and require less of the extremely costly and – if on a large scale – environmentally questionable 'vertical' segregation favoured by the report.

(4) There was no need to adopt *the same* transport strategy in close-knit older city districts and in looser-knit suburban districts, where both the financial and the environmental costs of road-building are much lower. Motorways can be built in outlying districts, while greater reliance could be placed on other methods in the inner areas with their denser and more 'close grained' pattern of development.

(5) Public transport – while it cannot displace the car – had an indispensable role to play, especially for commuting.

In the event, most British cities pursued neither the 'Buchanan' approach nor the economists' more eclectic approach of limited motorways and some decentralisation. London, in particular, has not followed the recommendations of the Thomson report to start on the outer ringways and abandon the inner ones. It has abandoned all the ringways and ceased to preserve the routes: the main policy has been to restrict parking facilities. The need to abandon the motor car has been stressed at innumerable meetings by GLC politicians – who have been known to arrive by car.

Most European countries have not experienced such sharp swings in transport planning. After the War, many countries modernised and extended a network of single-decker trams running on segregated tracks (a 'new' idea being investigated by the Transport and Road Research Laboratory!). Most of them also built successful suburban motorways, although they experienced a reaction against inner-city motorways.

In urban transport planning British performance, by international standards, can only be described as middling. The transport system in London does not compare too favourably with that in many European cities, whether one is travelling by car, public transport or on foot; even in countries with allegedly backward planning systems such as West Germany. The Layfield Report on the Greater London plan,

compared the status of the pedestrian with that of his counterpart in Frankfurt, Düsseldorf, Hamburg and Stockholm. In certain respects he is better off, thanks to zebra crossings, better regulated lights and the respect in which he is held by the motorist (*sic*) . . . But his European counterpart glides down shiny moving staircases into glittering halls enlivened with busy shops, including the basement floors of large department stores. He passes under large avenues along wide, gaily decorated corridors, admirably lighted both artificially and from abroad gently sloping ramps. These are often the gateway to a large network of pedestrian streets, to which wheeled traffic is only admitted up to 10 a.m. The contrast with the steep and narrow stairs and dingy dark passages, which are the normal fate of those crossing under roads in London is too obvious to need emphasis. (p. 490).

PLANNING AND THE FUTURE

The latest thinking of some leading members of the British planning profession on the 'crisis in planning' is provided in a report of the Royal Town Planning Institute, prepared by a committee representing all sides of the profession.[25] This document is, in parts, refreshingly frank about the failures of planning (e.g. in urban renewal) and the widespread questioning of its *rationale*. At the same time, the analysis is often fuzzy. The report makes a commendable, if not altogether successful, attempt to go back to first principles and provide a philosophical basis for town planning. It begins by listing 'the major goals of society'. Some of these, such as 'To respect the values of life and eliminate the causes of unnecessary physical and mental suffering', could mean anything. Others, such as 'To reduce inequalities not merely of opportunity but of material conditions of life', gloss over crucially important issues.[26]

The report proposes 'A new approach to planning' (prefaced by a quotation from Machiavelli!). It advocates reforming rather than abolishing the planning mechanism, but the proposed path to this end is not altogether clear. On the one hand, some of the ideas that have been put forward by critics of planning are accepted. It is recognised that it is impossible to take decisions in the public interest', without considering the consequences for gainers and losers. Smaller units of local government are favoured, and more consultation with industry, commerce and developers. On the other hand, most of the document is concerned with the need for a 'comprehensive planning strategy', but it is far from clear what this means in relation to land policy and the development process. This is hardly surprising, since the committee contained members with differing views; on the Community Land Act, for example, the committee contained severe critics and enthusiastic supporters. The debate on British town planning seems likely to continue.

SUMMARY

The modern town planning movement, which arose as a reaction to the unplanned towns of the early Industrial Revolution, contained a variety of philosophical approaches and took somewhat different forms in different countries. A 'Utopian' element, which was suspicious of individual rights, local action, and market forces was most apparent in Britain, where planning has been more divorced from development expertise or 'grass roots' movements than in some other countries. The British planning system is unusual in that it gives local authorities almost complete discretionary control, subject to a right of appeal to the Department of the Environment. Criticisms have often been made of delays, excessively detailed control and ill-informed policy decisions, although opinions differ on the extent of these defects. Two extreme approaches to the future of town planning are to abolish it, or to abolish any opposition to it through comprehensive state ownership. A more moderate approach – and one in line with planning systems in other countries – would be to limit discretionary power to more 'strategic' questions and to seek to correct the defects of market forces rather than opposing them. There seems to be an emerging consensus that control on minor matters should be relaxed, and that development should be allowed, unless there are clear reasons for refusal.

SELECT BIBLIOGRAPHY

Brian J. L. Berry, *The Human Consequences of Urbanisation*, Macmillan, 1973.

G. E. Cherry, *Town Planning in its Social Context*, Leonard Hill, 1973.

G. E. Cherry *The Evolution of British Town Planning* Leonard Hill, 1973.

M. Clawson and P. Hall.. *Planning and Urban Growth: An Anglo-American Comparison*. This incorporates the main conclusions of P. Hall (ed). *The Containment of Urban England*, 2 Vols. Allen & Unwin, 1973.

J. B. Cullingworth, *Town and Country Planning in England and Wales*, Allen and Unwin, 1970.

P. McAuslan, *Land, Law and Planning*, Weidenfeld and Nicolson, 1975.

Lewis Mumford, *The City in History*, Secker and Warburg, 1961.

D. J. Reynolds, *Economics, Town Planning and Traffic*. Institute of Economic Affairs, 1966.

Royal Town Planning Institute, *Planning and the Future*, 1976.

J. Michael Thomson, *Motorways in London*. Duckworth, 1969.
Traffic in Towns. The Buchanan Report, HMSO, 1963.

REFERENCES

1. Lewis Mumford, *The City in History*. Secker and Warburg, 1961.
2. Jane Jacobs, *The Death and Life of Great American Cities*, Jonathan Cape, 1962.
3. *Planning and the Future*, op. cit. p. 45.
4. The need to retain aspects of the 'rule of law' in town planning, while accepting that there must also be administrative discretion, has been eloquently argued by Professor J. Jowell. See 'The legal control of discretion' *Public Law* (1973) p. 178 and 'The Limits of law in urban planning' *Current Legal Problems* (1977) p. 16.
5. There are virtually no inter-European comparative studies. An Anglo-Dutch study is being undertaken by Oxford Polytechnic for the Centre for Environmental Studies.
6. *Expert Committee on Compensation and Betterment*. (Uthwatt Report). Cmnd 6386. HMSO, 1942.
   Report of the Committee on Land Utilisation and Rural Areas. (Scott Report). Cmnd 6378. HMSO 1942.
   Royal Commission on the Distribution of the Industrial Population. (Barlow Report). Cmnd 6153. HMSO 1940.
7. Hallett (1977), p. 124–6. The Uthwatt Committee drew a sharp distinction between 'undeveloped' and 'developed' land. For undeveloped land it recommended expropriation at existing use value. For developed land it recommended a system of taxing rises in site value as 'the only effective way of collecting betterment without hampering individual enterprise in the development of land' (para. 51).
8. W. Ashworth. *The Genesis of Modern British Town Planning*, London, 1954.
9. F. A. Hayek. *The Road to Serfdom*. London, 1944.
10. Samuel Brittan. *Capitalism and the Permissive Society*. Macmillan, 1973.
11. C. E. Lindblom. *The Decision Making Process*. Prentice Hall, 1968.
12. Lewis Keeble. *'Principles and Practice of Town and Country Planning'*. Estates Gazette, 1952.
13. Gordon Cherry. *Town Planning in its Social Context*. Leonard Hill, 1973. p. 129.

14. Richard Williams 'The Idea of Social Planning' *Planning Outlook*, 1977.

15. Brian J. L. Berry. *The Human Consequences of Urbanisation*, Macmillan, 1973, p. 72.

16. M. Clawson and P. Hall (eds). *Planning and Urban Growth: An Anglo-American Comparison*. Johns Hopkins University Press, 1973.

17. Some, possibly untypical, horror stories are related in *Planning for New Homes* by Nigel Moor and Robert Langton, London, 1978.

18. The Town and Country Planning Act, 1968, required local authorities to produce 'structure plans' which would purportedly be simpler and quicker to produce than the previous more detailed plans. By the end of 1977, of the 83 plans in England and Wales, only 39 had been submitted and of these, only 13 approved. Scotland introduced a system of simple, quick 'Regional Reports' which have worked well. They are 'provisional' and not *supposed* to replace Structure Plans.

19. Greater London Development Plan, *Report of the Panel of Inquiry* Vol. I. Dept of the Environment 1973 p. 27.

20. 'I must say frankly that I am angry at what is almost an abuse of town planning which some development control policies amount to – decisions which have trivial and sometimes detrimental effects on the quality of life which good planning should enhance. . . . Should it be a development control committee's business to decide on whether a property is converted into two or three flats simply by reference to whether it has a history of multi-occupation? – Should they concern themselves with the colour of roof tiles or the precise style of fencing or whether baths should be installed instead of showers? Or storm porches, or the use of lofts for living accommodation? Should they busy themselves with insisting that two large expensive family houses should be built in place of four smaller cheaper ones, simply because of a personal preference unrelated to need, demand, design or density standards?' This, surprisingly and encouragingly, is from a speech to the Town and Country Planning Association, 1, Dec. 1976, by Mr. R. Freeson, Minister of Housing. One is reminded of the control of manufacturers' specifications under the Mercantilist system.

21. General criticisms, and proposals for reform, are put forward in *Land for Housing*, The Housebuilders Federation, 1977. Some more limited administrative streamlining is advocated in *Review of the Development Control System* by George Dobry, QC., HMSO, 1975,

8th Report from the Expenditure Committee, House of Commons Paper 359, 1977, and a report on *Development Control* by a working party of the RTPI, 1978.

22. *Housing Land Availability in the South East*, Department of the Environment and Housing Research Institute, 1975.

23. M. Neutze. *The Price of Land*, OECD, Paris, 1973.

24. The defects of excessive concentration of activity are not cured by 'pedestrianisation' (an unavoidable word). Like many other urban layouts – motorways, rail transport, suburban shopping centres – pedestrianisation should neither be regarded as a panacea nor dismissed out of hand. It is one technique among many, all of which are needed. When the environment of a shopping street is being destroyed by heavy traffic, pedestrianisation provides a means of giving back its original function. But the street is best suited to small shops, selling 'shopping' rather than convenience goods. A pedestrianised city street lined by supermarkets lacks the virtues of either a 'shopping' street or a suburban shopping centre. This point is becoming clear even in West Germany, which has allowed some suburban shopping centres and produced central pedestrian precincts of superb quality. But when a pedestrianised street attracts too many people, it not only loses its advantages but also drains away the 'life' from surrounding districts, which can become a 'grey' zone of car parks, loading bays and increased vehicular traffic. There is a consequent fall in the number of small shops, and in the resident population. Interest is therefore turning to methods of reducing and slowing down traffic – by wider pavements, and 'sleeping policemen' – rather than eliminating it. Such an approach (as in Delft) encourages an extension rather than an intensification of the town centre, and the maintenance of mixed uses.

25. R. T. P. I. *Planning and the future*. London, 1976.

26. There is an important distinction between removing poverty and reducing inequalities (or differences, to use a more neutral term) in income or living standards. Very different results would, for example, be obtained by (a) taxing at 100 per cent all income over a certain level and distributing it among the rest of the population and (b) establishing a guaranteed minimum income financed by a slowly progressive income tax. But both would 'reduce inequality', possibly by the same amount (as measured by, say, the Gini coefficient). May there not be a case, in the British situation, for *increasing* the rewards for skill and enterprise? Similar issues arise more specifically in housing policy – e.g. in the 'levelling-up' approach of

ensuring that everyone is able to obtain a minimum level of housing as compared with the 'levelling down' approach which has underlain the argument for abolishing, tax relief on mortgages. On this and similar issues the RTPI clearly has no competence to pronounce. But if it is not *aware* of them, it might do better to stick to Professor Keeble's more limited, and lucid, definition of town planning.

9 Windfalls and Wipeouts

This Labour Government is determined that, whatever else it does, it will deal with the land problem once and for all.

The Rt. Hon. Mr. Anthony Crosland, 1974.

The relation between land values and public policy is a field in which strong passions have been aroused. On the one hand, critics of 'unearned increment' have demanded state intervention to prevent speculators making what they consider to be gains at the expense of the community; on the other hand, the 'speculators' often turn out to be ordinary households, and the policies adopted in the UK have caused hardship, desperation and at least one suicide. They have also had consequences in blocking development (e.g. the redevelopment of Victoria Station) which their framers never envisaged. The issues are therefore of considerable importance, although they have tended to be ignored by economists and smothered in detail by lawyers. One must begin by wielding Occam's razor. Many influential ideas are demonstrably based on logical confusion or untrue factual assumptions, which must be untangled before one can start to establish a workable basis for policy.

BETTERMENT

The subject under discussion has often been called 'compensation and betterment', although – as will be explained – the terminology and linking is questionable. 'Compensation' refers to the payment (if any) made by the state to the owner of real estate when it acquires his property for public purposes, undertakes public works which reduce the benefit he receives from his property, or prevents him from using his property as he wishes.

'Betterment' is a word the meaning of which has changed. In the 19th century it meant a specific benefit to a property owner – usually of agricultural land – resulting from public works: the cost of the public

175

works was therefore charged to owners in proportion to the 'betterment'. This method of financing public works proved unworkable when local authorities attempted to apply it to streets, sewers, etc., and it was replaced by local rates or user charges. Subsequently, the term began to be used in a different sense, based on a particular view of the land market. It was first argued that all development gains were 'unearned', being dependent on the growth of population and business rather than on individual initiative; hence it was proposed that they should be taxed away. As town planning (in the sense of development control) began to be introduced, the different argument was advanced that development gains were the result of planning permission. In 1942, the Uthwatt Commission defined betterment 'in the broader sense' as:

> any increase in the value of land (including the building thereon) arising from central or local government action, whether positive, e.g. by the execution of public works or improvements, or negative, e.g. by the impositions of restrictions on other land.[1]

However, it is quite impossible to measure betterment in this sense, since it is impossible to distinguish the influence of government action and that of the growth of population and income. It is also clear that not all development value is betterment, as defined above, since it existed throughout history in periods of urban growth, even though there was no negative government action and little or no positive action. Moreover, positive government action has pervasive effects which tend to *lower* land price in older urban areas: the decline in inner area land values is well known in the USA, but in a less marked form it has also occurred in European countries (Chap. 6). Thus it is impossible to measure betterment in the Uthwatt sense. The local and immediate effects of some types of public works can (roughly) be measured; the more distant effects cannot. Nor have any of the taxes imposed in Britain since the War been based on betterment. Even the 'betterment levy' was not based on 'betterment', as defined by Uthwatt, but on development value. As we have argued above (Chap. 3), development value can be in part a windfall gain – especially in the 'greenfield' situation which has attracted most attention – but it can be in part the payment for inconvenience, risk and initiative. It would contribute to rational discussion if the misleading term 'betterment' ceased to be used, and one spoke instead of the taxation of development value.

COMPENSATION

Most countries have legislation giving central or local authorities power to purchase land compulsorily in certain circumstances, although the rights of owners are protected by regulations concerning the purposes for which the land may be acquired, rights of appeal, and provisions for public inquiries. A differing balance is struck in different countries between the rights of individuals and the power of the state. Local authorities obviously need to acquire land from time to time for purposes such as roads,[2] and powers of compulsory purchase are necessary because, in their absence, someone who owned a small piece of land, for example, in the path of a proposed road, could either block construction or extort an exceptionally high price. Once compulsory powers are granted, it becomes necessary to lay down principles for determining the price to be paid.

The first question that needs to be asked is whether property owners should be compensated at all. In some discussions there is an underlying hostility to compensation, reflecting a hostility to private ownership of land; at a less extreme level, it is often argued that 'excessive' compensation will increase the cost of public works, and may prevent them altogether. If, however, the existence of private interests in land is accepted as economically and politically desirable, then the principle of providing (in some sense) 'full' compensation can be defended on grounds of both equity and efficiency. Most people would consider it inevitable if, given two householders, X and Y, X should lose a substantial part of the value of his house because the local authority decides to acquire X's house for building a road rather than Y's house. It can also be argued that generous – rather than grudging – compensations is worthwhile from the state's point of view, because the affected property owners will otherwise resist the whole project far more strongly (see Chap. 2). Moreover, there is the argument that public uses should be subject to the economic test imposed by charging the market price for land. The market price of a scarce resources reflects its value in alternative uses: charging a market price forces the public authority to examine carefully (a) whether the project is a worthwhile use of resources and (b) whether the same benefits can be obtained more economically. In assessing the value of expenditure on council housing, it is not necessarily a question of housing *versus*, say, candyfloss; it can for example, be a question of council housing *versus* owner-occupied housing, which is cheaper for the Exchequer and is what most people want. The argument for cheap land for public uses usually mentions cemeteries, playing fields, etc. But crematoria provide a land-saving alternative to cemeteries, and people who prefer to be buried can reasonably be asked to pay the cost. Similarly, it has long been questioned whether the traditional system of school playing fields used only on term-time afternoons is a rational use of resources. But in the absence of economic pressure there is less likelihood of 'sharing' arrangements being introduced.

Granted the principle of 'full' compensation, the 'market value' is the obvious basis for valuation (although 'market value' raises problems of definition). If there is a well-functioning market in the type of property concerned, the market value should be the owner to acquire a property of similar type, e.g. buy a similar house, shop or farm. But the move itself will probably involve him in expenses: this has long been accepted in British law, which in some cases provides for payment for 'disturbance'. However, even the payment of market value may still leave a displaced property owner worse off than he was before (ignoring for the moment the problems of assessing 'market value'). The value to the owner of a house (to take the most common case) may well be higher than the market value, although it cannot be lower. It cannot be lower, because he would *ipso facto* sell the house. But it can be higher, if the supply of a particular type of property is limited. A displaced householder may be able to obtain a physically similar house with the compensation payment, but perhaps in a different district, where he cannot, say, pursue his favourite recreations. He will thus be worse off, even though he has obtained market value. In other cases, it may be impossible to obtain even a physical equivalent. Small craftsmen dispossessed from old rented workships through 'urban renewal' have usually found it impossible to obtain similar property at similar rents, and have had to move into new property at much higher rents. Thus whereas 'market value' cannot be *more* than the figure needed to leave the owner equally well off, it may well be less.

The basis for 'open market value' in the UK has been spelled out in laws which – in marked contrast to the successive laws on the taxation of development value – have, on the whole, been clear, well-informed and workable. The *Acquisition of Land Act 1919* introduced 'six basic rules' which were incorporated into *The Land Compensation Act 1961*. The provisions are less generous than those in force before 1919, and seek to arrive at a 'normal' value.[3] Any special value for which there is no general market is excluded, as is any value arising from the scheme under which the property is being purchased. (Thus the common complaint that local authorities have to pay for values which they have themselves created is not true, in a direct sense). Property for which there is no market (e.g. a school) can be valued on the basis of the cost of equivalent accommodation. When there is development value, the question arises whether compensation should be based on current use value or the higher 'unrestricted' value (less any tax on development value). Under the New Town legislation, and the ultimate provisions of the Community Land Act, property can be acquired at current use value. Under the more general legislation, rules are laid down for the somewhat hypothetical assumptions on the type of development that would have been permitted.

A peculiarly unsatisfactory arrangement is when there is a dual market in land. This means that the price (net of any tax) received from a public authority is lower than if sold privately. This was the case in Britain from 1953 to 1959, as an aftermath of the development charge, and it is the system in countries where land can be compulsorily acquired for public housing at below market value. This is justified on the grounds that land for public purposes should be acquired as cheaply as possible. But there are three objections to this dual market; it provides a concealed rather than an open subsidy; it means that owners will do everything in their power to avoid selling to local authorities; and it can cause hardship if someone buys at the market price and then has his property expropriated at the lower price. It required a man to be driven to suicide over the threatened loss of his home before the Conservative Government in 1959 restored the principle of paying full market value.[4]

'UNFIT FOR HUMAN HABITATION'.

The main exception in Britain to the principle that property acquired compulsorily is paid for at 'open market value' concerns houses which are 'condemned'. In this case, the basic principle under the Housing Acts has been that local authorities are required only to pay for the bare site, with no compensation at all for the house. The local authority can also order the owner to demolish the house and clear the site, at his own expense. In 1969 the compensation for owner-occupiers was raised, but for owners of tenanted houses, compensation remains at site value.

The law originated in the 19th century, but at that time 'unfit for human habitation' meant a threat to public health. The standard has subsequently been raised from a sanitary minimum to a level of what, according to prevailing ideas, is considered desirable. This change has been defended by most British commentators on the grounds that it is politically unacceptable to permit 'slums' to remain. As against this, it can be argued that it is perverse to apply modern standards of, for example, natural lighting to old buildings.[5] Many houses which were found satisfactory by the people who lived in them, and would have sold (ten years ago!) for perhaps £2000 were condemned, and compulsorily acquired for a site value of around £200. This procedure caused severe hardship to a number of owner-occupiers before 1969 and greatly facilitated the policies of 'comprehensive redevelopment' which are now widely regarded as having been mistaken. If open market value had had to be paid, the balance would have been strongly tilted in favour of modernisation and gradual rebuilding. British experience might thus be considered to support Professor Hayek's warning:

Nothing ought to be treated with more suspicion than arguments used by town planners to justify expropriation below fair market value, arguments regularly based on the false contention that they can thereby reduce the social costs of the scheme. All that such a scheme amounts to is that certain costs will not be taken into account: the planners make it appear advantageous simply by placing some of the costs on the shoulders of private persons and then disregarding them.[6]

INJURIOUS AFFECTION.

The second form of compensation is for 'injurious affection'. This means that the value of property is lowered by public action on adjacent property. This question has assumed a far greater importance as a result of the growth of car and air traffic. The building of an airport or a motorway near a house can mean that the occupier suffers from severe noise if he stays, and finds that his house has dropped sharply in value if he tries to move.

In the early motorway and air age, the remedies for 'injurious affection' granted by British law were minimal. The common law right to sue public authorities for disturbance had been taken away by various statutes, and the principles laid down for compensation were implicitly based on horse-and-carriage conditions, where little disturbance was likely to be caused unless land was actually taken. Thus the earlier motorway builders could put an elevated motorway a few yards in front of a bedroom window without paying a penny in compensation. After considerable agitation for a widening of the scope of the law, the Government published a White Paper in 1972 which stated:

A better balance must be achieved in public development between provision for the community as a whole and the mitigation of any adverse effects on the individual citizen.[7]

It accepted that motorways should be built more expensively, with more regard to their surroundings. But it agreed that even the best designed motorways (and airports) would cause some disturbance, and proposed new principles for compensating householders. No compensation was payable for the use of an existing road or airport up to its planned capacity. But when a new road or airport was built, or the capacity of existing ones increased, affected householders could claim compensation based on a 'before and after' valuation. Although the Act did not altogether live up to the principles of the White Paper, it largely established (or re-established) the principle that houseowners should be compensated for clear-cut losses caused by official action. This removed a considerable injustice arising from early motorway construction. To some extent it 'internalised the externality' by charging the public authorities with the costs of disturbance; this should encourage more civilised design for urban motorways, and a more dispassionate discussion of the need for them.

REFUSAL OF PLANNING PERMISSION

The third form of compensation is for refusal of planning permission. The question has therefore arisen only with the introduction of planning laws in the 20th century. Between the Wars, local authorities in the UK had (in some circumstances) to compensate property owners for refusal of planning permission, and this, it was argued, prevented effective town planning. Since 1947, no compensation has been payable – except when permission is refused for some minor forms of improvement, or if the authority orders the owner to cease using the property for the purpose for which it is already being used. In most other countries, the position is similar, but permitted development is laid down in more objective rules, and compensation is often available when regulation is so severe as to come close to expropriation.[8]

A case can be made for the payment of compensation, on the ground that prohibitions cause an economic loss, not only to owners but also to consumers, which should be taken into account in public decision-making.[9] Such an idea deserves academic consideration, although 'whole hog' compensation is not a live issue in Britain. There are still, however, serious issues of both equity and resource allocation in cases where development which would normally be allowed is prohibited for 'historic' or local environmental reasons – e.g. a preservation order on an unusable old building or special restrictions in National Parks, etc. Forcing owners to do things that are *too* unprofitable is not likely to be an effective policy in the long run.

TAXATION OF RISES IN LAND VALUES

Over the past hundred years, land prices for the various categories of land – in real terms – have risen and fallen, and shown surprisingly little upward trend (see Chap. 5). However, there can be a sharp rise in land prices on major changes of use – notably when undeveloped land is used for building and when commercial development takes place on the edge of business districts. The size of such gains (in relation to national income) has often been exaggerated, and the topic has, for some people, become a secular religion. But there has been a widespread, and reasonable, feeling that such gains are often of a windfall kind, which should be taxed, possibly at a higher rate than other income.

The issues involved in this type of taxation can be illuminated by the 'canons of taxation' developed by economists from Adam Smith onwards. The tax system should be equitable, cheap to administer, cause as little inconvenience to the taxpayer as possible, and influence the allocation of resources as little as possible (unless this is specifically desired); the aim is not to find an ideal system but to strike a balance between different, and sometimes contradictory, objectives. British post-War experience would have been happier if these ideas had been appreciated.

There are three possible types of tax:

(a) Site value taxation.
(b) A tax on realised gains.
(c) A tax on development value, irrespective of whether the gains are realised or not.

Under site value taxation, an annual tax is levied, on the basis of the value of the site if it were not covered by a building. Assessment raises obvious difficulties, but the system has been introduced in Denmark, Australia and New Zealand (and to some extent in Germany) – with results that seem reasonably satisfactory, if not startlingly beneficial. One advantage of site value taxation, as compared with the other two types, is that, not being levied merely when development occurs, it does not discourage development. Excessive claims have often been made for the system, but it is unfortunate that it has never been seriously considered in the many British post-War experiments.

Of the two types of tax on development value, a tax on realised gains has the advantage that it is levied only when a clear monetary gain has been made, on an objective basis. A tax on *unrealised* gains raises problems of valuation, and can give rise to inequities – as became clear with the 1966 'betterment levy'. For both types of tax, there are two further issues; the rate of tax, and whether it should be universal or confined to designated districts. The advantage of confining the tax to newly-developed 'greenfield' districts (as proposed by the Uthwatt Committee, and envisaged in the scheme discussed in the West German Parliament between 1973 and 1976, for 'planning value compensation'), is that this covers the largest and most 'unearned' gains, without incurring the 'disincentive' effects of a universal tax on development value.

The *level* of the tax raises the same issues as other taxes on income. A tax of 100 per cent of development value (or over, say, 80 per cent) by definition removes the profit from development; it might therefore be expected to reduce sharply the amount of private development. The corollary of such a tax is that the state would have to use compulsory powers to acquire sites, and initiate all development itself. This was in fact the basic philosophy behind the Community Land Act.

BRITISH LAND TAXES

The history of the succession of hastily-conceived and hastily-abandoned taxes on development value imposed in Britain since the War can be summarised briefly.[10] The 1947 Town and Country Planning Act included a 100 per cent tax on development value. As this, by definition, made it unprofitable to sell land for development, and took all the profit out of development, it might have been expected to be unworkable – and this proved to be the case. But there was a widespread feeling that there should be some kind of tax on development gains. There was room for argument whether it would have been better to reduce the rate of the development charge, tax realised gains through the Inland Revenue, or perhaps institute a system of site value taxation. The Conservative Government of 1952 simply repealed the development charge. As there was no capital gains tax at the time, this meant that development gains were completely untaxed, which was widely regarded as unjustified.

In 1966 the Labour Government introduced a 'betterment levy', which was similar to a 50 per cent development charge. In principle, this could probably have been quite workable. In practice, the levy became an administrative nightmare because of its Byzantine complexity, and the way it was applied to the minutest or most notional of gains. This was eventually realised by the Government itself, which in 1969 exempted some small transactions from the levy. The 1970 Conservative Government could have continued the simplification of the betterment levy (and allowed the Land Commission to develop its land assembly functions). Instead, it abolished the Land Commission and the levy.

The repeal of the Land Commission Act differed from the repeal of the development charge in that realised gains were now subject to Capital Gains Tax. This arrangement came to an end, not because of sustained defects but as a result of panic reactions to the short-lived property boom of 1972–3. The main cause of the boom was inflationary Government policies, but it became politically necessary to take action against 'speculators'. At a time when the boom was already over, the Conservative Government imposed a series of penal taxes on development. The Development Gains Tax and the First Lettings Tax, plus a rent freeze, brought commercial development to a virtual halt for three years.

In Opposition, as a direct result of the property boom, the Labour Party had adopted a new policy of nationalising development land. The idea behind the Community Land Act of 1975 was that *all* development should, after a transitional period, take place on land owned by local authorities. In the Act, local authorities were given extended powers to acquire land for development, in particular the option of aquiring any property for which planning permission was sought. After the 'second appointed day' – to be decided at a future date – all such property would be automatically taken over, at existing use value. During the transitional period, there was to be a Development Land Tax – based on realised or unrealised development gain – at a rate of 80 per cent. Before examining the experience with this latest scheme, let us examine the general principles concerning the taxation of development value.

PRINCIPLES OF TAXATION

The discussion of taxes on rises in land value has been bedevilled by analytical confusions and factual misapprehensions. A tax of this type will not, as has sometimes been imagined, *lower* land prices to buyers (except when local authorities or other public bodies are allowed to purchase land 'net of tax'). As the simple economic analysis of tax incidence indicates, this type of tax is likely to *raise* prices to the buyer, although lowering them to the seller.[11] Nor are development gains significant in relation to national income. The experience with taxes of this type, in several countries since 1910, is that net receipts are invariably much lower than promised. None of this means that land values, or rises in land values, should not be taxed. It simply means that gains from land transactions, although they rise sharply in periods of rapid urban growth, are not of major economic significance; that this field is not exempt from the usual economic principles; and that the taxation of development gains raises the same problems of combining efficiency and equity encountered in the taxation of other types of income.

Two reports, by the Royal Institution of Chartered Surveyors and the British Property Federation, have examined the taxation of development value on these lines.[12] Both lay down lists of criteria for a satisfactory tax system, which largely overlap and include the following:

1. There must be an equitable division of development gains between the Treasury, the local authority and the landowner/developer.
2. The tax system should not discourage landowners from making land available for development.
3. The administration of the system should not overburden government, and should not be disproportionately expensive.
4. The system should be consistent with a mixed economy and permit an adequate rate of investment in development, especially from institutional sources.
5. It should be such as to command broad political support.

More technical criteria include:

6. The tax payable should be capable of quantification at the time development commences.
7. It should be calculated by reference to the increase in value of the land only.

8. The system should contain reasonably generous 'de minimis' provisions.
9. In the case of tax on unrealised gains, it should be possible to pay the tax out of income.
10. There should be an offsetting provision for losses.

These criteria would probably command wide support, but in any case they can be discussed and accepted or rejected if they are made explicit in this way. Both Development Gains Tax and Development Land Tax fail on several of these counts.[13]

The two reports made somewhat similar recommendations. Both recommended a tax on development gains of around 60 per cent although the Chartered Surveyors recommended confining the tax to realised gains, whereas the British Property Federation accepted (with some qualifications) a tax on unrealised gains. The more general conclusion must be that the taxation of real property should be based on this kind of utilitarian approach – not on the idea that there is a 'Solution' which will resolve all problems once and for all. Such a utilitarian approach involves a blend of simple economic theory, institutional knowledge, and a balancing of the likely revenue of various categories of tax against the cost of collecting it – a very different approach from that adopted in the framing of British post-War legislation in this field.

THE COMMUNITY LAND ACT

The only examination of the working of the Community Land Act published at the time of writing (June 1978) is a report by the Royal Institution of Chartered Surveyors (*The Land Problem Reviewed*), based on a postal survey of local authorities, developers and chartered surveyors. (Any official monitoring has been strictly confidential). It begins by examining the basic objectives of the Community Land Act, as outlined in White Paper.

(a) to enable the community to control the development of land in accordance with its needs and priorities;
(b) to restore to the community the increase in value of land arising from its efforts.

The first objective ('positive planning') was said to require that all land which was to be developed, or redeveloped, should pass into the ownership of the local authority. The second was said to require that all property should be acquired at existing use value.

The report questioned both assumptions. It argued that public landownership did not guarantee socially desirable development unless accompanied by the expertise, organisation and will necessary to achieve it. Indeed, many of the most striking cases of failure to develop land have involved publicly owned land. The report argued that socially desirable development could take place on either publicly or privately owned land, and that the flexibility, expertise and variety of privately initiated development should not be rejected.

The report distinguishes between 'economically motivated development' and 'socially motivated development' suggesting that, in the former case, the prime requisites are demand and an efficient development mechanism, while in the latter case the prime requisites are public funds and an efficient development mechanism. The report thus takes a fundamentally different view of the development process from the White Paper on *Land* (and Mr. Broadbent *op. cit.*)

2.5.3. The White Paper was, in our view, wrong in referring to land as the *planner's* resource. Land is certainly a national resource, but in the context of development it is primarily the developer's resource, whether he be a private individual or company, or a local authority. It is the developer who must have access to land, not the planner. The planner's role is, essentially, to decide where development of various kinds is desirable, and where it is not. In the allocation of land, he should take full account of probable demand, and of the economics of the development process. Then, if he does his job well, market forces will result in that economically motivated development taking place. Similarly, if plans involving public buildings and facilities are drawn with proper regard to the financial and other resources of the authorities concerned, they too will be implemented. No amount of legislation, no extra powers of acquisition or control, can make development occur where there is no real demand, or where the financial resources are lacking.

The report accepts, however, that extensive powers of compulsory purchase are necessary, not only for public uses, but also when imperfections in the land market necessitate changing the development which would otherwise have taken place. The corollary of allowing private development was to allow a sufficient margin of profit in development. Thus although it was legitimate to levy a substantial tax on development gains (by no means all of which arose from 'the community's efforts') some economic incentive was necessary: a tax rate of around 60 per cent of the gain was proposed.

In its review of the Act's operation, the RICS reports that it was unpopular with nearly all local authorities and developers (less so in the case of the Land Authority for Wales) and that there was little evidence that it was making a contribution to 'positive planning'.[14] In a few cases in which the threat of compulsory acquisition had been used to encourage or discourage a particular development, this was when such a policy could not be defended on planning grounds. Although the period since the passing of the Act was one of recession in the development industry, there was evidence that the Act was discouraging development. The main causes were the high rate (and complexity and uncertainty) of Development Land Tax, and the provision whereby all planning applications were examined to see whether compulsory acquision powers should be invoked. There was a widespread belief among private developers that, as demand recovered in 1978–9, the Act would contribute to a severe land shortage. The arrangements for sharing proceeds under the Act encouraged local authorities to acquire 'greenfield' sites, with a prospect of substantial development value, rather than less profitable, but socially desirable, development in 'inner areas'. The extended powers of compulsory purchase under the Act were considered helpful by many local authorities. On the other hand, many local authorities felt that the limitation on the disposal of land for commercial purposes to leases of not more than 99 years was hindering disposals on profitable terms. (A change in this provision had been recommended in the First, and so far only, Report of the Advisory group on Commercial Property Development; see Chap. 12).

After assessing the Act against the criteria put forward in an earlier report the report concluded that the Act did not meet the criteria, especially in its ultimate form. It then considered whether the Act could be amended in such a way as to meet the criteria, or alternatively, if the Act were repealed, what new measures would be needed. The necessary amendments would be substantial, and would include: repeal of the 'ultimate' provisions under which local authorities would be obliged to acquire all land for development at existing use value; repeal of the provisions under which, even now, all planning applications must be examined to see whether the local authority should acquire the land; changes in the arrangements for allocating any surplus on community land accounts so as to give a larger share to local authorities; a restoration of the right to challenge compulsory purchase orders. On Development Land Tax, the report concluded that the rate of tax was too high and the provisions too complicated; it repeated the view put forward in the earlier report that the rate should not be more than 60 per cent and that, ideally, a tax on realised gains would be preferable. However, given the desirability of greater stability in tax arrangements, it favoured modifying Development Land Tax rather than replacing it by yet another tax. Various detailed amendments were put forward to give a simpler and fairer assessment of taxable gain (and to exempt charities completely).

The alternative would be to repeal the Act and achieve any powers needed for 'positive planning' under other legislation. The report points out that the extensive powers of compulsory purchase under the 1971 Town and Country Planning Act had been unduly restricted by Ministry circulars (*sic*). It proposed that local authorities should be given greater compulsory purchase powers, but not *carte blanche*. The local authority should be required to justify the use of such powers – if necessary at a public inquiry.

The report went on to examine the basis of financing public infra-structure and repeated the argument often advanced by the RICS (and opposed by the Housebuilders Federation) for a formal system of infra-structure charges payable by developers. It pointed out that neither the Community Land Act nor its predecessors had done anything to solve the problem of the provision of necessary infra-structure being held up by shortages of funds.

On the issue of amending or repealing the Act, the report indicated that the amendments required would fundamentally alter the nature of the Act, and that there would be practical advantages in incorporating the extended powers of compulsory purchase into the Town and Country Planning Act. But it carefully left this issue open, ending with the hope that the proposals outlined will commend themselves to a wide cross-section of political opinion, and that 'the disruptive cycle of enactment and repeal will at last be broken'. This indicates a political argument in favour of amending rather than repealing the Act. Repeal would certainly be regarded by the Labour Party as 'sabotage', so that the cycle would be repeated. Even the proposed amendments would be hotly contested; several influential planners have argued that the problem is one of local authorities perversely ignoring the Act, and that its ultimate provisions should be introduced forthwith. There is thus no certainty that an Act amended on the lines indicated would fare any better than, for example, the 1972 Housing Finance Act. But the prospects for legislative changes involving a repeal of the Act would be even worse. Amendments to the Act, whatever their practical disadvantages, would at least offer a prospect of ending the disruptive and internationally unique cycle of British post-War land legislation.

SUMMARY

For over a century, there has been controversy over the taxation of development value (misleadingly called 'betterment') and compensation for property rights expropriated by the state. There is also considerable international experience with taxes and compensation arrangements of this type, which has usually been ignored in all countries in the framing of legislation.

An influential view in the town planning movement has been that it should be possible to take decisions on the basis of 'the public interest', with no reference to land values. The approach of mainstream economics, on the other hand, is that land values, and development value, play a crucial role in resource allocation, and cannot be eliminated without introducing a comprehensive 'command economy'; the relative virtues of a market economy and a command economy – or various combinations of them – should be examined in the light of the evidence. Taxes on land values, like other taxes, should be judged by the general principles of 'public finance'.

There are three possible types of tax on rises in land value: a tax on site value (which has theoretical advantages); a tax on realised gains; a tax on development value. On grounds of equity, a good case can be made for some type of tax, but its practical application must be examined to see whether it has undesired effects in hindering development. There is also a good case for the payment of generous compensation for property rights – including disturbance by motorways, etc., both on grounds of equity and of 'buying off' opposition.

Britain has had a damaging cycle since the War of hasty enactment and hasty repeal of legislation on the taxation of development value. Three major schemes have been introduced by Labour Governments, of which the latest is the Community Land Act; all have been based on an insufficient examination of their practical consequences, and have proved unsatisfactory in practice. On two occasions they have been repealed by Conservative Governments, with insufficient thought to retaining what was good in the original concept, if not its execution. There is a professional consensus based on the propositions that (a) there should be a substantial, but not prohibitive, tax on development gains (b) there should be *participation* by public authorities in the land market, but not a monopoly. This approach would seem to offer the basis for a bi-partisan policy, but in 1978 both the Conservative and the Labour Party seemed to be a long way from such a policy.

SELECT BIBLIOGRAPHY

British Property Federation, *Policy for Land*. 1976.

Commercial Property Development, First Report of the Advisory Group on Commercial Property Development, (Pilcher Report) HMSO, 1975.

Graham Hallett, *Housing and Land Policies in West Germany and Britain*. pt. 3, Macmillan, 1978.

Donald Hagman and Dean Misczuski *Windfalls for Wipeouts: Land Value Capture and Compensation*. American Society of Planning Officials, Chicago, 1978. A legal study of the USA, UK, New Zealand, Australia and Canada.

Royal Institution of Chartered Surveyors, *The land problem; a fresh approach*, 1974; *The Land Problem Reviewed*, 1978.

D. M. Turner, *An Approach to Land Values*, Geographical Publications, 1977.

REFERENCES

1. *Expert Committee on Compensation and Betterment*. Cmnd 6386. HMSO, 1942, p. 105

2. Most compulsory purchase in the UK, however, is for public authority housing or 'urban renewal'. In these cases, the need for compulsory purchase arises only because of particular systems, the need for which, at least on a massive scale, can be questioned.

3. Some German valuers criticise 'market value' as being too volatile, and have developed a concept of '*gemeine Wert*'. However, this seems to be very similar to 'open market value' as assessed under the provisions of the British legislation.

4. J. B. Cullingworth. *Town and Country Planning in England and Wales*. Allen & Unwin, 3rd ed. 1970, p. 156.

5. I would have taken the following case to be from one of the more desperate TV 'sit-coms', if I had not experienced it myself. An

elderly lady was the owner of a Georgian cottage, in which various changes specified by the Public Health Inspector were required to avoid 'condemnation'. One concerned the upstairs landing, which gave on to two bedrooms; it had no window and was lit by electric light. The Inspector said that the landing would have to have daylight, and the only practical way of achieving this was by means of glass panels in the bedroom doors. The owner suggested frosted glass, but the Inspector replied that this would not provide sufficient illumination; the panels in the bedroom doors had to be of clear glass! The owner pointed out that she had curtains behind the doors. The Inspector, who was not an unreasonable man, said that the curtains only had to be drawn back when he made his inspection.

6. F. A. Hayek. *The Constitution of Liberty*, p. 357.
7. *Development and Compensation – Putting People First*. Cmnd. 5124. H.M.S.O. 1972. p. 70.
8. Hagman & Misczynski *op cit* p. 256ff.
9. B. Bracewell-Milnes. "Market Control over Land-use 'Planning'" in *Government and the Land*, Readings 13, Institute of Economic Affairs, London, 1974, p. 81.
10. It is examined in more detail in the author's *Housing and Land Policies in West Germany and Britain*. Macmillan, 1977, Pt. III.
11. P. Samuelson. *Economics* 9th ed. p. 386, Chapter 28. It is often assumed in the economic textbooks that the supply of land is completely inelastic, so that a tax would leave prices unaltered. But it is in practice unlikely that owners will sell for development or undertake development, without any 'sweetener' for risk and inconvenience. On this more realistic assumption, the supply of land will to some extent be elastic, so that a tax will raise the market price.
12. *The Land Problem – a fresh approach*, R.I.C.S. 1974. *Policy for Land*, British Property Federation, 1976. See also *Land for Housing*, The House Builders Federation, 1977.
13. *Policy for Land*, op. cit. Appendix.
14. The report makes only passing reference to the difference between the English system, where local authorities operate the Act and the Welsh system of a 'Land Authority for Wales'. Most independent observers have concluded that the Welsh system has worked better than the English, by being freed from local authority control ('Community Land?', by Malcolm Grant, Centre for Environmental Studies, Urban Law Conference, 1978) The abol-

ition of the LAW would be a clear loss from a repeal of the Act.

This is not to say that there are not potential advantages in some participation in the land market by local authorities, provided that competent 'estate management' departments were set up, and allowed a measure of professional autonomy. Experience in West Germany, where there is participation in the land market by both local authorities and 'provincial 'homestead companies' suggests that there may be scope for both types of organisation.

10 Problems of the Inner City

When you walk through the smoke-dim slums of Manchester, you think that nothing is needed except to tear down these abominations and build decent housing in their place. But the trouble is that, in destroying the slum you destroy other things as well.

George Orwell, *The Road to Wigan Pier*, 1937, p. 69.

In many cities of Western Europe and the Eastern USA, the central districts (outside the often renovated central business district) were built during the period of rapid city growth before 1914. These districts, once young and vigorous, have in recent years begun to exhibit the debility of old age. Housing has often deteriorated and, even if physically sound, is often unsuitable for modern living. Arrangements for access and parking are ill-suited to the age of the motor vehicle; new industries have preferred to settle in the suburbs where there is more space and better facilities. At the same time there has been an exodus of younger and more vigorous people to the suburbs.

The housing being thus located has often been filled by 'alien' groups: in the USA, black people from the rural South; in Britain, immigrants from the 'New Commonwealth'; in West Germany, 'guest workers' from the Mediterranean countries. These physical, economic and social trends often react to each other to produce a cumulative process of decline. Governmental arrangements have in some cases accentuated the decline. Rent control has in some countries caused the dereliction of older housing, and policies of 'slum clearance' have often done more harm than good. A special problem in the USA is that the 'central city' is usually a separate local government area from the suburbs and both rely heavily for local services on local property taxation; thus the central city, whose needs are greater, has a narrower tax base.

The picture is not one of unrelieved gloom. Conditions vary considerably from country to country and are far more serious in

194

Britain and the Eastern cities of the USA, than, for example, in West Germany, the Netherlands or Canada. And even in Britain (especially London) and the USA there are districts which have been rejuvenated, mainly by owner-occupiers, and have once become 'desirable residential areas'. Nevertheless, in spite of the differing extent of the problem, its characteristics are so similar in so many countries that there are clearly general processes at work.

AMERICAN AND BRITISH EXPERIENCE

The problems were incipient in the USA between the wars (*cf* Burgess and Hoyt) but came to the fore in the 1950s, when programmes of 'urban renewal' were initiated. There followed a flood of academic studies of 'the central city', most of which were critical to a greater or lesser degree, of the prevailing type of 'urban renewal'. But – in spite of local successes in cities where decay had not gone too far – no alternative type of renewal was widely implemented. The problems have remained, and have become even more serious in the 1970s, especially in New York (which, possibly not without connection, has pursued a somewhat 'British' policy of rent control and public housing).[1] Some observers now detect signs of hope in current demographic trends. The virtual end of the great rural-urban migration that began in the 1940s, together with the fall in the birth rate, will soon mean a reduction in population pressure in the central cities and a sharp drop in the 15–25 age group, which has the highest rates of unemployment and crime.

In contrast to the extensive and soul-searching American examination of the problems of the central city and 'urban renewal', few detailed studies were, until recently, undertaken in Britain. It was conceded that some British cities had 'slums', dating from the 19th century, but these, it was argued, were rapidly being eliminated by the 'slum clearance' programmes initiated by local authorities in the 1930s. In the 1950s, 'slum clearance' was taken up vigorously again. Some sociological studies questioned its social effects but on the whole the social scientists ignored the question, while the planners and architects enthused over the new steel and glass towers. The problems of American cities were dismissed, not without *Schadenfreude*, as typically American.

A gradual change of opinion began in the mid-1960s. One of the few economists who, at the time, advocated 'cellular renewal' has dated the change to a 1963 proposal to extend 'slum clearance' to housing which was structurally sound but in 'depressed residential areas'.[2] This threat aroused local residents (often owner-occupiers) to take a stand against the bulldozer.

Once the acquiescence in 'comprehensive redevelopment' was ended, a cumulative counter-movement began. Academics and journalists began to take an interest, and studies by private developers indicated the superior economics of partial re-building and improvement. But it was not until the 1970s that gradual re-building was accepted by the Government as preferable to 'comprehensive redevelopment', and this view has still not permeated all local authorities. But even if 'comprehensive redevelopment' is out of favour, it can reasonably be doubted whether the official attitudes which produced it have completely changed. Moreover, even correctly recognising a problem does not solve it, as the American experience illustrates only too well. It may be illuminating to review the attitudes and policies towards urban renewal in the USA before discussing the recent evidence on Britain's problems.

'COMPREHENSIVE REDEVELOPMENT'

The policy of 'urban renewal' initiated in the USA in the early 1950s was supposed to be wider in scope than 'slum clearance', providing new communications and facilities of all kinds as well as housing, but in fact it was largely confined to housing. In any event, it meant bulldozing an area and buildings on a clean slate, which was allegedly the only statisfactory procedure. The results were rarely successful in social or environmental terms, and 'the federal bulldozer' came under increasing criticism.[3] The challenge to the urban renewal orthodoxy came from various directions. Sociologists who had actually lived in 'slums' pointed out that the picture of uniform degradation was as incorrect as the romanticisation of the slum. One sociologist who had lived in it wrote about a district of Boston which was later brutally destroyed:

> The West End was not a charming neighbourhood of "noble peasants" living in an exotic fashion, resisting the mass-produced homogeneity of American culture and overflowing with a cohesive sense of community. It was a run-down area of people struggling with the problems of low income, poor education and related difficulties. Even so, it was by and large a good place to live.[4]

A less judicious, but more influential, book was Jane Jacobs' best-seller.[5] This was a slightly romanticised and generalised version of the

Italian 'North End' of Boston. There is considerable doubt about Miss Jacobs' equation of 'over 100 dwelling units per acre' with urban 'life' and a sense of community. The new public housing developments had similar high densities and were often social disasters. But her pithy and entertaining pilloring of conventional planning attitudes, and in particular her praises of an urban environment in which housing, shops, workplaces, were cheek-by-jowl rather than clinically segregated, struck a responsive chord at a time when the defects of 'the federal bulldozer' were becoming too obvious to be overlooked. The history of urban renewal and public housing in the USA, while not without a few successes, contains a large number of disasters, of which one complex in St. Louis became internationally notorious when it had to be demolished within a few years of being built. British experience is less well-documented, but several studies have revealed cases in which comprehensive redevelopment has *reduced* both the housing stock and employment in the area.

The problems inherent in any comprehensive redevelopment were aggravated by the type of housing built. The 'modern' housing built by public authorities in the 1960s may have been more sanitary than the housing it replaced, but it was often even less adapted to human needs. It is now widely accepted that it was a mistake to build monolithic and impersonal tower blocks with poor thermal and accoustic insulation, dangerous and dirty 'public' corridors and high maintenance costs. But even good housing – which was produced in a few renewal schemes – does not necessarily solve social problems. As one 'close student of New Yorks' slums' put it over two decades ago,

> Once upon a time we thought that if we could only get our problem families out of those dreadful slums, then papa would stop taking dope, mama would stop chasing around, and junior would stop carrying a knife. Well, we've got them in a nice new apartment with modern kitchens and a recreation center. And they're the same bunch of bastards they always were'.[6]

The policy of 'comprehensive redevelopment' was not based on any coherent economic or sociological analysis. It did not ask *why* people in the inner areas were poor, housing deteriorating, and the area 'going down'. It did not ask how much of the housing was capable of renovation at an economic cost. Nor did it examine whether some, at least, of the districts had communities which should not lightly be disrupted. The approach was a crudely physical and parternalistic one which accepted without question that slums had harmful effects which would be removed by the provision of new housing.

'Urban renewal' in continental European countries benefited by coming later. West Germany, in particular, has engaged in a most detailed discussion of urban renewal policies since the mid-1970s, the outcome of which was the 1971 'Act to Promote Town Planning'. Under this Act, some 500 schemes are currently being implemented (mainly in small, historic towns), and the programme bids fair to become the most successful urban renewal programme yet seen in the present century. Whereas the West German programme is based on a 'socially responsible market economy', the long-established British policy of 'slum clearance' has been based on local authority ownership, and this philosophy has been retained in the suddenly fashionable interest in the 'inner area'. Before examining the West German policy and the still tenuous but philosophically very different policy proposed for Britain, let us examine in general terms the main approaches that are possible.

FOUR APPROACHES

Four main approaches to the problem of urban decay have been suggested in the academic discussion, which can be crudely summed up as:

(a) 'There is no problem'.
(b) 'Improve and dilute the slums'.
(c) 'The problem is capitalism, and the solution is socialism'.
(d) 'Self help'.

The first argument (which might be termed 'extreme liberal') has been put forward in a general way by Professor Hayek, and in a detailed statistical way by Professor Muth. It is a coherent, sophisticated argument which, even if it is in the end rejected as inadequate, makes a number of telling points. According to this view, the problem of the inner areas is that their inhabitants are poor and the poor quality of the housing is a consequence of this poverty. Poor people cannot afford expensive high quality housing; it is therefore in their interests that owners provide cheap housing which they can afford by cutting down on improvements and maintenance. A policy of slum clearance removes this reservoir of cheap housing, and forces the previous inhabitants into more expensive accommodation, thus intensifying their poverty, or into public institutional care. To bring the price of new housing down to the level of the old, most of the cost would have to consist of subsidy. This money would be more effectively spent in other ways, such as income transfers to the poor. Moreover, urban renewal eliminates 'sordid' but useful functions like rooming-houses and hostels for destitute men, which can find a home only in rather run-down areas.

On this view, the 'zone in transition' meets a need, and should be allowed to do so. This does not imply complete *laissez-faire*. The liberal economists who adopt this approach have also pioneered the concept of a 'guaranteed minimum income' or 'negative income tax'. The direct relief of poverty in this way would enable some of the inhabitants of inner areas to move to newer housing. Similarly, a reduction in the institutional discrimination against the (often coloured) inhabitants of these areas which lowers their earning ability – e.g. poor schools – would raise their incomes and so assist people in the most effective way. On the 'extreme liberal' view, therefore, there is a problem of poverty, but no problem of urban decay. The housing stock adjusts itself to any given level of local income, and should be allowed to do so. Provided that new housing construction is not restricted, so that there is an ample supply elsewhere, it is in the interests of the poor to allow obsolescent housing to become cheap and low-quality. Eventually, the value of some of the housing will fall so low that redevelopment becomes profitable; the area will thus be redeveloped in a gradual way suitable to its new circumstances. This was the view put forward in an extreme form by Professor Hayek in *The Constitution of Liberty*, but sympathetic critics of urban renewal had already made similar points. As an American urban economist has written, in a survey of early European urban renewal efforts:

. . . the pioneer effort in the United States was premature in starting, as it did, at a time of severe shortages of housing and other real estate facilities which made site acquisition expensive and relocation extremely painful. The more proper strategy would have been to concentrate after the war on soundly planned suburban construction and the building of new towns beyond the pale of existing urban agglomerations. Such a policy would not only have accommodated growth most rapidly but would also have provided 'reception stations' for the people and activities to be dislocated later by urban renewal. Moreover, the exodus from built-up areas induced in this fashion would have held down central property values and made a later renewal program much less costly. By initiating urban renewal as early as 1949, we were trying 'to do the right thing at the wrong time'. The European lag in commencing urban renewal has come close to meeting this prescription.[7]

Similarly, the enthusiasts for New Towns – who as successors to the 'land reform' movement tend to be at the opposite extreme of political economy from Professor Hayek – take a somewhat similar line when they advocate the continuance of the New Town programme rather than switching resources to the 'inner cities'.

But other students of urban affairs, while accepting the arguments against merely pumping huge sums into 'urban renewal', and ruthlessly bull-dozing whole districts, are not prepared to go to the other extreme of letting the inner areas rot. Provided that there is ample new housing available, and hence no overall shortage, would it not, they ask, be desirable to remove the worst housing in the inner areas, (which cannot economically be renovated) while encouraging renovation, assisting environmental tidying-up and generally seeking to prevent the social and physical decay of inner areas reaching a stage when it is virtually irreversible? If essential maintenance is neglected, the cost of renovation rapidly escalates. This 'uneconomic' type of cost-saving can be brought about by rent control, but it can also happen when, as a result of the social disintegration of a district, owners who take a long view of property management leave or die out. The physical condition of inner areas interacts with its social composition, and these areas typically have a high proportion of the unemployed, single-parent families, etc., and an exodus of the more stable and enterprising families. There can then be a process of cumulative decline to a situation going far beyond that of cheap, shabby districts, which can indeed serve a useful purpose.

Professor Gunnar Myrdal's theory of 'cumulative causation' seems to apply to urban areas rather better than to the national regions in connection with which he put it forward.[8] Although some trends – such as lower population densities – probably cannot and should not be resisted, there is no inevitability about decline to the level of, say, New York or Liverpool. It seems justifiable for the state to assist the processes which could establish a new, and more satisfactory, equilibrium. These ideas lead on to the second policy, which is:

the idea that the most effective attack on slums will involve both improving and diluting them, i.e. providing better living conditions and more jobs in the slums and at the same time removing barriers to out-migration. A given aggregate amount of poverty and ignorance, according to this idea, is socially less serious and more quickly curable if it is scattered than if it makes up a solid mass.[9]

This approach obtained widespread acceptance among students of urban affairs in the USA. It is in accord with the swing towards 'cellular' redevelopment which has taken place in all countries in the 1970s, and it underlies the recommendations of all the recent 'inner area' studies in London, Liverpool and Birmingham. Another change which began in the USA in the 1960s was the realisation that the problems of old residential areas could not be tackled *merely* by improving housing. To be effective, policies had to involve employment, traffic, recreational facilities, historic buildings and the whole 'ambience' of an area.

The third approach is that of state socialism (see Chap. 7). On this view, the root cause of the problem lies in the continued existence of private firms, and the continued private ownership of land and housing. The solution lies, on the one hand, in such a degree of state ownership or control that any required employment can be directed to the inner areas. On the other hand, privately owned housing and land would be brought under municipal ownership. This approach finds the strongest support in Britain, which has already gone a long way to implementing it. The Community Land Act gives local authorities the right, and ultimately the responsibility, of buying *all* land for which permission to develop is sought. At the same time, private tenancy has been made unprofitable by the Rent Acts, and private rented housing is rapidly passing into the ownership of local councils.

The fourth policy, 'self help', suggests that national funds are likely to be limited, and that the inner areas must help themselves. Associations of local people, for example, can organise and supervise playgrounds, assist old people, put pressure on local schools to improve their performance, etc. This kind of 'community action' can be quite important – it often is in American suburbs and, in some American central districts with a stable black population, similar movements are in evidence. But community action is unlikely where the composition of the population is changing rapidly or where it is 'a residuum of the defeated, leaderless and helpless'. What can be expected in the long run is the rise of 'immigrants' to positions of economic power ('black capitalism') and local political influence. It is a source of complaint in many American cities that, whereas most of the inhabitants are black or Spanish, most of the posts in local government are held by Irish or Italian-Americans (who were the blacks and Spanish of three generations ago). This will probably change within a generation, so that this element of 'colonial rule' will be ended. The 'central cities' might then be in a better position to tackle their problems, even if in a way contrary to the 'melting pot' philosophy. American cities could thus conceivably benefit from their 'unreformed' boundaries.

These, then, are the four main approaches. But this categorisation is, in practice, not clear-cut, since each can be interpreted in different ways, and some combinations are possible. The 'improve and dilute' approach could, to some extent be adopted under a socialist system. However, state ownership and development seems to favour a bulldozing approach, and a lack of variety and interest in a district. Physical and social variety, intimacy, and effective management are – on the basis of international experience – more likely to be achieved by at least 'social ownership' with a number of different landlords, interspersed with owner-occupation, than by the traditional British system of council housing. These questions will be discussed in more detail later (Chap. 12). Let us first turn to the case-studies which are now available on the nature and extent of 'inner area' problems in Britain.

BRITISH 'INNER AREA' PROBLEMS

Remarkably few independent surveys of 'inner areas' were conducted in Britain in the 1950s and 1960s. Only in the 1970s were detailed case studies initiated, but a number of reports are now available – in particular, studies of districts in Liverpool, Birmingham and London sponsored by the Department of the Environment and carried out by professional consultants. A Ministerial summary states that:

> The chief centres of this urban deprivation include the inner areas of the major conurbations, London, Glasgow, Tyne-Wear, West Yorkshire, Greater Manchester, Merseyside and West Midlands. In 1971 they contained nearly four million people, one fourteenth of the country's population but an eighth of its unskilled workers, a fifth of its families living in some form of housing stress and a third of its new commonwealth immigrants. . . . The picture is one of exceptional concentrations of poverty and deprivation. Even so, only a minority of those living in the inner areas are below the poverty line.[10]

Although there are differences in the scale of problems in the three areas, the most striking feature of these studies is the similarity of their analysis and conclusions. Not only do the reports make clear that British inner areas face serious problems, they are also unanimous in arguing that the traditional type of 'slum clearance' has been unsatisfactory, and that 'regional policies', as well as local planning policies, have often had harmful results. All three reports make points which were made years ago about American 'central cities': the concentration of the poor, the unskilled and immigrants; the decay of old housing; the decline of business activity; the suffering caused by 'the municipal bulldozer' combined with neglect in other fields; the failure of the schools.

The three areas studied were central Liverpool, Small Heath in Birmingham and Lambeth in London. Of these, the Liverpool district has had the greatest fall in population, numbers having halved between 1921 and 1971. Thus, although there may be some further decline in numbers even in Liverpool, there is not the same need to reduce total numbers that exists to some extent in Small Heath and clearly in Lambeth. Small Heath is rapidly becoming an Asian community; although it poses problems for the indigenous population, this is in some ways a source of strength. Lambeth is unusual in having, together with the typical large proportion of unskilled people, a small body of professional people. This is the result of the nearness of central London and the distance of the suburbs from central London.

In all three areas, the problems pinpointed as the most important are the poor quality of housing and the environment, and low incomes. In Liverpool, 'the most striking impression is physical decay'; one-tenth of the total area has been cleared, with the idea of building schools, open spaces or highways which have not yet been built, and are unlikely to be built for years. In Small Heath:

It is the obsolescence and deterioration of the housing stock – even more than employment conditions – that have led to a downward spiral. Housing conditions, rather than jobs, have determined where people live. Poor occupants of the houses have found their maintenance too costly, and the relatively better off have been able to take the option of moving out altogether. The less skilled labour force has found it more difficult to take advantage of such employment opportunities as do exist; in turn, the absence of skilled labour has made the area less attractive to employers.

Later the report comments that:

Low incomes are the centre of the problem.

The same problems are observed in Lambeth, but the density of population is much higher, and housing is dear in relation to its quality, whereas in Liverpool and Small Heath (as in the American ghettos) it is noticeably cheap. The cheap housing in Liverpool and Birmingham to some extent meets a demand. However, as the Small Heath report points out, this is 'for some (particularly among Asians) an opportunity, for others a trap'.

The decline in employment in the three areas was in all cases initiated by structural changes which could hardly have been prevented, but has subsequently been accelerated both by the deterioration in the local environment and by mis-directed planning policies. In none of the areas was the decline caused by firms moving out, but by existing firms dying, and new employment not being created. In Liverpool, the initial downturn was caused by the decline of the port and the elimination of central warehousing. Mereseyside has been a 'development area' since the War, and 100,000 new manufacturing jobs have been created, but these have all been located on the edge of the conurbation. Central area employment has declined faster than population, and the rate of unemployment is several times the national average. In Small Heath, factories have become outmoded, and have closed down in dispropor- tionate numbers. The creation of new employment in Birmingham and London has been hampered by regional policy. Both cities have been treated as areas where there was supposedly *too much* employment, which could be diverted to the 'development areas'. In Lambeth, the unemployment problem is partly the result of the run-down in local manufacturing, but also of a mis-match of job opportunities and skills. There has been a national shift from less skilled to more skilled jobs, especially in central London, which is virtually part of the Lambeth labour market. But the Lambeth labour force is largely unskilled, and with few opportunities to acquire skills.

The three reports are agreed that the policy pursued in these areas since the 1930s – bulldozing whole streets and putting up council housing – has been unsatisfactory. The Liverpool study speaks of the 'brutal uprooting of communities' which has accelerated the exodus of skilled people. The council estates are 'poorly maintained and heavily vandalised'. It groups together council estates and rooming houses as having the worst social and environmental conditions, but also points out that the area contains considerable diversity; there are still stable working class neighbourhoods and multi-racial communities with a potential for recovery. The Small Heath study speaks of the 'avoidable misery' caused by council re-development; the imbalance in

Birmingham's housing expenditure between new construction (which in 1975–6 still took the lion's share) and the improvement of older property; and the failure of the current system of housing subsidies to help those most in need. In Lambeth, one of the main social problems is 'the constant shifting of families, exacerbated by council redevelopment schemes and the decline in privately-rented housing', although the report also points out that, in a situation where half the population are council tenants, there is no clear link between poverty and poor housing, and that many of the problems are the result of excessively high population densities. The Lambeth report is clear that 'There is no justification for further large-scale redevelopment in Inner London. The "housing gain" this sought to achieve has proved illusory: such gain is better sought further out'. At the same time, it warns that not all housing is worth retaining, and that some new construction will be needed: the precise 'mix' can be determined only on a 'house-to-house' basis. The recent policy of designating 'Housing Action Areas' or 'General Improvement Areas' is supported in principle, but the reports suggest that a disproportionate amount of the funds allocated are being used up in administration.

Finally, all three studies express an underlying disquiet with the organisation and attitudes of local government. The city authorities have intervened too much with 'bulldozer' policies (which are largely paid for by the national Government) but have otherwise devoted relatively few resources to these areas, and have neglected their employment problems. The Liverpool and Small Heath reports suggest that the city government has been remote, and insensitive to local needs. In Liverpool,

> Land use planning has reflected the priority given to housing, applying standard practices with little recognition of local conditions. Resources have not been available to carry out plans. Decisions are firmly based in the main committees and little responsibility is delegated to local officials . . .

The Small Heath report comments on 'a widespread lack of confidence in the area and in its government', but is reluctant to advocate a major reorganisation of local government 'so soon after the recent upheaval with its attendant increases in costs and bureaucracy'.

THE REPORTS' PROPOSALS

Just as there is a striking similarity in the diagnosis of the three reports, so there is *mutatis mutandis* a striking similarity in their proposals. All believe that improvements are possible and that, as the Small Heath report puts it, 'What is essential is that action to set revitalisation under way is taken – now, while retrieval is still possible'. But all the reports accept that policy must accept the economic forces which have led to a decline in inner city population and employment, and should concentrate on encouraging adjustments to a new equilibrium. On total population, the different recommendations reflect the different densities. The Liverpool study argues that the aim of revitalisation 'cannot be equated with any long term target population'. If a decent environment is to be achieved, with new private, as well as public housing, densities may have to fall further. The Small Heath study also argues against a pre-determined population target. Only in Lambeth does the report advocate reducing the population by making it easier for unskilled workers to move out, in particular by facilitating movement of council tenants from one authority to another.

All three reports outline basically similar policies under the broad headings of (a) economic development, (b) the alleviation of poverty, (c) education and training, (d) the reform of housing policy and (e) the decentralisation of administration. In most cases, the policies that require change are national rather than local. All the reports advocate measures to attract or retain viable employment, especially in small firms, which fit better into the small sites available in old districts. The reports for Birmingham and London advocate the abolition of IDC's and ODP's. All three reports advocate a rethinking of planning policies which, in the pursuit of an excessive segregation of housing and workplaces, have contributed to the flight of industry. They also advocate a policy of making land available for new industrial premises, or rehabilitating old premises.

All three reports express a dissatisfaction with the performance of the existing 'welfare state', and attach high priority to alleviating poverty by direct cash transfers. Many of the numerous existing allowances are not claimed, and the Lambeth study advocates a national income-support scheme, operated through the Inland Revenue. Some services that are particularly important in these areas, such as more child day-care, simply need more money, but there is also a suggestion that the welfare services are too remote and impersonal.

The third element in the suggested programme is training and education to reduce the mismatch between job opportunities and available skills. The Lambeth report advocates more emphasis in schools on 'basic academic skills and vocational preparation'. It also points out that opportunities for school-leavers to undertake vocational training are very limited compared with many other European countries.

The fourth element concerns housing policy. All three reports suggest that the administration of council housing is unsatisfactory, being too remote and bureaucratic, while the criteria for allocation is not sufficiently based on need. Tentative suggestions are made for a more decentralised system, with more tenant participation. In the same vein, the Lambeth report stresses that if, as is likely under existing policies, private tenancy is largely eliminated, it should be replaced by 'social ownership' based on a variety of non-profit enterprises (which have lower costs than councils), and that the level of 'fair rents', which now bears no relation to costs, should be raised by means of an explicit formula giving a 'fair' rate of return on capital, which would then be indexed for inflation. Besides assisting housing associations, this would enable some resident landlords to remain.

On the physical pattern of housing, the reports all favour small-scale improvements rather than massive schemes. The Lambeth report also points out the social and environmental dangers of having the large impersonal areas of space that have been one of the hallmarks of public housing projects: it advocates the concept of 'defensible space'.[11] 'Every space should look as though it belonged to someone', or be supervised. Finally, the reports suggest that revitalisation requires a more decentralised system of public administration, in which local people do not feel that their views are ignored, and that City Hall wishes to forget about them.

WILL THESE PROPOSALS BE ADOPTED?

The proposals in the 'inner area studies' are a coherent and logical response to the analysis given of the problems. But they require major changes at the national level; some of these are already incipient, others run counter to deeply established attitudes and organisational interests. On economic development, the Government has accepted that manufacturing industry in inner areas should be encouraged, and asked local planning authorities to bear this need in mind. But the proposals in the Birmingham and London reports to abolish IDCs and ODPs would require a radical change of official attitudes on regional policy. Nevertheless, such a change is in the air.[12]

On the 'welfare state' proposals, there would be relatively little difficulty in providing more money for more services such as day-care. But the idea of alleviating poverty through tax credits rather than innumerable special allowances for which people must apply, and be means-tested by visits from social workers, is, at present, opposed by the social work profession and the Supplementary Benefits Commission. The outlook is more hopeful on education and training. It remains to be seen how effectively the problems of discipline and teaching in inner-area schools and inadequate vocational training will be tackled, but at least they have now been recognised.

On housing policy, the ideas on physical layout are more likely to gain acceptance than those on organisation. Concepts like 'defensible space' and 'the human scale' were unfashionable in the age of Le Corbusier, but studies of geese and monkeys are now helping us to rediscover old truths about humans. How far they are likely to be influential under council ownership and management in its present form is less certain. The ideas in the Lambeth report for a varied pattern of 'social ownership' and for giving 'fair rents' a meaningful economic interpretation are a very different matter. In particular, any proposals to base 'fair rents' on capital value, or to alleviate the restrictions even on resident landlords, would run completely counter to the policies implemented over the past decade. More likely to be acceptable are modifications of the subsidy system so as to favour renovation as against new council construction, supported in the 1977 'Green Paper'.[13]

VACANT LAND

In addition to the general studies by the inner area consultants, more specific studies have recently begun to be made on issues such as the area of vacant land. Britain is not well provided with land statistics.[14] There is a survey of 'derelict land' covered by mine workings, industrial debris, etc., and which is 'so damaged by industrial or other development as to be incapable of beneficial use without treatment'. There are 137,000 acres of derelict land in England and Wales. But these figures do not exclude undamaged vacant land, on which there are no published official statistics. One diligent researcher, however, has unearthed unpublished statistics indicating that vacant land accounts for around five per cent of the land area of British metropolitan authorities or major cities, rising to eight to twelve per cent in inner areas. Glasgow and Liverpool are in a class on their own, with the figure in the East End of Glasgow rising to nearly 20 per cent.

TABLE 11. Vacant land in four British cities 1974

| | Total | | Inner areas | | |
	Area vacant land ha	% of all land	Area vacant land ha	% of all land	% of all vacant land
B'ham	839	3.1	262	7.3	31.4
Glasgow	1562	7.7	418	11.9	26.7
Liverpool	648	5.6	359	10.3	55.5
London	7727	4.9	1885	5.6	24.3

Source: John Burrows, 'Vacant Land – a continuing crisis'. *The Planner*, Jan. 1978.

The average size of site is around one hectare, but the distribution is highly skewed, with a few large sites and many small ones. The limited available evidence suggests that the division of ownership, in acreage terms, is broadly: local authorities, a half; nationalised industries, one quarter; private owners one quarter. Local authorities and nationalised industries tend to own the larger sites.

In general, some two-thirds of this vacant land is outside 'inner areas' (somewhat arbitrarily defined) although the percentages are higher in inner areas than elsewhere. The percentage figures tend to follow a curve from the centre outwards: highest in the inner area (outside the CBD), lowest in the main suburban belt and rising again towards the rural fringe.

In addition to vacant land there is land which is 'under-used'. This is a more ambiguous and less easily measured concept, but it clearly applies to decaying warehouses or factories, partially used by transient merchandising firms. The impression is that this underutilisation is concentrated in inner areas.

Vacant or under-used land on a similar scale is found in the older cities of the USA. In other cities of North West Europe (e.g. the Netherlands, West Germany, and Scandinavia), on the other hand, there is very little vacant or under-used land. (a partial exception being some cities in the Ruhr where steelworks have closed). The initial symptoms are often there – as any picture display on 'urban renewal' in the Hague or Hanover will make clear – but their extent bears no comparison with the situation in Liverpool, Glasgow or New York.

WHAT IS THE PROBLEM?

The first question to be asked about vacant land (using this to include grossly under-used land) is whether it constitutes a problem. In an area experiencing changes in buildings or land use, *some* vacant land is inevitable. Nor is it desirable that all land should be covered with buildings: even 'wilderness' has its value. But litter-strewn sites do little good, and considerable harm to people's 'image' of an area, and hence to the prospects of regeneration. Although it is impossible to lay down any figures of the 'optimum' amount of vacant land, most people would probably agree that there is too much in Glasgow and Liverpool.

Granted that there is a problem, the next question is 'What causes it?' A conspiracy theory is often employed here, and the conspirator is usually the private landowner. A few American urban economists have attributed the decay of inner cities (of which vacant land is an aspect) to massive speculative withholding of land by landowners, and this view is echoed by some British commentators. But there are considerable difficulties, discussed above, in the explanation which attributes such an extensive and enduring phenomenon to speculation. And these difficulties seem greater in a country like Britain, in which most of the vacant land in inner areas is owned by public authorities. A different analysis seems called for, which explains both the similarities of the phenomenon in various countries, and the differences in its extent. The following ideas are based on those of Mr. John Burrows, the leading authority on the British situation.

Vacant land is a phenomenon of *change*. A picture of the situation at one moment is not useful unless it is put in the perspective of what has happened in the past and is likely to happen in the future. The process can be divided into (1) reasons for the cessation of former land uses, and (2) reasons why new uses do not emerge. The situation is somewhat different at the urban fringe and in the 'inner city'. On the fringe, vacant land can arise for several reasons. It can be 'derelict' in the official sense, the costs of reclamation may be currently too high to make development possible; it may have been by-passed by development; vandalism from the extending suburbs may have caused agricultural use to cease. Views on the question range from denunciations of planning for falling away from post-war standards of compactness to the view that 'scatteration' is not without virtue.

The more visually obtrusive and probably economically (although not quantitatively) significant type of vacant land is in the 'inner city' Here, the characteristic sequence is illustrated in Fig. 14 (which is a

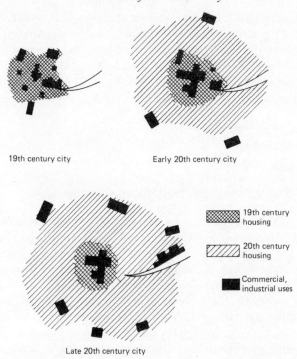

19th century city   Early 20th century city

19th century housing

20th century housing

Commercial, industrial uses

Late 20th century city

FIG. 14. The emergence of vacant land

development of the 'classical model'). The 19th century city was dense and compact. Embedded in the housing was an inner-ring of small manufacturing, railway stations, etc; on the edge of the city were larger land-users such as sewage works and generating stations. Port cities had large areas of land in warehousing alongside the docks. In the 20th century, many of these facilities have become obsolete, and have been replaced by larger plants situated towards the edge of the expanded city. Thus substantial areas of land are being freed. In addition, there is the process of decay of older housing, sometimes accelerated by rent control. When official 'slum clearance' schemes have been implemented, the initial effect is to create vacant land.

The fact that many land uses in the inner city were *declining* was for a time disguised by the expansion of central business uses. With the slowing-down in this type of expansion, the problem of vacant land – incipient for a long time – has suddenly become obvious. However, there are striking differences – between countries, and between cities in one country – in the extent to which new uses have emerged.

This raises the second question. Why is it that in some cases the emergence of new uses is so delayed as to create a problem? The reasons can be grouped in three catagories. New uses may not arise because the land is

(a) not available
(b) not in demand,

or because

(c) development is delayed for administrative reasons

Situation (a) arises when, for example, a port or railway authority no longer uses land but does not dispose of it; when a local authority owns land but has not decided on a use for it; or when potential development (e.g. for owner-occupied housing) is not allowed by the planning authorities. Situation (b) arises when, because of the site's characteristics (physical problems, location, general environment) potential developers are not interested, even at a low or zero price, or when land prices are allegedly 'too high'. Situation (c) arises when a scheme which has received general planning approval is delayed by, for example, disagreements between various interested parties (e.g. London's dockland). These three situations can be combined to any city, although the combination can vary. In central Liverpool or Glasgow, although there is so much vacant land, very little is available for sale to developers. Even if it were, it is doubtful whether there would at present be many takers. In London, many boroughs are equally reluctant to sell land, but there would in most districts be a demand for private house-building.

'TOO HIGH' LAND PRICES?

One argument which raises many of the basic principles of land economics is the argument recently put forward that land prices in inner areas are 'too high'. This implies either:

(a) that there are defects in the operation of the land market (eg 'speculation') or
(b) that the compensation code (or the way it is implemented) has an upward bias.

These issues are discussed in a report by a working party of the Royal Town Planning Institute.[15] This report is in part an 'agreed statement' of differing views. There were differences between members of the working party on whether incentives or expropriation should be relied on; this was reflected in disagreement as to whether Development Land Tax should be raised to 100 per cent. Moreover, a brief introductory discussion of 'value' seems to reflect the continuing confusion of economic thought among town planners.[16] But the body of the report is a competent examination of the costs of acquisition and preparation, and possible upward bias in the compensation code.

The report points out that when most of the land in an inner area is in the hands of public bodies (which, as a map strikingly shows, is the situation in Liverpool) and when very little property has changed hands in recent years, there is a very 'thin' market. Data is sparse, and valuation becomes subject to an unusually large range of error. Values based on feasible new uses – in real terms – are well below those based on previous uses; thus valuation procedures partly based on original uses may fail to reflect the current situation.

The report makes some minor proposals for amending the compensation code – notably a proposal, which seems very reasonable, that land uses which have been discontinued for more than five years should not be considered as a basis for valuation. However, the working party also conclude that the problem is 'not simply one of high land costs impeding development'. As several case-studies illustrate, preparing old urban areas for new uses is very expensive, and sometimes unprofitable under *any* compensation code. Several of the recommendations concern the land market. Planning surveys should 'include outlook of investors and developers, influences and trends in the market, ways of encouraging desirable private and voluntary sector contributions—and ways of avoiding unnecessary hindrance of this'. The need for a public Land Register is stressed, and it is proposed that information on the workings of the Community Land Act should be published, both to monitor the Act's workings and to obtain information on the land market. Such ideas are not new, and they are probably not universally held in the planning profession, let alone among politicians, but they strike a relatively new note in British planning.

It looks as though 'too high' prices are, at most, a minor element in the problem. As Mr. Burrows put its: 'The important question to pose here is not why inner city land values are so high but why the land is valued so low by potential users. The answers will inevitably point to courses of action'. For example, if the physical condition of the site makes preparation expensive, central or local government could finance acquisition and preparation. When the problem is the generally discouraging urban environment, local authorities should consider what changes would make people *want* to live in these areas. This latter approach runs counter to the policy recently pursued in most British cities. Most plans provide predominantly for council housing; little provision is made for owner-occupied housing, at least where it would be in demand. To retain people who have a choice, and choose to remain, it may be necessary to zone substantial amounts of the more desirable districts for owner-occupied new housing. There are examples in London where developments of this type have been surprisingly successful. In a seriously decayed district, however, this approach may necessitate a minimum size so that a new 'micro-environment' is created. (A figure of 100 dwelling units has been suggested). The argument advanced against such policies is that they encourage *embourgeoisement* and are social divisive. However, it has been argued above that it is *district-wide* social segregation which is really divisive, and this is precisely what is likely to result from turning the inner city into a council estate.

An atmosphere of confidence is necessary if private capital is to be attracted to inner areas, if the more able inhabitants are to be encouraged to stay, and owner occupiers encouraged to improve their housing. Other policy changes needed include a better co-ordination of local authorities' land use plans and available resources and a greater readiness to rezone vacant land for an alternative acceptable use, or for temporary uses (the Civic Trust report gives examples of beautification by local groups). But all such policies presuppose considerable changes in official attitudes. As Mr. Burrows puts it

Vacant urban land is already a political issue and an issue about which the public, the politicians and the press might reasonably expect planners to be well informed and active in solving. As our cities stand today, however, one is forced to question the current priorities of a system of planning which spends so much time and energy exercising strict controls over the extensions of individual houses and minor changes of use, while allowing whole areas to be demolished and laid to waste for years, even decades, at the heart of the most populous cities in the country.

THE WHITE PAPER

Enough has been said to suggest that effective policies towards the British inner city areas may conflict at several points with deeply entrenched policies and attitudes. This conflict is reflected in the White Paper *Policy for the Inner Cities* (Cmnd. 6845) published in June 1977. It accepts the serious condition of the inner areas, and the need to arrest their decline. This represents an important change. On the other hand, the analysis of the areas' problems is cursory, and the detailed policy recommendations are bitty and obscure, revealing, to those experienced in textual exegesis, differing attitudes within the Government and civil service.

The 'nature of the problem' is analysed – reasonably enough – as a loss of jobs in traditional industries, physical decay, and a concentration of poor and socially handicapped people. The discussion of the causes of decay, however, is far from searching.

The bulldozers have done their work, but the rebuilding has lagged behind. Sometimes this has been caused by changes of plan as more people left the cities than expected. In other instances, it has resulted from reductions in the allocation of resources, central and local. Whatever the explanation, there is a wide extent of vacant land in some inner areas, mainly in public ownership: and there is much under-used land and property, with shops boarded up and sites and buildings neglected.

The possibility that comprehensive redevelopment schemes, planning powers exercised by councils hostile to private ownership of housing or business, and rent control, may have contributed to the problems is not explicitly conceded, although it seems implicit in some statements. Public investment 'must be on a more human scale, with less disruption of community ties'. 'The resources of small and medium size firms are essential if real progress is to be made and the diversity and vitality, for so long characteristic of inner cities, is to be restored'. 'Controls over the expansion of light industry in residential areas can be relaxed where this can be done without serious objection on noise or nuisance grounds'. 'The state of the private rented sector is especially significant in some inner areas. The current review of the Rent Acts will be particularly relevant to the needs of these parts of cities' (a hope which anyone who has studied the history of British rent legislation must view with some scepticism).

On the other hand, the 'Conclusions' echo the historically question-able view that post-War policies have helped to clear up the mess left by the Victorians. 'The current state of the inner areas has its roots in social and economic events reaching to the last century and beyond. Much has been done to ease their problems since the Second World War . . .'.

The preliminary discussion reaches the conclusion (which many people, including the author, would accept) that, although 'some of the changes which have taken place are due to social and economic forces which could be reversed only with great difficulty or at unacceptable cost' nevertheless, 'the inner parts of our cities ought not to be left to decay'. Vacant or under-utilised land in these areas should not be abandoned, and it should be possible to 'achieve a more balanced structure of jobs and population within our cities'.

A section on 'The agencies for action' dismisses the idea of replacing local authorities by nominated bodies. It comments favourably on self-help and community effort, and stresses the role of the private sector, with the public sector creating opportunities and under-pinning con-fidence. The specific proposals are that more money should be channelled to the inner areas, at the expense of New Towns, and that small-scale industrial development should be encouraged rather than discouraged. 'Partnership arrangements' would be entered into by the central government with a number of local authorities under which money would be provided and a 'unified approach' to inner areas adopted. Local authorities would be given money and powers to build advance factories and provide initial 'rent holidays' for incoming firms. They would be encouraged to improve employment prospects by allocating more land to industrial and commercial activities. At the same time, regional policy would be given an 'intra-regional emphasis'. Inner London and Inner Birmingham, instead of being 'white', non-assisted areas, less favoured than the 'black' or 'grey' Assisted Areas, would in future be 'blacker-than-black' islands in a white sea, with precedence over the Assisted Areas.

An annex goes into more detail on some points. The brief section on land policy suggests a change from the White Papers of the Heath and Wilson Governments, with their emphasis on the evils of 'speculation' and the need for local authority ownership of all development land. It openly states that much of the vacant, under-used or derelict land is owned by local authorities or other public bodies. The Community Land Act receives only a passing mention. No very clear policies are spelled out, but it is accepted that tidying-up the environment and bringing vacant sites into use – commercial, recreational or residential – is a prerequisite for the regeneration of the areas. One section (paras. 10, 11) contains opposing views on land prices. It mentions the argument, that land prices in these areas are 'too high', and then gives counter-arguments. 'Land prices respond to market demand but at times when market activity is low they tend to respond slowly'; the main discouragement to development is lack of confidence in the future of the area.

Policy for the Inner Cities (which was promptly translated into an Inner Urban Areas Bill) marks an essential first step in tackling a problem – recognising that it exists. On the other hand, the only concrete proposals are to spend more public money and relax the planning restrictions on industrial development. But for new employment to emerge there will probably have to be radical changes in both local planning attitudes and in national policy towards small firms and the development process. Similarly, there are many aspects of current social, housing and educational policy which are particularly harmful in districts where people have less opportunity to either go outside the state system or influence it.

THE INDUSTRIAL DEVELOPER'S VIEWPOINT

A very different perspective from that in the White Paper is obtained from a report by Mr. G. W. Mobbs, a director of one of the most experienced and reputable factory developers.[17] It argues that, although the White Paper diagnoses the problem correctly, it does not spell out how industry is to be attracted back, and glosses over many of the policies which have contributed to the decline of inner-city employment. The inner city has lost most of the locational advantages it once possessed. There has been a decline in both the physical and social environment, aggravated by government policies. The environment must be improved, and the bureaucratic obstacles to development reduced, before progress can be made. Among the environmental handicaps are the reduction in the supply of skilled labour – resulting from immigration and the decline in the supply of private tenanted housing caused by the Rent Acts – and unsatisfactory road access. Some British cities – most notably London – have not built urban motorways, and have started to restrict motor traffic in towns, with the idea of bringing about a switch to public transport. But this can be disastrous for manufacturing firms: many of their employees cannot use public transport geared to 'radial' routes, and products have to be dispatched by lorry. Thus it is essential for new industrial zones to be served by good roads, so that goods vehicles are not forced to use residential streets.

Many small business houses have been destroyed by comprehensive redevelopment, while the emergence of new firms has been inhibited by 'planning blight' (i.e. the designation of long-term uses without adequate consideration of the effect on medium-term uses) and by excessively restrictive regulations for industrial premises. The report complains that planners do not understand the needs of industry, and have aggravated the situation by seeking to impose ill-informed and unrealistic plans.

Changes that have occurred in the nature and character of business have clearly affected the balance of a community. Unfortunately, planners have not been agile enough to anticipate these changes and they have often sought to reverse the cycle of change rather than attempting to move ahead of it and create the new structure that will benefit from the change. This problem arises because planners tend to work in a vacuum, with little or no preliminary contact with industry at the formative stage of policies.

It suggests the appointment of local advisory boards containing representatives of industry, commerce and other interests to advise the planning authorities. In other countries, there is greater trust and co-operation between the public and private sector, planning delays are shorter, and because planning is less authoritarian, new ideas can be discussed and tried out more readily.

Small industries are particularly suited to inner-city locations. In the past, they were often accommodated in backstreet workshops, railway arches, etc., which were at least of the right size, and cheap. Legislation on working conditions has often prevented this type of building being used, and the provision of new accommodation has been prevented by IDCs (in the South and Midlands) and by inappropriate building regulations. Before the War, multiple 'nursery' units were built, and are still being built in Canada and Australia. These consist of a shell containing 'modules' let on short leases: a firm could take one or more according to its needs. If it became so successful that it needed larger premises, it would move out. This type of building cannot be built today because permission is rarely granted for (private) speculative industrial building. (It should be added that *some* local authorities, especially in the North-East, have attempted to fill the gap with nursery factories).

The report argues that renovation of pre-1914 factories is rarely possible. The costs are high and the results unsatisfactory for modern operations: in most areas, redevelopment is necessary. (There are, of course, cases where these often splendid buildings can be put to other uses: the chocolate factory which now houses boutiques in San Francisco is an internationally famous example).

The report is critical of the assumption in the White Paper that local authorities should play the major role in developing industrial premises, arguing that they are ill-suited to undertake all the tasks in this specialised field. It advocates partnership arrangements between local authorities (who may have to exercise compulsory purchase powers when ownership is fragmented), financial institutions, and developers. Developers include both the publicly owned English Industrial Estates Corporation and private developers. In order to facilitate the provision of the necessary infra-structure, new factories should be grouped rather than scattered, and the report suggests the creation of special boards for the planning of such industrial areas. (The use of organisations like the German 'homestead companies' would, however, be an alternative with the advantage of maintaining an experienced team for use elsewhere).

Mr. Mobbs finally makes the point that Government must allow development to be profitable if it is to take place. He reflects the bitterness and disillusionment resulting from recent legislation by both Conservative and Labour Governments, even among industrial developers, which were never the main target of criticism.

Because of the implication of recent legislation on the taxation of development values and the community ownership of land, confidence has been eroded to a point where the private sector suspects the sincerity of government in seeking a solution to the problems of the urban areas.

SUMMARY

The extent of the physical and social decay of older, inner city districts varies considerably from country to country and has been influenced by national policies such as rent control. However, the phenomenon is to some extent international. The initial response, begun in the UK before the War, was a purely physical approach of bulldozing whole areas and putting up council housing. A similar policy was adopted in the USA in the 1950s, but was soon discontinued when its socially and environmentally disruptive consequences were realised. In Britain, the consequences were similar, but were not publicised.

In the USA, there was an open debate on the appropriate policy for these districts. Some economists argued that deteriorating areas served a useful purpose as reservoirs of low-cost housing. The more widely accepted view was that a positive policy was needed to 'improve and dilute' these districts by making out-migration easier while at the same time undertaking *partial* rebuilding and renovation. But the racial and social problems of the 'central city' were considerable, and only patchy progress was made.

In Britain, 'comprehensive redevelopment' remained without serious challenge or discussion until the 1970s. The problems of the 'inner city' have now been highlighted in a series of officially sponsored studies. These all attribute the problems of the districts to a decline in traditional industries combined with ageing housing and a high concentration of the poor, the socially handicapped and immigrants. The various policies proposed in various fields are for the most part contrary to those which have been pursued up till now. Similarly, unofficial studies of vacant land have high-lighted both the decline in demand for inner areas land and the inefficiencies in the land management policies of public bodies.

As a consequence of the belated recognition that 'slum clearance' was not solving the problems of inner areas, Government policy has recently undergone a change of emphasis: the New Town programme is being curtailed, while considerable sums of money are to be made available to selected local authorities for the regeneration of inner areas. This public money is necessary: whether by itself it will be sufficient seems doubtful.[18]

SELECT BIBLIOGRAPHY

AMERICAN

B. J. Frieden *"The Future of Old Neighborhoods"*. Cambridge, Mass., M.I.T. Press, 1964.

Issues in Urban Economics (H. S. Perloff and Lowdon Wingo Jr., John Hopkins Press, 1968) – especially the article by Edgar M. Hoover.

Internal Structure of the City (L. S. Bourne, ed. Oxford University Press 1971) Parts V and VII.

Paul R. Porter, *The Recovery of American Cities*, Sun River Press, 1976.

INTERNATIONAL

Leo Grebler, *Urban Renewal in European Countries* 1964, University of Pennsylvania Press, Philadelphia, U.S.A.

BRITISH

Inner London: Policies for dispersal and balance. Final report of the Lambeth Inner Area Study, 1977.
Change or Decay. Final Report of the Liverpool Inner Area Study, 1977.
Unequal City. Final Report of the Birmingham Inner Area Study, 1977.

These three reports are well summarised in: *Inner Area Studies: A Summary of Consultants' Reports.* 1977.
All are published by HMSO for the Department of the Environment.

John Burrows, 'Vacant Land—a continuing crisis', *The Planner*, Jan. 1978.
Urban Wasteland, The Civic Trust, 1977.

REFERENCES

1. 'A survey of New York City', p. 10. *The Economist.* 25–31 March, 1978.
2. Robert McKie, 'Social objectives and citizens' participation in urban renewal in the United Kingdom', in *Urban Renewal in the Netherlands.* International Federation for Housing and Planning. 1975.
3. M. Anderson, *The Federal Bulldozer.* Cambridge, Mass. M.I.T. Press, 1964.
   J. Q. Wilson, *Urban Renewal: the Record and the Controversy*, Cambridge, Mass. M.I.T. Press, 1966.
4. Herbert Gans, *The Urban Villagers*, The Free Press, N.Y. 1962.
5. Jane Jacobs, *The Death and Life of Great American Cities.* Penguin Books, 1964.
6. D. Seligman, 'The Enduring Slums', *The Exploding Metropolis.* Doubleday Anchor Books, Garden City, N.Y., U.S.A. 1957, p. 106.
7. Leo Grebler, *Urban Renewal in European Countries.* Philadelphia U.S.A., 1964.
8. Gunnar Myrdal, *Economic Theory and Underdeveloped Regions*, London, 1957.
9. Edgar M. Hoover, 'The Evolving Form and Organisation of the Metropolis', in *Issues in Urban Economics, op. cit.* p. 275.

10. *Inner Area Studies: A Summary of Consultants' Reports*. Department of the Environment, HMSO, 1977, p. 3.

11. *Inner London: Policies for Dispersal and Balance*, op. cit., p. 156, Oscar Newman, *Defensible Space*, Architectural Press, 1973.

12. The Conservative Party's proposal to abolish ODP's was not welcomed by all development companies, since ODPs have benefitted those enjoying political favour. The case against such government intervention (as with development – restricting taxation and rent control) lies in its effects on *consumers*, not necessarily producers. As one Chairman of a property group candidly put it, 'I would rather have our planning restrictions than open competition'. (*Financial Times*, July 7, 1977, p. 19).

13. *Housing Policy: A Consultative Document*, Cmnd, 6851, HMSO, 1977.

14. Scotland, in contrast to England, has had a Land Register since the 17th century. It has not been used to produce published statistics, partly because of the complicated ledgers used (a situation that will soon be changed by computerisation). Even so, the administrators in St. Andrew's House appear to be better informed on land use and land ownership than their colleagues South of the Border.

15. *Land Values and Planning in the Inner Areas*, Royal Town Planning Institute, London, 1978.

16. 'Many economists define value as only that which is produced by human effort. In this sense, land itself, needing no production, has no value. . . . Other economists . . . are inclined to equate value and price . . . (*op. cit.* p. 9)

17. G. N. Mobbs. *The Inner City – a location for industry?* Slough Estates Ltd., 1977.

18. It is even disputed whether there is really more money. The London boroughs, at least, maintain that existing funds have been given a new name.

11 Urban Renewal

The *City in History*, incidentally, replaces the limited historical
sections of *The Culture of Cities*: parts of those four original chapters
now lie embedded in the eighteen chapters of the present
work . . . The material thus retained should give the book an organic
continuity and solidity that would have been lacking, perhaps, had I
ignored the earlier structure and, like a speculative builder with a
bulldozer, levelled the whole tract.

Lewis Mumford, Preface to *The City in History* New York, 1961.

Urban renewal is not a new phenomenon. If it were, the centres of
London, Paris or Cologne would be the same as they were in the Middle
Ages. Change takes place when individual buildings are redeveloped or
modernised, when new streets are built, when whole districts are
demolished in war or when public urban renewal programmes are
initiated. Perhaps it is worth remembering that cities were renewed – not
always without success – before 'urban renewal' or 'town planning' was
invented. Nevertheless, the renewal of urban districts poses two
technical (among other) problems. Firstly, the existing property boundaries may not be suitable; e.g. larger sites may be needed. Secondly,
there is a need for some co-ordination at a level above that of the
individual site. The London squares of the early 19th century required
planning of the terraces, roads and the central garden; a comparable
type of small-scale planning is needed today.

In the past, ground landlords sometimes exercised these functions.
Some of the most attractive parts of central London and some of the few
attractive parts of Birmingham (the Bournville and Calthorpe estates)
were the outcome of sensitive management for over a century by ground
landlords who were able to take a long view. These ground landlords
included both non-profit enterprises and private families and trusts.
Under the leasehold system, covenants were imposed during the term of
the lease: at the end of the lease redevelopment or extensive modernisation became possible. This system was virtually ended by the

Leasehold Reform (Enfranchisement) Act, 1967. Estates which qualified as 'well managed' were allowed to retain certain powers, although their ability to recover possession and redevelop at the end of the lease was severely restricted, but no new estates could be added. Alternatives to the leasehold system will have to be found.

The modernisation and redevelopment of old urban neighbourhoods can take place at three levels: (a) individual sites, by individual owners, (b) small areas, e.g. by a ground landlord and (c) small to moderate size areas, under a public 'urban renewal' scheme. The last method can take forms ranging from 'comprehensive development', where the whole area is bulldozed and replanned from scratch, through varying combinations of modernisation and redevelopment.

COST-BENEFIT ANALYSIS

If modernisation or redevelopment took place as and when necessary, there would be no problem. The fact that there is so much discussion of the problem of 'urban decay' is a reasonable indication that there is in fact a problem, although one which varies enormously from country to country, and city to city. If there is a problem of 'urban decay' – and one not caused by uncertainty about local authority policy – this implies that redevelopment or modernisation which is desirable on broad social grounds is not taking place because it is unprofitable. In the terminology of cost-benefit analysis, the 'private' return is less the 'social' return. One type of renewal strategy is to bridge this gap by subsidies, e.g. modernisation grants; in districts where decay has not gone too far, and the basic layout is suitable for modern housing, this can have a marked effect. In more decayed or obsolete districts, a more organised renewal strategy may be necessary. Any scheme embracing more than a single site – whether carried out commercially, on some local cooperative basis, by a non-profit 'trustee' in the German manner, or even by the 'municipal bulldozer', should have the advantage of 'internalising the externality'. In most cases, however, some public expenditure will be involved, ranging from simple alterations to access and parking arrangements to massive expenditure on redevelopment. But there are always alternative uses for a limited supply of public finance. Is expenditure on urban renewal justified? Should it be concentrated in certain districts or spread more thinly over a larger area? What should be the mix of redevelopment and renovation? These are the kind of questions which cost-benefit analysis is supposed to answer, and attempts have been made to apply this method of analysis to urban investment.

The issue, however, has often been clouded by a confusion over the treatment of land prices, especially in the issue of 'greenfield' development *versus* urban renewal (although one can, of course, have both). Land on peripheral greenfield sites is often cheaper – at market prices, not to mention current use prices. (But the differential in market prices is falling, and in countries with extensive urban decay, such as the UK and USA, land prices in many 'inner areas' are no longer higher than in more favoured suburbs).

It has frequently been argued that, in a comparison of re-building old districts and taking the 'easy' course of greenfield development, market prices for land should be ignored (from which it is not a long step to arguing that market prices should not be paid). A survey of early urban renewal in European countries (by an American economist with whose substantive conclusions the author agrees) argues that:

> from a national accounting point of view, the prices paid for land represent merely transfer payments. When the input of real resources is considered exclusive of land the saving from the use of existing overhead facilities in urban renewal cannot be ignored. On this kind of reckoning, urban renewal may well emerge as a resource-economising device compared to the building of new major cities.

This argument purports to be an application of the concept of 'opportunity cost'. It seems, however, to be a theoretical misunderstanding based on a kernel of truth. It is true that, whether a public authority pays a high or a low price, or no price at all, for property acquired for a development scheme will not in itself affect the optimum allocation of resources. Bygones are bygones. On the other hand, property prices *do* reflect the value of actual or potential uses. If they are ignored, serious misallocation of resources can occur: only the more extreme critics of 'over-development' would think it sensible to grow wheat in Oxford Street, but if land prices were ignored there would be no reason for not doing so. Similarly, the current use value of buildings, even in a run-down area, may be considerable, and should not be ignored. If the site value exceeds the current use value, this indicates the value of possible new uses, which also should not be ignored.

If it were possible to devise a *complete* cost-benefit analyis, land prices should be ignored because they *reflect* the costs and benefits of different locations. But a complete cost-benefit analysis would have to cover a huge range of costs and benefits, often impossible to quantify, for large numbers of people affected both directly and indirectly. A comparison between renewing an inner area and building on a 'greenfield' site would have to include a comparison of: public authority costs for construction, demolition and infra-structure; householders' housing costs and an assessment of the relative 'quality' of housing; the indirect effects on householders of nearness-to-work, 'amenities' etc.; lower receipts from rates and possible under-utilisation of resources in inner areas; the 'brain drain' of younger and more vigorous people; and, on the other hand, the advantages of lower densities. Even this incomplete catalogue indicates the virtual impossibility of a complete and quantified cost-benefit analysis. And an *incomplete* cost-benefit analysis, confined to readily quantifiable costs and benefits, or merely to public expenditure can be grossly misleading.[2] This is obviously a blind alley.

The most detailed examination of cost-benefit analysis in urban renewal adopts the simple and common sense approach of estimating the 'private' (i.e. financial) cost to the public authority, and then the 'social' benefits which may justify this expenditure.[3] The inclusion of the costs of property acquisition (minus land sales) in the 'private' calculation indicates the extent to which demolition will cause a loss of houses, shops or industrial buildings which still have a useful life. This study was implicitly based on the 'federal bulldozer' type of programme, which has little support now. And even in this methodologically clear-cut case, Professor Rothenberg exhibited a refreshing modesty

> It is indeed possible that the benefits from using cost-benefit may not be worth their cost (p. 258)

Professor Lichfield's approach emphasises the comparison of alternative policies, and the costs and benefits to *particular groups*: rate-payers, shoppers, motorists, etc.[4] The 'cheapest' scheme for ratepayers is unlikely to be the best for ratepayers wearing other hats. On the other hand, an expensive scheme is not necessarily a good one from many points of view. This disaggregation of benefits brings out an important point implicit in welfare economics (Chap. 2). Different schemes may well be capable of being ranked differently according to their effects on different groups or from different viewpoints. The large margins of error involved should rule out any pretence of being able to calculate precise values for all costs and benefits. However, it would be useful, before any preliminary decisions were taken on renewing either town centres or 'inner areas', if the local authority were given – on a single sheet of paper – a list of a large range of alternatives (including currently unfashionable ones) with both a 'price list' and some indication, quantified only when it makes sense, of their benefits. This is not 'sophisticated' cost-benefit analysis, but it is probably the sort that can be of some use.

APPROACHES TO URBAN RENEWAL

The approach to urban renewal first adopted in the USA and Britain in the post-War era was 'comprehensive redevelopment'. Such an approach was supposed to overcome the problem of 'externality'. The argument was that it would not pay an individual owner to redevelop, or even improve, his property unless his neighbours did so as well. Since everyone would wait for everyone else, the district would remain trapped in a vicious circle. A comprehensive scheme would break the vicious circle by 'internalising the externality'. This theory therefore attributed 'urban decay' to a failure of the market mechanism. An often overlooked corollary is that, if the urban decay is *solely* caused by externalities, the market value of the reorganised land will be greater than the market value of the existing property. The public authority would thus make a profit from urban renewal, even if market value were paid.

It has not worked out this way. Urban renewal is not profitable: it is usually highly unprofitable. This does not necessarily mean that it should not be undertaken; it does, however, seem to weaken the argument which attributes urban decay to externalities. Moreover, the bulldozing physical approach with which comprehensive land acquisition has been associated (and for which it is most appropriate) has been shown to be socially and economically, as well as architecturally, disruptive. If the aim is not comprehensive redevelopment, there is not the same necessity to acquire the whole area. If a 'cellular' type of renewal is adopted, state intervention can be more limited; at one extreme, it can confine itself to reorganising roads, playgrounds and other public facilities and assisting the adjustment of private boundaries where needed, but relying on private owners to undertake the redevelopment or renovation of buildings. This approach has the practical advantage that it greatly reduces the public capital needed. However, this approach is possible only when the process of decay (physical and social) has not gone too far. When decay has passed a certain point, there is *some* truth in the 'externality' argument: it may be necessary for a single developer to take over an area of a certain size in order to 'internalise the externality'. But this area does not have to be huge, nor does everything in it have to be flattened.

There is thus a spectrum of types of urban renewal. At the one extreme is compulsory acquisition of the whole area by a public body; at the other is a policy of encouraging modernisation by subsidies or tax allowances, perhaps tilting the tax balance in favour of *occupying* older housing,[5] and giving older areas a higher priority in public spending, but otherwise relying on private initiative to modernise or redevelop when the time is right.

Which policy can most effectively be adopted depends on the physical and social capacity of a district for regeneration. Whether modernisation is feasible can be decided only on a street-by-street or even house-by-house assessment. Similarly much depends on whether the district contains stable families, or has become a 'Skid Row' and on whether the owners of housing, shops and businesses are in a position to finance improvements or are old and impoverished.

But it would be an error to imagine that there is general agreement on 'ends', and that the only question is the character of the particular district (and the funds available). In spite of the international swing against 'comprehensive redevelopment', there are profound differences in attitudes to urban renewal. On the one hand, there are those who favour state ownership and control and distrust dispersed ownership, competition and market forces. On the other hand there are those who accept the need for state action to guide major changes in urban structure but who favour the maximum possible dispersal of ownership and control, not only on grounds of efficiency but because they believe that such a system is in Mill's words, 'consistent with the greatest amount of human liberty and spontaneity'[6] and, in its physical manifestations, to a greater variety of townscape. Defenders of the 'unplanned', the un-uniform, the spontaneous, have begun to challenge the 'planning' orthodoxy of the post-War era, but have rarely examined the implications for landownership. Some important indicators can, however, be obtained from two countries which have recently attempted urban renewal not based on bulldozers or comprehensive state ownership – the USA and West Germany. In the USA, the defects of 'urban renewal' as practised in the 1950s led to the 'Model Cities Program' of 1966. This was based on a realisation of the defects of both the 'federal bulldozer' and indeed of any programme purely concerned with housing. In a specified, limited, area a 'City Demonstration Agency' (working alongside the fragmented and by no means unbureaucratic government agencies) was entrusted with developing a plan embracing all aspects of public action over a number of years. This plan would then be broken down into yearly instalments, with corresponding subsidies from the Federal Government. The idea sounded fine, but the programme produced more reports than results on the ground. Various explanations have been given. Some suggest that the trouble was the decline in interest under the Nixon Administration, and the inadequacies of American planning law. But it has also been suggested that the Americans succumbed to the recurrent temptation to produce plans that were too elaborate, rather than concentrating on establishing simple guidelines and an effective administrative system.

URBAN RENEWAL IN WEST GERMANY

The basic ideas of the American programme were taken up by West Germany, in an Act passed in 1971, and implemented far more effectively. But this was merely the last of three stages of urban development. There was first the rebuilding of the bombed central cities, then the development of 'greenfield' sites; only in the 1970s did attention turn to the renewal of older areas not destroyed in the War. In all three phases, development has been based on dispersed ownership, with the non-profit housing movement playing a substantial role, and a market economy operating within a framework of state action. This reflects the philosophy of a 'socially responsible market economy', which was originally conceived by the Christian Democratic Party but was later adopted, and developed, by the Social Democratic Party.

Saturation bombing of the main cities destroyed not merely the central business districts but huge areas of pre-1914 housing. The destruction was so complete that in some cases the authorities seriously considered abandoning the old cities and building on a fresh site. When it was decided to rebuild the bombed areas, it was also in some cases proposed to rebuild on a clean slate by buying out all existing interests and rebuilding on a centralised basis to a new plan. This was not generally done. Instead, existing owners were encouraged to develop themselves, and an elaborate organisation was built up by local authorities to reorganise boundaries, and facilitate land transfers where major changes were necessary. (These functions had been conducted on a small scale since before 1914). Property owned by local authorities often played an important role in reorganisation; for example, if one owner wished to buy out a neighbouring owner, the local authority was sometimes able to facilitate the transfer by offering an alternative site to the owner being bought out.

Critics argued at the time that such a system would be grossly slow and inefficient compared with a radical centralised reorganisation, and would recreate an obsolete layout. This has hardly been borne out by events. The speed of the West German reconstruction had no parallel in any other country. It is also noteworthy that it was carried out under pre-War laws (the inadequacies of which had often been argued), and some *ad hoc* provincial legislation. The German equivalent of the 1947 Town and Country Planning Act (The Federal Building Act) was not passed until 1960. Similarly, the 'failure' to replan the city centres was often their salvation. The most satisfactory results were obtained where a medieval street plan was recreated for pedestrians, supplemented by urban motorways and an underground tram system. The poorest results have been where land ownership became centralised and was replanned according to the best precepts of the late 1940s. This is not to deny that mistakes were made. In some cases shop or office buildings were put up which took little account of their surroundings (and which would not be possible under the stricter – and slower – procedures in force today).

The second phase of development was large-scale suburban development. In the third phase, attention was turned to the older, undamaged, areas. It began to be realised in the mid-1960s that attention was needed both to the historic centres of small towns, where many buildings dated from the 17th century and earlier, and also to large areas of late 19th century housing. This housing was generally structurally sound, but street arrangements pre-dating the motor car were no longer adequate. Traffic noise and congestion, in particular, were damaging the environment and causing an exodus of population and commerce.

The renewal legislation, embodied in the 1971 'Act to Promote Town Planning' after some five years of detailed discussion, was based on an appreciation that the planned renewal of old urban areas required a delicate exercise in partial rebuilding, and that there could be no question of 'bulldozing'. There was general agreement that great care should be taken to preserve existing property, if at all possible; to allow both owner-occupiers and tenants of housing to remain in the area; and also to allow landlords, shopkeepers and small businesses to remain. There was none of the desire to use redevelopment – as has been a factor in British policy – to advance public ownership. However, there was a strong feeling (stimulated by the continuing property boom in the late 1960s) that property owners should not benefit from public expenditure.

The 1971 Act laid down four principles:

(1) The area selected for renewal should be sufficiently small for the programme to be carried out in a reasonable length of time, such as five years (which, in practice has had to be extended).

(2) Subsidies for intra-structure investment should be provided by the national and provincial government, but the capital for the modernisation or redevelopment of buildings should normally be provided by private owners.

(3) A non-profit planning organisation should be appointed as 'trustee' to organise the scheme, or the local authority could undertake the scheme itself.

(4) A 'betterment levy' should be imposed on the basis of property values before and after the scheme (but at one date, so as to exclude the effect of inflation).

A key role in this type of renewal scheme is played by the 'trustee', which is either one of the provincial public development companies ('homestead' companies) or the planning section of a large non-profit housing enterprise such as *Neue Heimat*. Although empowered to develop in its own right, or on behalf of the local authority (for public buildings etc.) the trustee mainly acts as intermediary between the local authority and local residents and businesses. The trustee is specifically required to begin by preparing a 'social plan' which lists existing 'interests' and seeks to preserve them. It then draws up a physical plan, embodying the general requirements of the local authority but tailored to the needs and capabilities of the owners. It reorganises boundaries, buys out owners where this is necessary (or provides alternative property), organises construction (which is generally undertaken by small building firms) and generally supervises the renewal until the plan has been completed. The 'renewal area' entry in the Land Register is then removed, and all the special legal provisions for renewal areas cease to apply.

As none of the schemes have been completed, no 'betterment levy' has yet been imposed. It is, however, becoming apparent that, in the more balanced property market which has succeeded the boom of the 1960s, the levy will not be a major source of finance. It was conceived (like all the other such taxes imposed in both Germany and Britain since 1911) at a time when it was thought that a property boom would continue for ever.

Although it is too early to give a final judgement on the German renewal schemes, the results so far are promising. New buildings – which have been built only where renovation was impossible – have been on a scale, and often a style, which fits in well with the old buildings. The renewal areas will contain a mixture of residential and commercial uses which is modern and functional and yet retains the original intimacy and charm of the district. The criticism has been made that the renewal districts are a small proportion of the total older area, and that the very high costs of the system rule it out for general use. There is truth in this criticism, but the districts chosen have been often both central and of considerable historic importance. It is perhaps reasonable to use an elaborate and expensive procedure in these cases while relying on cheaper and less comprehensive programmes for more run-of-the-mill districts, where modernisation is now being encouraged by general subsidies.

It might seem a reversal of popular ideas about 'socialist' Britain and 'capitalist' Germany that the 'homestead companies' and the non-profit enterprises play such a major role in urban development in Germany, whereas speculative property companies, which have been subject to so much criticism in Britain play no major role in Germany. But it is quite explicable in terms of the philosophy of a 'socially responsible market economy', which has underlain the policies in office of all three parties in West Germany. This philosophy is not egalitarian: it has been more concerned to pull the poor up than to pull the rich down. German policy towards asset creation by individuals and small firms has been consistently more favourable than British. This has the important implication for urban development that there are now affluent individuals and small firms able and willing to invest directly in real property. On the other hand, the prevailing philosophy, while not wishing to eliminate the market, believes in assisting and correcting it by the participation of public (or non-profit) bodies alongside private firms and individuals.

'CELLULAR' RENEWAL

British policies for urban renewal have been very different from those in West Germany. They fall into two distinct categories: 'inner area' and town centre schemes. The inner area schemes have consisted in declaring houses 'unfit for human habitation', acquiring them compulsorily at site value, and – sometimes after considerable delay – putting up council housing. Rather late in the day, the effects of this policy are beginning to be documented, and require no further comment.

There is as-yet no consensus on the type of renewal that should replace it. One of the leading British authorities on this question recommends an approach markedly different from that of most post-War British planning.[7] Professor McKie starts from a 'liberal utilitarian' basis that urban renewal should respond to people's demands, but he stresses the 'organic' nature of society – a point appreciated by the German proponents of *soziale Marktwirtschaft* but often overlooked by English-speaking economists who postulate a universe of 'atomic' consumers. A city should be regarded as an organic structure of partially interdependent neighbourhoods. Neighbourhoods change their character and function over time but, if a planner arbitrarily destroys or abruptly changes a neighbourhood without regard to its wider function – e.g. by reducing the supply of cheap housing too rapidly – this can both harm individuals and upset the functioning of a city.

Within neighbourhoods are what Professor McKie calls 'cells' made up of differing social groups, different types of housing, groupings of workplaces, shops etc. In inner city areas, some cells will have 'died' and require major surgery, such as the redevelopment of obsolete industrial premises. Others may require adaptation to enable them to perform better their original functions, such as the conversion of tenements with shared facilities into self-contained flats. Others are best left alone, or rather left to be improved by individual owners (perhaps assisted by general modernisation grants or allowances). This often occurs on a generation change: a 'liberal utilitarian' will not be inclined to drive old people out of their homes and familiar surroundings, or to *force* owner-occupiers to improve their homes unless they become an eyesore or a threat to public health.[8]

On this view of the urban system, the objective of urban renewal is to maintain the functions of neighbourhoods within the town, while responding to clear, local, pressures for changes in function. This can be achieved by gradual renewal, combining small-scale redevelopment, with rehabilitation to varying standards geared to the needs of the local community. 'Crisis' approaches may be needed in some areas of severe social stress, but the underlying approach should be continuous, rather than a series of finite schemes.

Professor McKie points out that:

Gradual renewal thus requires a number of dramatic departures from the conventional wisdom of planning. Firstly, gradual renewal is the opposite of the traditional action area or local plan. At the outset of a programme of gradual renewal it may be possible to predict a future service grid, a probable street pattern and even alternative scenarios for change and development, but it would and should be quite impossible to produce an architectural design of the area as it is intended to be in, say, thirty years time.

He goes on to comment on 'participation' and planning surveys. His recommendation is, in essence, to start with small and immediate problems. There is not going to be much participation if the man in the street is presented with an elaborate plan of what a transformed neighbourhood will be like in the year 2000. But if he is asked for his views on the desirability of closing a particular street to traffic, he will give the planner useful views and information. Similarly, renewal as a continual process requires that the planning authority has a continuing, rather than sporadic, concern with the area. But although the planner should bear long-term objectives in mind, his main concern should be with small-scale issues. In this 'incremental' way, a process of steady improvement can be achieved, far superior to the neglect and wholesale disruption resulting from successive conventional planning strategies.

In maintaining continual contact with neighbourhoods, a useful role can be played by independent consultants and community groups. Independent consultants may be necessary for a reason which is a comment on British planning – the need to regain the confidence of residents.

All too often an independent consultant knocking on a householder's door gets the suspicious response: 'Are you from the local authority?' But experience shows that once a suitable disclaimer is made, initially hostile residents are only too pleased to talk about their problems.

PROPERTY COMPANIES

Before discussing town centre planning schemes as such, mention must be made of one of the most publicised participants in such schemes – the property companies. There were companies which built offices and shops speculatively. Originally, they retained ownership, letting the property on long leases. As the difficulties of financing grew, it became more common to sell rather than retain ownership; sometimes it was sold to a financial institution and leased back on a long lease, before being sub-let on shorter leases.

The larger of these companies – Land Securities, British Land, MEPC, etc. – were, and still are, substantial organisations in terms of

Stock Exchange quotations, although their market value has fluctuated enormously. They have been represented in many journalistic and Marxist treatments as bestriding the urban world like a Colossus and representing the most developed form of capitalist organisation. It is now possible to see them in a different perspective. They were largely confined to Britain, to one section of the urban development market, namely offices and shops, and their heyday was a period which can be dated fairly precisely, from the abolition of the post-War building controls in 1953 to the property slump of 1973. Companies of this type had not existed on a large scale before the War, and never became common in other countries. They came into being partly because their founders – a collection of swashbuckling entrepreneurs – were quick to perceive the emerging demand for office space and built up efficient organisations for supplying it. But their rise and decline owed much to the peculiarities of the British tax system. The absence of a tax depreciation allowance for shops and offices worked against owner-occupation, while the combination of high rates of income tax and (before 1965) no tax on capital gains meant that the only way an entrepreneur could make money was to build up a company and sell out. But the introduction of Corporation Tax in 1966 was a severe blow to property companies, while at the same time the financial institutions, which enjoy tax advantages, were becoming more adventurous, and starting to invest in property more directly. The new system of corporate taxation was particularly harmful for property companies, which distributed all their income. But the effects were temporarily masked by the 'Brown ban' on office development in Greater London in 1964. The consequent scarcity caused rents to soar, and increased the income of many property companies. By the end of the 1960s, as shortages eased and profits from development fell, the underlying economic conditions were moving against the property companies, but this was once again masked by the 'Barber boom' of 1972–3, which brought floods of surplus cash into their hands.

During the slump of 1973–7, the property companies which did not go into liquidation remained fairly dormant, in some cases selling off a few properties to restore their balance sheets, but undertaking little new development. Some of them may undertake a more active role as the property market improves, but for the most part they will probably remain as survivors of a past age, no longer playing the dominant role that they did in the late 1950s and 1960s. In future, the financial institutions are likely to invest more directly, making use of development agencies or straightforward builder/contractors. If this happens, it will be, in one sense, return to the situation which prevailed before 1939 and has always been the rule in most other countries. But it also opens the way to the development of non-profit development agencies which – as German experience suggests – could retain much of the commercial acumen of profit-making enterprises, while avoiding the resentment they tend to attract.

BRITISH TOWN CENTRE SCHEMES

British town centre schemes have mostly been conducted on the basis of 'partnership' arrangements between private development companies and the local authority. The local authority generally supplies the land; the developer supplies the capital and the development expertise. A plan is drawn up in conjunction with the local authority planners, and an arrangement is made for sharing future profits, generally by linking ground rents to changes in rack rents. This arrangement was designed to get the best of both worlds. The developer supplies the commercial expertise which a local authority staff, which had never before tackled a town centre scheme, could not hope to possess. On the other hand, the local authority would – it was argued – provide the sensitivity to social and aesthetic considerations which might be ignored by a developer acting independently. And at the same time the local authority would share in the profits.

These arrangements have often been criticised by 'anti-developer' groups. The main argument up to 1974 was that the developers made enormous profits, and that the local authority should take *all* the profits, not only a proportion of them, by supplying the 'risk capital' itself. (There was, it was argued, no risk). The property slump put this argument in a rather different light. Had local authorities in general adopted the policies advocated by critics of the development companies, they would have suffered serious losses. But even if this criticism of the role of property companies in partnership schemes is questionable, there is bound to be suspicion of a profit-making organisation closely linked with a local authority, and benefitting from the exercise of statutory powers. Although the usual criticism is of 'carve-ups' putting money into private hands, there is fragmentary evidence of a different, and potentially more serious type of abuse, and one which would still apply if the local authority undertook the whole investment itself. This is that the local authority, as planner, suppresses developments which could compete with 'its' scheme, even if the competition is superior in terms of both 'private' and 'social' returns. This usually means that suburban shopping developments – which are what people want, are cheaper, and create less traffic problems – are suppressed in the interests of a planned town centre scheme (which does not always materialise).[9]

In considering the future of the development industry, Britain might do well to think less in terms of 'speculators' on the one hand and local authority monopoly on the other. In West Germany, the main initiators of development and renovation have been the owners of individual sites – individuals, firms and non-profit housing enterprises. But large-scale development has been coordinated by non-profit planning organisations. A system on these lines, however, requires a variety of owners – personal, corporate or non-profit – with the financial resources for development. There is now a marked difference in this respect between Britain and most other Western countries. In Britain, private landlords have, for the most part, been eliminated or impoverished; non-profit housing is still a poor relation of council housing; and small businesses, under the impact of tax systems inimical to growth, have shrunk in a way with few parallels in developed countries. Given the political will to do so, many of these trends could be reversed. Something could be saved from the wreck of private tenancy, non-profit housing could be given the same subsidy treatment as council housing, and the tax system for individuals and small companies could be made comparable to that in other industrial countries. Whether such changes are desirable – or likely – is an issue on which opinions may differ, but these questions have important implications for urban development.

A further requirement for a move towards a less speculative development system would be the availability of competent and reputable development *agencies*. There are already several private firms of this type in Britain, and a modified Community Land Act could conceivably be used to develop organisations similar to the 'homestead companies'. Indeed, beneath all the political rhetoric which has accompanied the boom-and-slump, considerable change has been taking place in the organisation of the development industry. It is now far more variegated; alongside the property companies there are now building contractors, funding institutions, agencies of govenment and major retailers. The shake-out resulting from the slump has also produced a more realistic and professional approach at all levels, public and private.

Partnership arrangements when they are retained, could be reformed so as to make their operation more satisfactory. This applies particularly to the method of selecting partners. There are two main methods. The traditional one is for a 'developers' brief' to be issued to be interested developers who are invited to submit proposals containing both a financial offer and an architectural scheme. The disadvantages are (a) it is difficult to make comparisons when both 'price' and 'product' are variable, e.g. between a mediocre scheme which (apparently) is very profitable for the local authority and a brilliant scheme which is less profitable; (b) there is a long, laborious sorting process which can cause frustration and undesirable political pressures; and (c) once a developer has been chosen he has the whip hand in the process of spelling out the details of the scheme. Because of these disadvantages, a second method is increasingly being favoured. A developer is chosen at an early stage, with whom a financial and architectural scheme is then worked out. This avoids delay and wasted effort but also has disadvantages. The basis of selection is unclear, and there is no guarantee that the best scheme will emerge, since there is every incentive to submit a superficially attractive scheme in order to obtain the contract.

Both methods have the disadvantage that the scales are weighted in favour of financial gain to the local authority (often of a short-term kind) as against 'quality' (i.e. the intangible gain to users, which often gives the best financial return in the end). An alternative method has recently been suggested.[10] Under this, the first stage would be for the local authority to devise the broad outlines of a physical scheme – the volume and type of buildings, access arrangements, etc. The second stage would be for the local authority estates department to decide the amount, and details, of the lease, using normal valuation procedures. Only then would developers be invited to submit detailed architectural proposals, from which the choice would be made.

The advantages claimed for such an approach are that it would concentrate the attention of the public and politicians on the choice between different architectural schemes and eliminate the suggestion that public sites are being auctioned to the highest bidder to the detriment of architectural merit.

SUMMARY

The renewal of old urban areas poses far more complex problems than 'greenfield' development. Sometimes renewal is profitable, and is undertaken – well or badly. Sometimes it does not readily occur in the absence of public subsidy; older areas then suffer from a cumulative process of decay which goes beyond the type of decline in status and value which may be inevitable and even serve a social purpose. Subsidised renewal may well be justified on wider social grounds, but it does not necessarily mean the type practised in Britain since the 1930s. There are many ways in which public action, and public subsidy, can be utilised.

The defects of 'comprehensive redevelopment' are now widely accepted – even in Britain, where the policy was continued longer, and on a larger scale, than in any other country. The most successful results have been achieved under a system in which a planning authority adopts a sensitive and flexible approach to the desires of residents at a very local level, facilitating gradual redevelopment and improvement but relying on owners (individuals, private firms or non-profit enterprises) to finance development. This 'cellular' approach involves radical departures from a great deal of recent British town planning orthodoxy.

The dominant role which the property companies exercised in British town centre development in the 1950s and 1960s has already given way to a more variegated system. There is perhaps scope for the creation of non-profit development agencies, and for improving the arrangements in 'partnership' schemes.

SELECT BIBLIOGRAPHY

John Holliday (ed.), *City Redevelopment*, Charles Knight 1977.

R. M. Kirwaun and D. B. Martin *Economics of Urban Renewal*, Working Paper 77, Centre for Environmental Studies, London, 1972.

Charles McKean, *Fight Blight*, Kaye & Ward, 1977.

Robert McKie, 'Cellular renewal: a policy for the older housing areas' *Town Planning Review* Vol. 45 No. 3 July 1974.

Robert McKie, *Housing and the Whitehall Bulldozer*, Hobart Paper 52 Institute of Economic Affairs, London, 1971.

David M. Muchnick, *Urban Renewal in Liverpool*, Occasional Papers in Social Administration 33, Bell, 1970.

J. Trevor Roberts, *General Improvement Areas*, Saxon House, 1976.

REFERENCES

1. Leo Grebler, *Urban Renewal in European Countries*, Philadelphia, USA, 1964, p. 103. A similar point is made in *Land Values and Planning in the Inner Areas* Royal Town Planning Institute, 1978, p. 10.

2. see G. H. Peters, *Cost-Benefit Analysis and Public Expenditure*, Eaton Paper 8, Institute of Economic Affairs, London. p. 71.
3. J. Rothenberg. *Economic Evaluation of Urban Renewal*, Brookings Institution, Washington D.C. 1967.
4. Nathaniel Lichfield, 'Evaluation of Methodology of Urban and Regional Plans: A Review', *Regional Studies*, August 1970.
5. Tax and subsidy arrangements affect the costs of occupying, or modernising, housing in different areas, and can sometimes discriminate against older areas. It was a common complaint that the post-War American system of mortgage assistance was, in effect, confined to the 'white suburbs'. In West Germany, the depreciation allowance on houses was, until 1977, confined to new houses, when it was extended to older houses as an 'inner area' policy. The British rating system, being based on a 'rental' concept which is no longer realistic, *may* discriminate against older areas.
6. J. S. Mill, *Principles of Political Economy* Bk. II Chap. 1:3. p. 210.
7. Robert McKie 'Social objectives and citizens' participation in urban renewal in the United Kingdom', in *Urban Renewal in the Netherlands*, International Federation for Housing and Planning. 1975.
8. In 1966 a Ministerial advisory group recommended that owner-occupiers should be compelled to provide the 'standard amenities' in their houses (or be dispossessed). At the time, the 'standard amenities' included a 'ventilated food store', in an age of refrigerators! *Our older homes: a call to action.* HMSO. 1966.
9. In one city known to the author, with an Edwardian centre of some charm, redevelopment or modernisation by individual owners was held up for twenty years (leading to considerable 'blight') because of the Council's grandiose plans, which seemed about to be implemented in 1972. Under a partnership with a development company, a mini-Manhattan was to be created. The scheme seemed to the author to be as environmentally undesirable as it was financially questionable. But it was 'sold' in a way which would have created an outcry if adopted by a soap manufacturer. (The author was invited to write a report showing its economic benefits). The massive subsidising of central multi-storey car parks out of local rates was justified on the grounds that 'We must learn to pay for the motor car' – which meant that its use would be subsidised in the one field in which pricing presented no technical difficulties. The scheme was abandoned in 1975, because of the property slump. But a new scaled-down scheme, in partnership with a different developer, was announced in 1977. The worst aspect has been that, since the early

1960s, the local authority has severly restricted all suburban shopping developments, propably in order to protect 'its' town centre scheme. There are either no, or inadequate, off-street parking facilities, and in some of the new housing areas there are no shops at all.

10. V. Linacre, 'Choosing ways of choosing developers' *Estates Gazette*, March 4, 1978.

12 Public Land Acquisition

In 1918, communal land policy was given a new direction under the administration of the then Mayor, Dr. Adenauer. Till then it had primarily been influenced by revenue considerations; the emphasis now shifted to land banking, the provision of parks, and the development of suburban housing and industrial districts

One Hundred Years of Land Policy in the City of Cologne, Cologne, 1975 (author's translation).

In all countries, the state participates in the urban land market, either at the minimal level necessary to purchase land for roads and other public works, or more extensively. A radically different system is one in which the state undertakes all development, or (in some sense) owns all land. We will first examine public participation in the land market before examining 'nationalisation' and the rather untypical British post-War experience.

EXPERIENCE WITH PUBLIC LAND ACQUISITION

Public bodies can assemble land – either undeveloped land or obsolete building in urban areas – and sell or lease it to developers, public or private, or both. They can take a more active role by acquiring land and seeking to interest potential developers. They can buy land for fairly immediate development, or they can buy it speculatively. Finally, they can go beyond land transactions and engage in development. Further questions are whether the public body or bodies should be given the powers to handle *all* land, or all land in specified districts, or should not be given monopoly powers; and should these functions be undertaken by local authorities or by specialist bodies?

The greatest corpus of practical experience on these questions is in continental European countries, especially West Germany. One of the proposals of the German 'land reform' movement before 1914 was that suburban land should be bought well in advance of need by local authorities. This 'land banking', it was argued, would lower land prices and facilitate good planning. The proposal has been widely implemented in West Germany since the 1920s. An active role in development by the 'provincial development companies' (*Heimstätten*) goes back to 1918, and municipal landownership even further; neither has been a serious issue of controversy under the Federal Republic. There has been, and (despite the controversies stimulated by the short-lived property boom of 1971–3) still is, a consensus that, within a market economy in which ownership of real property is primarily in the hands of individuals, non-profit enterprises and private firms, active participation by public bodies is necessary. Thus large-scale developments on the edges of conurbations (the German equivalent of New Towns) have been organised by non-profit enterprises, often the 'homestead companies', which have acquired land at market prices and carried out development for potential owners or disposal of land to other developers. It is perhaps a measure of the success of German (and Dutch) arrangements for public participation in the land market that they are taken for granted. In Canada and the USA, the subject of suburban 'land banking' has attracted some controversy in recent years, although of rather a hypothetical kind. Let us briefly examine the economic issues, bearing in mind what is known of the practical experience in this field.

The fact that land is divided up into physical 'parcels' and 'bundles of rights' means that assembling land in built-up areas for (even partial) redevelopment is a complex process requiring specialist skills. These can be supplied by private development agencies, but there is a case for having public bodies, without prohibiting private initiative. This is partly to assure all concerned that the agency has no prejudicial financial interest, and partly because a public organisation can also carry out the closely related functions of supervising the land market, giving information to planners from a practical 'estate management' point of view, and identifying sites where development would have 'public' benefits. Similarly, land can be bought in advance of new public uses – motorways, airports, etc. If a public body can acquire sites well in advance of need, and use buildings for explicitly short-run purposes, this avoids both 'planning blight' and the hardship of abrupt expropriation. In all these ways, public bodies can ease the problems which arise in a market economy when changes in land use become necessary.

NEW TOWNS

A wider type of land acquisition is when large areas are bought up before development, often using compulsory powers. This can be done either for 'greenfield' districts or for urban renewal. In the case of urban renewal, however, it is normally linked to 'bulldozing' redevelopment, which has produced unhappy results. 'Greenfield' land buying can take the form either of purchase for planned development or of purchase for possible future development ('land banking'). In Britain there has been virtually no 'land banking', but in areas designated as New Towns the whole area is expropriated at current use (e.g. agricultural) values. The claims made for land banking are (a) that it facilitates better planning, (b) that it enables land to be obtained more cheaply, and (c) that it enables the public authority to make large profits. Before examining the economic logic of these claims, let us examine the history of the idea, which owes much to its Victorian origin.

To Ebenezer Howard, land acquisition was linked with ideas of a new urban form to replace the compact, densely populated Victorian city. By building new self-contained communities of about 30,000 inhabitants away from the great cities, it would, he hoped, be possible to obtain the virtues of town and country life without the defects of either. If population increased, new Garden Cities would be built. The whole process would be undertaken without compulsory powers. A co-operative 'Garden City' association would buy the necessary land at the market price and organise development according to a strict geometrical plan. Occupiers would be granted long leases, so that any rises in land values would ultimately accrue to the 'Garden City', which would be the sole ground landlord. Letchworth and Welwyn, after considerable difficulties, were established by private action. After 1945, they were taken over by the New Town Corporation which, using government money and powers of compulsory purchase, went on to found other New Towns.

Reading Ebenezer Howard today, one is struck on the one hand by the far-sightedness of some aspects of his vision, on the other hand by its paternalism. He indeed pointed the way to a new urban form, although his description of how the inhabitants would amuse themselves in whole-some pursuits, his discussion of whether alcohol should be allowed, etc., has more than a touch of the Victorian boarding school about it. These ideas, *mutatis mutandis*, have carried over to the arguments, advanced for the British New Towns and put forward in the USA today, that ownership by the administering authority of *all* the land in the proposed new town, or suburb, is necessary for good planning. As one American writer puts it:

> The most important advantage of such a system, which alone justifies its adoption, is that it would provide effective control over the strategic elements of urban growth – the location, the design, the sequence, and the tempo of development. Our present control mechanism, relying chiefly on the police power regulations (such as zoning and building codes) does not.[1]

The strength of this argument – or at least the case for a monopolistic system – depends on the type of planning envisaged. There is a spectrum of planning philosophies, with corresponding implications for land acquisition, ranging from the approach which mistrusts market forces and private initiative to the 'market correcting' approach which seeks to guide and supplement the market process. From this latter point of view, it may be desirable to acquire land for purposes which fall outside the market economy (e.g. recreational areas, public buildings) or to provide alternatives to private developers, with an emphasis on experimental housing, low-income housing, etc., but it is not necessary to buy *all* land in the proposed settlement. Alternatively, if all the land is bought up by a development agency, as in the German 'new towns' (or the suburbs of many Dutch towns), the agency can immediately dispose of all the land not needed for public purposes to a variety of developers – on a freehold or a leasehold basis. Professor Marion Clawson, after his study of the purely private suburban development of the USA, advocates a measure of public land acquisition. He rejects, however, the idea of a public monopoly.

> A public agency with a monopoly on developable land could readily fall into serious errors. If it really had a monopoly there would be no private market to provide a measure and a corrective. A bureaucracy with a monopoly would be under strong temptation to fall into unprogressive, insensitive and inefficient ways of operation.[2]

The economic consequences of the public acquisition of all land in the proposed settlement do not need to be considered in purely a *priori* terms, since the British New Towns provide practical case studies. Until recently, the literature on them was mainly confined to enthusiasts who regarded them as the New Jerusalem. More recent studies reach a more balanced assessment. The monumental study by Professor Peter Hall and associates brings out an interesting point. A number of towns in the South-East, which had none of the powers of the New Towns, have developed very similarly, in terms of population and employment.[3]

The British New Towns (at least the 'first generation' ones) were based on the idea of a town as a compact monocentric entity, designed on a clean slate without the complications of existing built-up areas. This is precisely the idea underlying Ebenezer Howard's specimen plan, even if the layout of Welwyn or Stevenage has little in common with his, 'central park', 'Grand Arcade', or 'circular railway'. The German 'new towns', even though they have a greater variety of investors and developers, have also been very 'tightly' planned. There is a danger that a town of this type may suffer, in the long run, from excessive rigidity. In the past, towns have had to be adapted to changes which were not foreseen, and it is highly likely that this will continue to be the case. Some layouts have proved remarkably adaptable to different ways of life – London squares, the spacious terraces of middle-class Victorian districts or the restored canal district of Amsterdam (a delightful combination of residential, commercial, academic and red-light land uses).

Similarly, London and Amsterdam themselves have been enlarged and modified over the centuries – with varying degrees of success. On the other hand, towns like Cumbernauld or Nord-West-Stadt, Frank-furt, are virtually incapable of being modified, and this could contain the seeds of eventual decay. A town, a suburb, which contains a variety of housing types is more likely to be able to adapt successfully to change than one which has only a single type. Some recent 'planned' European settlements – even ones as technically superb as Nord-West-Stadt or Neu Perlach – have everyone living in flats, even though, by cutting out some grass areas of questionable value, a substantial portion of houses could have been included at the same overall density.[4] This uniformity – on such a large scale – could well be storing up social problems for the future. These dangers are much less in districts where the planning has been less of a piece, and less of one time. Perhaps a more 'strategic' type of planning, which allowed a variety of approaches by different developers, could achieve the best of both worlds. But one iconoclastic Munich planning official, after showing a British party round Neu Perlach, proposed a self-denying ordinance, 'Never build for more than 10,000 people at a time'.

NEW TOWNS: CONCLUSIONS

Both Britain and Germany have thus acquired considerable experience of centrally planned 'new towns' based on comprehensive land purchase – in one case purchased compulsorily at current use values, in the other case at market values. In both cases, the 'new towns' have accounted for only a very small proportion of new construction. In Britain, where London was of a size and predominance with no European parallel apart from the equally problematical case of Paris, there was a good 'structural' case for a New Town programme. But the British New Towns also have defects arising from centralised ownership and control. It is an open question whether a looser system would have produced better results. More generous compensation to the dispossessed British farmers would certainly have reduced hardship – and opposition.

In any case, this discussion is somewhat academic since, because of the fall in the birth rate and the shift in emphasis to the renewal of old urban areas, there are unlikely to be any New Towns (of the traditional type) for at least another generation. This applies not only to Britain but to most of Western Europe and the USA (Canada, with its rising population concentrated in a few large metropolises may – or may not – be an exception). The only type of 'New Town' likely to be started in Britain is the linking together of the scattered settlements in districts dominated by early industrial development, reclaiming derelict land, tidying up the environment, and developing a new 'urban system'. But such a 'new town' will inevitably be of a loose-knit type, and will retain existing communities. In such a situation, selective purchase of land by public authorities can play an important role, but the approach needed is more akin to that of 'cellular' renewal in large cities than the traditional New Town approach.

CHEAPER LAND?

So much for the planning arguments for public land acquisition. Other arguments for it are that it enables users to obtain land more cheaply, or that it enables the public authority to make large profits, which would otherwise have gone into private hands. On these points, economic theory and empirical evidence point to certain clear-cut conclusions. If a public authority obtains land more cheaply than the prevailing market price – either because it bought land very cheaply in the past or because it has expropriated owners at below market price – it has the choice of passing the land on to buyers at this low price, or of selling at the market price. The original 'land reform' argument was that, if public authorities bought land on the outskirts of cities, they could obtain it at a fraction of the price it would command when ultimately developed. This would enable the price, or the rents of housing, to be lower, and would also make lower density housing possible. This view was put forward before 1914, when housing densities, and urban land prices (in relation to incomes) were higher than today. The same argument has been continued up to the present day, even though the low-density development to which the land reformers looked forward has taken place to such an extent that some planners now complain about densities being *too low*.

But there was a fallacy in the 'land reform' argument, even before 1914. House prices determine land prices, not *vice versa*. In the Victorian city, land prices and densities were high because large numbers of people had to live within walking distance of their work, which was also concentrated, generally near rail terminals. Given these technological conditions, high densities were necessary and desirable. Lower densities, and lower land prices in real terms, were made possible only by the introduction of modes of transport which made a more dispersed city possible. Making land cheaper on the edges of Victorian cities would not have reduced rents or house prices but merely have given a windfall gain to whoever obtained the cheap land.[5]

Land prices do not depend on private ownership; they reflect scarcity, either inherent or created by planning controls. Thus if land acquired at below the market price is made available at this low price, but houses can still be bought and sold, this will not lower the price of houses, it merely gives a windfall gain to the purchasers, who might well not be particularly poor or deserving of special assistance. Even if the land is for subsidised housing for poor or elderly people, hospitals, cemeteries, etc., there is a strong case for charging the market price, so that subsidies are open rather than concealed. This enables a correct comparison to be made between different methods of reaching the same objective. At least at the margin, there is the choice between council housing and giving assistance to people to buy or rent their own housing, between looking after people at home or in institutions, between burial and cremation.

The point that cheap land gives cheap houses only to the first buyer is illustrated by the British New Towns. The land was acquired at agricultural value, but long leases for houses, shops and offices are now bought and sold at prices which reflect current market conditions; the fact that the land was originally purchased for, say, £50 an acre is irrelevant. An interesting comparison can also be made between Canada and the USA, which are very similar in most ways but have recently pursued different urban policies. Many Canadian cities have adopted 'land banking' but also planning controls which can lead to far longer delays in development than in the USA (although not as long as in Britain). These Canadian cities may be better planned than comparable American cities, but they have far higher land and house prices.

The conclusion is that neither 'land banking' nor expropriation at below market price would lower house prices; this can be brought about only by an increase in the supply of land or a reduction in the demand for it. This conclusion does not mean that the German land reformers were wrong to advocate 'land banking'. The acquisition of land by German municipalities unquestionably assisted the planning of some towns (e.g. the Cologne 'park ring' in the 1920s) and provided useful opportunities for 'horse trading' in the reorganisation that accompanied the reconstruction after 1945.

'SITTING ON A FORTUNE'?

This leads on to the third argument, that 'land banking' can bring large profits to the public authority, because land anywhere near cities is eventually bound to rise enormously in value. The same argument was applied to investment in new commercial property by several journalists and politicians in Britain in 1972–3, who argued that local authorities should undertake commercial development themselves, so as to obtain *all* the huge gains of property development. These arguments were put forward during a sharp upswing in property and land prices which was immediately followed by a slump; if this policy had been widely adopted, local authorities would have shared in the serious losses suffered by property firms and the Crown Agents. This experience brings home the cyclical nature of property prices, and the high risk involved in the speculative purchase of potential building land. The evidence cited of the allegedly huge gains to be made from holding land is usually based on particular parcels which rose sharply in price during a period – the 1950s and 1960s – when land prices in real terms were recovering from the fall between the Wars, and when inflation was accelerating, but interest rates had not yet been pulled up. Theoretical considerations – as well as a long-term view of land prices and property yields – suggest that the average return on landholding is unlikely to differ greatly from the return on other investments.[6]

Both theory and experience in many countries therefore suggest that land acquisition or land banking by public authorities can play a useful role in coping with the imperfections of the land market – both in the renewal of old urban areas and in greenfield development. But the purchase of all land in renewal districts is unnecessary and even undesirable if a 'cellular' type of renewal is desired. On large greenfield developments, even if all land is acquired, most of it then has to be disposed of (either freehold or on long leases) so that there is no subsequent influence on land prices. In general, land acquisition is irrelevant to the question of land prices, and is not a means for local authorities to make an easy fortune.

LAND NATIONALISATION

Britain has taken a different course on land policy from Germany and most of the North-West European countries. In the 19th century, it had a more concentrated pattern of private landownership, which gave rise to a more vehement socialist reaction. The type of land banking and municipal landownership found in Germany, Holland and Scandinavia, which has become an uncontroversial part of their land markets, was not developed. This useful, limited aspect of public policy has been frustrated because of attempts to impose more sweeping and – in the event – unworkable schemes.[7]

The nationalisation of land raises the same general issues as the nationalisation of industry, commerce or agriculture, but the nature of land results in certain peculiarities. The subject can be divided into two parts: first, the economic and social consquences resulting solely from the replacement of the previous owners; second, the principles on which the nationalised enterprise or enterprises are to be run. Is there to be competition (within the nationalised sector, or between it and a private sector) or a monopoly? Is the nationalised enterprise (or enterprises) to be operated on 'market' principles? If not, on what principles?

Land nationalisation first became a serious issue in British politics, and a part of the programme of the Labour Party, in the years before the First World War. It was major element in the *Fabian Essays*, published in 1889; the 'keynote' essay on *The Economic Basis of Socialism* by G. B. Shaw is a colourful account of the Ricardian spectre of a growing shortage of agricultural land, leading to steadily rising food prices, farm rents, and landowners' incomes (in real terms) while wages are forced down to a subsistence level.

A more documented and moderate *critique* was made by the Liberal Party in a report on *Towns and the Land* published in 1925.[8] Together with a parallel report on agricultural land, this represented the final flowering of the Liberal concern with 'The Land Question'. The report argued that 'Without foresight or control our towns have grown up in a blind struggle against the land monopoly'. But it diverged from the Labour Party in supporting 'the free operation of private enterprise' and 'private and individual tenure of land'. It gave a good survey of the 'landbanking' policies of many Continental European countries, and concluded that:

> . . . it is abundantly evident how far this country lags behind many of its Continental neighbours in regard to public acquisition and control of land. . . . The Local Authorities of Norway or Holland or Germany have a freedom undreamt of by us in regard to this question. (p. 200)

The report also praised the site-value method of taxation adopted in Germany. But it noted that Germany, which had such an admirable land system, had a worse housing situation than Britain.

The report's recommendations were primarily concerned with land acquisition and taxation – as well as improving, rather than abolishing, the leasehold system, and encouraging regional planning and the decentralisation of industry. The report recommended that large-scale landownership by towns should be encouraged, 'not by sudden and indiscriminate purchase, but by a judicious policy of steady acquisition in advance of actual development'. It also recommended a system of site value taxation and a betterment levy, where land values had been increased 'by virtue of any specific improvement of a public character carried out in the vicinity'. (p. 263)

There are weaknesses in the report. It glosses over the reason why the famous 'increment value duties' in the 1910 Finance Act 'fell into abeyance' (p. 107) (the reason being the fall in land prices after the War). And the arguments for a betterment levy (in the old sense of 'betterment') ignored the evidence over the previous half-century that this method of allocating the benefits of specific urban improvements was usually unworkable. But, as a whole, the report is impressive in its marshalling of facts and arguments and in its carefully considered detailed conclusions. It pointed the way to a policy of public participation in the land market which, in Continental European countries, had already been shown to be feasible, and was further developed after the Second World War. In Britain, this approach was overwhelmed by the Fabian ideas which developed after the Great Depression. There has been little trace of it in the British land legislation since 1947 – either the ill-considered, unsuccessful, legislation of Labour Governments or the purely negative repeals of Conservative Governments.

It is well known that little thought had been given to the practical problems of administering nationalised industries before the Labour Government came to power in 1945. The same applies to the far more complex problem of land nationalisation. The nationalisation of development land was decided on by the Labour Party in 1972 with very little thought for the way in which it would be implemented in practice. Only when the Bill carrying out this type of nationalisation had been passed through Parliament was a professional committee appointed to examine the practical implications (The Pilcher report, see below).

Both the Liberal programme and the more influential Fabian programme were responses to a highly concentrated pattern of land ownership. At around the turn of the century, about 80 per cent of agricultural land was tenanted, much of it being in the possession of several thousand large personal landowners. And although landowners had lost overt political influence, they still possessed considerable social power. In the towns, most housing was let on weekly tenancies; although there were large numbers of leaseholders, the ground landlords were far more limited in number. In some ways therefore, land ownership was more concentrated in Britain than in other countries of Western Europe, where farmers had generally obtained freehold possession, and where owner-occupancy was usual in the towns until rapid urbanisation produced a new class of landlords (although the leasehold system was uncommon).

Nevertheless, arguments could be made for the English system. The agricultural landowners had consolidated farms, and thus obviated the fragmentation from which agriculture in West Germany suffers to this day. The existence of a ground landlord for urban property was in many cases either unimportant, or a means of ensuring good estate management. (In the Netherlands, the leasehold system has gained ground as a means of land management, and has never aroused the antipathy which it produced in Britain: this was because the ground landlords were public bodies and because the problem of reversion was dealt with in good time). But in Ireland, Wales and to some extent Scotland, the concentration of ownership was greater, the virtues of the prevailing system less, and its defects greater than in England. The Irish system of agricultural land tenancy had none of the virtues of the English. And in the Welsh mining valleys the mineowner was not only the sole employer but also the sole ground landlord and sometimes the sole owner of rented housing. It is not surprising that such a monopoly position – which continued into the 1930s – was sometimes abused, and always aroused resentment: a noticeably high proportion of early socialist leaders were of Welsh or Irish origin. The early literature on land nationalisation is pervaded by a desire to eliminate the concentration of ownership and control in the hands of a largely hereditary class, echoes of which were still heard in the debate on the Community Land Act.

However, having dispossessed the previous owners, the state has to decide how the development and management of real property is to be organised. The arrangemens that are feasible depend on the arrangements in other sectors of the economy. In a Stalinist economy, in which the allocation of all resources was centrally controlled, it would be feasible to operate a system in which property rights were limited to very short periods. All housing would be rented on short-term arrangements from state bodies, and shops, factories would be state-run, by organisations not possessing any independence but merely implementing the central plan. If, on the other hand, there was to be private investment in development, long transferable leases would have to be created. This would even be necessary if the organisations operating shops, offices, or factories were independent commercial bodies, or if owner-occupied housing were to be allowed. In other words, property rights would be *recreated*.

Traditional socialism was hostile not only to private ownership but also the price system. It was assumed that the allocation of resources would be carried out 'in the public interest'. A very different type of socialism is the 'market socialism' which accepts the 'liberal' principle that the economic system should be designed to satisfy the preferences that consumers indicate by their spending, although it rejects private ownership. It seeks to lay down certain rules for socialist managers based on the 'optimum conditions' of conventional economic theory: this would mean selling or letting to the highest bidder, just like any 'capitalist'. The obvious question is whether, in this case, it is necessary or desirable to eliminate private ownership. Would a state monopoly be inclined to recreate a competitive market? Would not a public (and a non-profit) sector alongside private firms achieve most of the social results hoped of nationalisation, while providing a better guarantee of maintaining the benefits of competition and a variety of approaches?

Does not the British experience of industry-wide nationalisation, as against the more usual continental approach of 'competitive public enterprise' point in the same direction?

The context of these questions has been radically altered by the changes in the pattern of ownership that have taken place in Britain since the idea was developed at the end of the 19th century. These changes in some ways make land nationalisation less applicable, in some ways less important. In agricultural land, the great estates and the social power of their owners have gone. As far as housing land is concerned – the major urban land use – over half is now owned by owner-occupiers, while the ground landlords have either gone or are being bought out under the 1967 Leasehold Enfranchisement Act. Nationalisation could take the form of granting existing owner-occupiers long leases. Although this would mean that nothing much would change for, say, 99 years, one of the main arguments for nationalisation in general (and the New Town arrangements in specific) has been that the state would recover the rise in land value at the end of the lease. However, this argument has usually been based on an exaggerated idea of long-term price rises, and the importance of land values in relation to national income (see Chap. 5). Moreover, in the case of housing, the state is – on recent experience – unlikely to recover possession. When the 99-year leases granted in the 1870s and 1880s began to come uncomfortably near their end, the lease-holders campaigned for the rules to be changed, and they were: it is highly unlikely that the state as ground landlord could revert to the pre-1967 situation. The Leasehold Reform (Enfranchisement) Act has, for good or ill, ended the leasehold system for single-family housing as a continuing system. Even land acquired for housing under the Community Land Act is normally being sold freehold.

For commercial and industrial property, on the other hand, the leasehold system still functions; if the state bought the reversions, it would obtain possession at the end of the existing lease. But even in this case, there would not necessarily be the advantages often claimed. If there is any kind of mixed economy – or even any kind of market economy – in which shops, offices, factories, theatres, universities, etc., are operated by independent agencies, they have to be assured of a long lease (say 100 years), in order to justify the cost of initial development, as well as all the subsequent investment in equipment, or human capital. If only a short lease is offered, firms will either decline to undertake investment, or will be able to offer only a sharply reduced price, thus defeating the objective that the state should gain financially. Thus the state, having acquired the land, would have to dispose of it on long transferable leases, and the problems of private ownership would reappear.

This point appears not to have been grasped by those who have advocated land nationalisation as a means of freeing planning from the financial constraints imposed on it by the need to buy property at market prices. These writers appear to imagine that once land was 'publicly owned' the planner could say, 'There will be houses here instead of factories, and factories here instead of houses' and have his instructions promptly carried out, with none of the cost, negotiation and paperwork needed to buy out existing 'interests'. This is an error, as the New Towns illustrate. All the land was originally acquired compulsorily at agricultural value. But long leases have been granted to shops and offices, so that the situation is in practice the same as in central London.

Thus land nationalisation in a comprehensive sense would not, in a mixed market economy, bring the planning or financial advantages often claimed for it. The original argument for breaking the grip of the 'hundred families' have been overtaken by events in Western Europe and North America, even if the argument still has some validity in Latin America. On the other hand, there is in principle no reason why a market economy should not operate perfectly well under a system in which the state was the universal ground landlord, with leases of around 100 years. This has in fact been the system under which some of the best (as well as some of the worst) housing in Britain has been managed. (And all the newer districts of Amsterdam have been developed under a leasehold system, with the municipality as ground landlord). This system would not – any more than site value taxation, or a betterment levy, or any other purported panacea – fundamentally alter the nature of the urban property market. But it might have helped to defuse many unprofitable arguments about the 'land question' and it could perhaps have assisted in urban renewal, if operated with the sensitivity shown by the best London ground landlords. But this latter qualification raises one of the crucial defects of a state monopoly in economic activity; if a mistaken policy is adopted, the unfortunate effects are magnified. It is becoming a commonplace that the record of British local authorities in urban renewal over the last 40 years has been a dismal one. In these circumstances, it is perhaps fortunate that they did not take over the leasehold estates as well.

NATIONAL PARKS

Let us turn to nationalisation in more limited senses, and to British post-War land policies. A type of nationalisation is involved – in most countries – in the creation of National Parks (or smaller recreational areas nearer cities). In the USA, West Germany, etc., a National Park involves the purchase of the land by a public body and its administration primarily for recreational purposes (which does not necessarily exclude forestry or some pastoral agriculture). In Britain, the land in the National Parks is largely privately owned, mainly by farmers, and covered with 'Keep Out' notices. This is perfectly reasonable from the owners' point of view. It is difficult enough to make a living from hill farming without having people damaging crops and disturbing live-stock. But it is unsatisfactory to describe such land as a National Park. If the primary aim is recreation for town-dwellers, the land needs to be owned and administered by a body primarily concerned with 'amenity'. This need not always be a state body, as the National Trust illustrates so well, but the state will normally have to play a major role. Some land could conveniently be left in private freehold if financial compensation was made for allowing public access, and limiting reclamation. To a large extent, however, the creation of National Parks requires the acquisition of freehold interests. But this is very different from 'land nationalisation'.

THE NATIONALISATION OF DEVELOPMENT RIGHTS

The land policy of the 1945 Labour Government can be summarised as 'the nationalisation of development rights', in two senses of the term. The more limited sense is that a planning authority can prohibit development without paying compensation. This power was introduced in the 1947 Town and Country Planning Act, and has remained ever since. Certain powers of this type are usual in most, although not all, developed countries. (Britain is unusual, however, in that the local authority possesses completely arbitrary power over development and even minor alterations – subject to appeal to the Department of the Environment).

A case can also be made for paying compensation for refusal of permission, to bring home to planners the costs involved (Chap. 9). But this case has few advocates; it is generally accepted that the planning authorities should have powers to control the main lines of development, by being able to prevent certain types of development without paying compensation.

The second sense in which the 1947 Act nationalised development rights was that in future landowners (in return for proposed once-for-all-compensation of £300m.) would be deprived of all development value. A 'development charge' equal to the difference between 'existing use value' and market value would be imposed, so as to skim off all the profit from any change of land use. This provision was repealed in 1953 (see Chap. 9).

The 1945 Labour Government did nothing to introduce public participation in the land market, of the kind Germany and the Netherlands had had for over half a century. The emphasis was on taking the profit out of land transactions rather than on facilitating good land management. This emphasis remained when the Labour Party returned to power in 1964 and passed the Land Commission Act (which was, in fact, more concerned with the 'betterment levy' than the Land Commission). However, the Commission's first Chairman, Sir Henry Wells, hoped to make it an agency for land assembly, and possibly development, very much on the lines of the German homestead companies. This was not at all how the Commission's role had been put over in Parliament. It was also a thoroughly 'market economy' approach, which may well have enjoyed surreptitious approval in high places.

> I think the Ministry of Housing has rather welcomed us. They see us as a body which will introduce into the whole planning machine what you might call a sense of commercial responsibility, which I think was lacking. If you get planners working entirely on their own, without continually being reminded that they are using national resources, they sometimes go absolutely haywire. (Sir Henry Wells, *The Economist*, 1 April, 1967).

In the event, the Land Commission's achievements are perhaps not too unfairly summed up in the common verdict that it acquired 2000 acres and 10,000 civil servants. The subsequent Conservative Government could probably have transformed the Commission into the body envisaged by Sir Henry and modified the betterment levy to make it a workable and acceptable tax. Instead, it abolished both.

THE COMMUNITY LAND ACT

Finally, there is the 'nationalisation of development land'. This was the policy adopted by the Labour Party during the property boom of 1972–3. Prices were rising sharply and large profits were being made in some land deals. When several property companies revalued their assets, thus producing large – and as events soon showed – spurious profits, there was a chorus of denunciation, not confined to the Left. It was widely believed that these conditions would continue indefinitely, and that the existing arrangement of subjecting realised gains to Capital Gains Tax, or even the previous Betterment Levy, was inadequate to deal with the situation. It was therefore proposed that *all* property for which planning permission was given for major development should be acquired compulsorily by local authorities at current use valuation. The local authority would undertake development itself or lease the land to a developer. In this way, the state would recover all the development value. It was also suggested that this arrangement would hold down prices. And the use of the leasehold system would enable the community to recover the long-term rise in land values.

A secondary consideration, which had considerable influence with the planning profession, was a desire for what was called 'positive' rather than 'negative' planning. In spite of the enormous powers given to planners (or local authorities) in Britain, they did not have the power to produce a certain type of development on a particular site, if no potential developer thought it would pay. But if the local authority owned all development land it could, it was argued, remould this sorry scheme of things nearer to their heart's desire. Thus the White Paper on *Land* received enthusiastic support from many planners.[9]

The main argument against this policy – put by the RICS –[10] was that it would not work. Most development consists of small projects, based on the vigilance of private enterprise in identifying investment opportunities and pursuing them. Under the proposed system, this driving force would be lost. All initiative for development would have to come from local authorities, which have inherent defects as developers, especially of small-scale projects – bureaucratic sluggishness and some-times pressure from sectional interest to resist development. Such a system would, it was argued by the RICS, seriously retard socially desirable development.

These arguments had little apparent influence on the Community Land Act. Government spokesmen made it clear during the passage of the Bill that its aim was to ensure that *all* development took place on land owned by local authorities, so that the state obtained the benefit of all development value. Local authorities (and in Wales the Land Authority for Wales) were given the right, which would ultimately be made the duty, of buying – at current use value – any land for which planning permission for development or redevelopment was given, and of leasing or selling it. As a transitional measure, land sold privately was to be subject to a Development Land Tax at a rate of 80 per cent of development value, which would eventually be raised to 100 per cent.

This is not how it has worked out. As relatively little money has been available during a period of financial stringency, local authorities have bought very little land. Some concessions have been made in Development Land Tax – an extraordinarily complicated tax – and some private sales are taking place, although the low level of building activity means that total land sales are low. The Land Authority for Wales, in particular, has shown how the Community Land Act could be implemented in the way that Sir Henry Wells hoped the Land Commission Act would be. It has the double advantage over England of covering a larger area than that of one local authority and of being free from direct political control, being thus in the form chosen for the German 'homestead companies' half a century ago. It operates as a commercial organisation with a social slant, buying and selling land for both public or private developers. Its functions are far removed from the rhetoric which accompanied the Act.

It has also begun to be recognised that buying land with compulsory powers and selling it is not necessarily an easy way of making large profits. It was originally envisaged that the leasehold system offered this opportunity, both through the eventual recovery of the whole site at the end of the lease, and by increasing the ground rent at intervals. Under the Act, land for commercial purposes may not be disposed of except on leases of not more than 100 years. But some local authorities have proposed relatively short leases and/or the right to alter the ground rent arrangements. The ground rents would in any case be subject to periodic reviews, as has been standard practice for many years. The request by some authorities goes beyond this, and involves the right to alter the *proportion* of rack rent going in ground rent, if (in the local authority's opinion!) public action has raised the value of the property. The fallacy in this argument is pointed out in a report on commercial development under the Act, prepared by a Ministerial advisory group.[11] The Pilcher report points out that, in the vast majority of cases, the finance and expertise for commercial property development will have to come from organisations other than local authorities, which are ill-suited to such a specialised, and risky, business. If organisations are to invest millions of pounds in property, they need the certainty of a clear legal title for a long period of time and (especially since current British tax law does not allow depreciation for commercial property) certainty about the level of ground rent in relation to rack rent. If the lease is shorter than, say, a hundred years, or the ground rent arrangements are uncertain, the institutions will either be reluctant to invest at all, or will be able to offer the local authority a very much reduced price for the lease. Instead of leases shorter than the 99 years common in the Victorian era, the report recommended leases of 125 years, with arrangements for negotiating a new lease if redevelopment took place before the end of the lease. It also recommended that freehold sale should be allowed in some cases. The report implicitly indicates why the Community Land Act does not (as had been widely expected) provide a means for local authorities to 'get rich quick'.

SUMMARY

Some continental European countries have had long experience of municipal land-banking and of participation in the land market by public bodies. This type of participation can play a useful role in certain types of urban development but it is largely irrelevant to the question of land prices, while the acquisition of *all* development land is unnecessary and even harmful, especially given the lower level of development likely in the foreseeable future in most Western countries. The various land policies implemented in Britain since 1947 have been based on a more sweeping type of nationalisation and have proved unworkable in practice. The Community Land Act, 1975, has been shown to suffer from various defects. However, with modifications it could perhaps be used to provide a degree of public participation in the land market, thus ending the see-saw in land policy which Britain has experienced.

SELECT BIBLIOGRAPHY

H. Darin-Drabkin, *Land Policy and Urban Growth*, Pergamon, 1977.

REFERENCES

1 J. Reps, 'The Future of American Planning: Requiem or Renaissance', *Planning*, 1967, Chicago, p. 50.

2. Marion Clawson, *Suburban Land Conversion in the United States*, Johns Hopkins, 1971, p. 359.

3. Peter Hall (ed) *The Containment of Urban England*. Vol. 1. Pt. 3.

4. Neu Perlach is a satellite town of 80,000 inhabitants near Munich, planned by the non-profit organisation *Neue Heimat*. The quality of design and construction is extremely high, and the provisions for cyclists and pedestrians, for recreation and shopping, are exemplary. Everyone lives in flats – in attractive blocks of 6–8 storeys with large green areas between them. This represented the 'sound planning' of the mid-1960s in Germany, when high-rise was under criticism but 'houses' were frowned upon. There is likely to be a continuing demand for flats, which are favoured by certain groups, such as working childless couples, and old people. But German families with children are following the Anglo-American trend towards 'houses'. A mixture of houses and flats – which would have been possible without even lowering the moderate density (a floor area/site ratio of 1) would have better matched even current demand from a cross-section of the population. Ironically enough, *Neue Heimat* built a lot of excellent terraced housing in the 1950's, of the kind that is now coming into fashion again.

5. The point, as is well known, was originally made by Ricardo in relation to agricultural land.
'Corn is not high because a rent is paid, but a rent is paid because corn is high . . . no reduction would take place in the price of corn, although landlords should forego the whole of their rent.' (David Ricardo, 'On the Principles of Political Economy and Taxation', Third Edition, 1821, in *The Works and Correspondence of David Ricardo*, edited by Piero Sraffa, Cambridge, Cambridge University Press 1951, Vol. 1, pp. 74–75.
A failure to understand this point is widespread. It was shared by one British building society chairman, who advocated cheap sales of land during the 1972 boom as a means of bringing down house prices. It underlies several recent Canadian and American reports. 'It is the price of land which determines the sales price of units to be built. An average $4567 lot would most likely mean a home selling for $22,500–$25,000 . . . So the increase in the cost of land is a factor in pricing much of the public out of the market'. A. Allan

Schmid, *Converting Land From Rural to Urban Use*. (Baltimore, Resources for the Future, Inc., 1968) pp. 3–4.

6. The only empirical study I know bears this out. E. R. Heaton, *Optimisation of Land Stock: a policy for management engaged in private housebuilding*. Unpublished M.Sc. thesis. University of Aston in Birmingham, 1971.

This study of the 'land banks' of building firms in the 1960s, concluded that the average annual appreciation in land value – 10 per cent – was almost exactly the same as the interest charged by merchant banks in this period. By obtaining equity capital more cheaply, and operating with an above-average degree of financial skill, it was possible to obtain a gross return on equity capital of 16 per cent. But this rate of return was possible – with above average skill – on building operations alone. The study concluded that land holding could only be justified by the need to maintain a steady flow of work. The 'land bank' should therefore be carefully tailored to prospective demand, and kept to a minimum rather than a maximum. Mr. Heaton can claim a probably unique empirical verification for his conclusions: he went into the housebuilding business and kept his firm going through a slump which bankrupted many competitors.

7. See G. Hallett. *Housing and Land Policies in West Germany and Britain*, London, 1977, Pt. 3.

8. *Towns and the Land*. Urban Report of the Liberal Land Committee. *Land and the Nation*. Rural Report.

9. 'I believe that land and housing are the two desperately important elements of social policy in the United Kingdom, Lord Goodman said the other day. 'One of the unsolved mysteries of our time is that we have not controlled the price of land within the last ten or sixteen years. I do not think it is due to sinister capitalist motivation, I think it is due to sheer idiocy.' Let us put an end to idiocy." Ewart Parkinson, Senior Vice President, Royal Town Planning Institute. R.T.P.I., Conference on 'The Future of Land', October 1974.

10. *The Land Question: a fresh approach*, Royal Institution of Chartered Surveyors, 1974.

Royal Institution of Chartered Surveyors, *The Land Problem Reviewed*, 1978.

11. *Commercial Property Development, First Report of the Advisory Group on Commercial Property Development*. (Pilcher Report). HMSO, 1975.

Concluding Thoughts

Market economy, price mechanism and competition are fine, but they are not enough.˙. . . . Market economy is one thing in a society where atomisation, proletarianization, and concentration rule; it is quite another in a society approaching anything like the 'natural order' . . . In such a society wealth would be widely dispensed; people's lives would have solid foundations; genuine communities, from the family upward, would form a background of moral support for the individual; there would be counterweights to competition and the mechanical operation of prices; people would have roots and would not be adrift to life without anchor; there would be a broad belt of an independent middle class, a healthy balance between town and country, industry and agriculture. The decision on the ultimate destiny of the market economy, with its admirable mechanism of supply and demand, lies, in other words, beyond supply and demand.

Wilhelm Röpke, *A Humane Economy*, trans. Elizabeth Henderson, 1960, Chicago, U.S.A.

The economic philosophy which was dominant in the English-speaking intellectual world from the 1930s to the 1960s lauded the virtues of central direction and control, and decried market forces and local initiatives. This was even more marked in the discussion of urban policy than in other branches of economics. These ideas were widely implemented in Great Britain whereas in other countries they encountered more vigorous opposition; namely in the USA from a sturdy belief in free enterprise and local autonomy and in West Germany from a sophisticated philosophy of a 'socially responsible market economy'. Many writers, both in Britain and abroad, argued that what was being implemented in Britain – the sweeping powers of development control, the 1947 'development charge' and later the Land Commission, 'slum clearance' and New Towns, rent control and council housing – was a model for the world. But an increasing number of people began to feel that the Emperor's clothes did not warrant such adulation. 'Planning' was frequently oppressive in detail and unimpressive in its total results; the various development taxes did not work well in practice; 'slum clearance' brutally destroyed neighbourhoods; council housing had its defects.

There are now signs of an intellectual revival of what Mr. Samuel Brittan calls 'liberal utilitarianism'; he suggests three 'main guidelines' for economic policy.[1]

(1) Individuals should be regarded *as if* they are the best judges of their own interests, and policy should be designed to satisfy the desires that individuals happen to have, excluding desires to coerce or downgrade other people.

(2) Policy should be governed by a preference for impersonal general rules with a minimum of discretionary power by publicly appointed officials – or private bodies engaged in backstage pressure – over their fellow men.

(3) We should try to *limit the domain of political activity* even though we cannot mark out exact boundary lines in advance.

Mr. Brittan adds a couple of 'rule-of-thumb maxims': 'look for any self-adjusting mechanisms, whether natural or contrived, wherever possible: if the mechanisms you find are unsatisfactory, seek to modify their operation rather than replace them by directives and prohibitions'. 'It is safer to rely on people's private interests rather than their professed public goals.'

These guidelines have implications for urban land policy, guideline (1) implies that if people show a clear readiness to pay for a certain type of residential development – e.g. a house in the suburbs – this is *prima facie* evidence for letting them obtain it. One can argue that the execution of suburban housing is poor, and set up publicly supported 'demonstration projects' or public development companies to improve the quality of design. There *may* be an argument on transport grounds for maintaining a higher density (and higher land prices) than the market would provide – although this is arguable. What one would not do is to adopt the unsympathetic, not to say condescending, attitude exemplified in a caption in a recent article in a planning journal (over a picture of admittedly boxy-looking houses). 'Sick culture produces the cancer of suburban sprawl.' Similarly, one would view with considerable scepticism a housing system which produced expensive dwellings which no one would dream of buying.

In Britain, in contrast to most countries, guideline (2) was abandoned in town planning in the 1947 Act. The consequences have been attracting increasing – if as yet unavailing – criticism. Some discretionary power is involved in any decision to allow development in some rural areas, and not in others, but there is considerable scope in Britain for planning to make greater use of general rules, and thus reducing the scope of discretionary power.

Guideline (3) indicates, for example, a preference for *participation* by public bodies in the land market (as discussed above) as against the acquisition of *all* development sites by local authorities – the original idea behind the Community Land Act.

The three guidelines together indicate a preference for income support of the 'guaranteed income' kind as against rent allowances: rent allowances as against subsidised housing; and subsidised housing by a variety of bodies, alongside unsubsidised private tenancy, as against a local authority monopoly of rented housing. Admittedly, one has to start from the existing situation – which in the field of British rented housing is almost the opposite of that indicated by our guidelines. This could not be changed quickly, even given the inclination to do so. However, a greater emphasis on principle rather than on what is 'politically possible' could indicate a number of steps that could be taken.

Many important aspects of current urban problems, however are not economic. A writer who deals with urban economics – and especially one who defends the role of markets, as against commands and prohibitions, in resolving economic problems – should perhaps conclude with a few words on the wider context.

We live in an age which lacks the optimism of the Victorians, and in which it is fashionable to represent urban civilisation as heading for an apocalypse of one sort or another. No one – except professional optimists like Mr. Herman Kahn[2] – disputes that (unlimited) atomic war would be apocalytical, but there are other dangers. Some writers paint a picture of deteriorating housing, growing poverty, worsening traffic jams, increasing pollution, and general, international, decline – often with an implicitly Marxist eschatology. Others point to the rise in crime and violence, and loss of 'urbane' qualities, the excessive size and impersonality of organisations – as well as probable future energy shortages – and argue that we must all become smallholders. Some moves in this direction – a renaissance of the small vegetable garden or more solar heating systems – are quite compatible with the spread-out form of the modern city. But to abandon completely urban life and its associated technology would both require the death of a largepart of the present population and sacrifice the great cultural and social virtues of city life.

However, the prophecies of doom depend on the evidence selected. Professor Banfield – whatever the weaknesses of his positive proposals – has argued cogently that urban conditions are in fact better than they have ever been, and that the trouble is simply excessive expectations.[3] Most of the statistics do not indicate universal decline. Despite the problems of the inner city, and self-inflicted wounds in rented housing in some countries, housing standards have *improved*. Traffic congestion is not getting worse everywhere. In many cities in North America the number of cars crossing the city boundary has *fallen* in recent years. Some pollution has worsened, but the air of London or the water of the Thames is *cleaner* than it was twenty or even a hundred years ago. The intensive research which has begun only recently is opening up possibilities for recycling, cleaner and quieter transport, and energy conservation which are only beginning to be tapped. This does not mean that there is not a serious long-term energy problem, or that there is not a good case, on health grounds alone, for simpler techniques in some cases – more bicycles in towns, perhaps. But this neither indicates the need for a more centrally planned economy nor disproves conventional microeconomics. There are some things that only central goverment can do – such as developing new sources of energy – and some that only local government can do – such as supplying more cycle tracks. But too much central planning can be counter-productive. The fashionable intellectual view of the 1960s in Britain was that France and Britain, with their highly centralised political and economic systems were the examples to follow, and not decentralised countries like West Germany, Switzerland or the USA. There seems to be a growing questioning of this view, reflected in the success of the late Dr. Schumacher's slogan.[4] But the 'small is beautiful' approach is not, as Dr. Schumacher suggested, an alternative to conventional economics. Most of his conclusions can be reached on the basis of conventional economic theory. (And a similar idea, 'spaceship Earth', was invented by the author of a long-established textbook of traditional economic theory).[5]

On the population front, there are also grounds for hope as well as concern. The population of the world is increasing by about the population of the UK every year. In the opinion of many observers – apart, of course, from Mr. Herman Kahn[6] – this raises serious problems for the mushrooming cities of the Third World, as well as for the supply of natural resources. But there has been a general fall in the rate of increase; in European countries and the USA, population growth is now zero or quite low. Population stability is likely to dominate urban development in these countries over the next generation.

Greater cause for concern than the economic and technical prospects for urban society is the growing social disorganisation, accompanied by increasing crime and violence. But perhaps some comfort can be gained from a study of history, which indicates ebbs and flows, rather than steady progress or steady deterioration. Descriptions of Manchester or Boston in the 1840s paint a picture of extreme squalor, violence, ignorance and crime. The Victorians and Edwardians tackled these problems with moral fervour, and by 1914 had eliminated most of them. Since then, much has been gained. Opportunities previously confined to a few have been extended to most of society, and a new form of suburban living developed which most people demonstrably prefer. But, equally, a great deal has been lost. Under the Victorians, it became safe to walk the streets at night: this is no longer so in many British and American cities. Vandalism, litter, terrorism, national strikes, inflation, broken homes – the list of modern ills is familiar. Only slowly is it beginning to be realised that this degeneration is not merely due to the difficulty of coping with changing technology and life-styles but also the result of the teaching of false (or misrepresented) prophets. Dr. Spock did *not* say that children should not be stopped from smashing up the china, any more than Dr. Freud said that people would become ill if they *consciously* repressed anti-social tendencies. When 'law and order' has for a generation been used as a pejorative term, is it altogether surprising that law and order begins to break down? The 'permissive society' has its admirable side, in its enlargement of personal liberty which does not harm others, and writers like Mr. Samuel Brittan are right to stress the curiously misunderstood point that its corollary in the economic field is the market mechanism, not state monopoly. What even as percipient a thinker as Mr. Brittan stresses insufficiently, and many 'liberal' writers ignore, is that in any society the desires of individuals have to be restrained when they conflict with the desires of others. If this is not done, life rapidly becomes 'nasty, brutish and short'. The simplest alternative to anarchy – and the one which people have always chosen when there seems to be no other choice – is dictatorship. To combine order with freedom requires an elaborate structure of law and convention, based on a consensus that freedom under the law is desirable and possible. Western civilisation has alone succeeded in creating such a structure, and it has been under steady attack for several generations from what a recent book (significant at least for being written by an ex-editor of *The New Statesman*) has called 'enemies of society'.[7]

There are signs that the tide of intellectual opinion is turning, and that old truths are beginning to be rediscovered. Some intellectuals have begun to argue that children need a stable family background, that the police should be supported, and suchlike recently unfashionable ideas. It may well be that things will get worse before they get better, but the change in the intellectual climate provides some ground for long-term hope.

To develop cities where a satisfying life can be lived by the whole community requires the social, political and moral conditions which permit the delicate combination of public order, psychological security and personal freedom, together with a viable market economy (with non-profit participation), an efficient supply of 'public goods' and an efficient, limited, planning system. It may be that the modern city will never again have the jewel-like charm of some pre-industrial cities. However, as Professor Kevin Lynch has argued, it can have its own beauty and interest.[8] Moreover, in cities which retain extensive older areas, the new and the old can, given sensitive planning, exist alongside each other. This does not mean preserving older areas unchanged, which in the end means death. With modest improvements, older areas can be made suitable for modern living while retaining much of their original character. But styles of transport, and shopping in particular, have to be different in old and new areas. It is as foolish to destroy older areas with supermarkets or too many urban motorways as it is to prevent supermarkets or urban motorways in loose-knit, newer suburban areas. Munich, Amsterdam and other cities in West Germany and the Netherlands point the way. Even in cities which lack historic cores of the European type, modern suburbs can co-exist with older areas which are well maintained, full of 'life' and with no more crime than the suburbs. In North America, the example of Toronto is well known, but there are also cities in the USA – such as Seattle – which deserve mention.

Britain differs from most other developed countries in many aspects of urban policy: the virtual elimination of private tenancy; the large size of its council housing and the small size of its non-profit housing sector; the extent and uniformity of its comprehensive redevelopment; and its discretionary controls over development (and in the level of taxation of higher incomes and small businesses and – not perhaps without connection – the small size of the small-business sector). These are all aspects of a 'social engineering' philosophy which has dominated the intellectual discussion of urban affairs. Only recently have a number of intellectuals begun to realise (what non-intellectuals had known from the beginning) that theory and reality are poles apart. Polemics against planners, architects and officials are – as far as they go – salutary. But the more constructive task is to isolate what was good in the original movement for town planning, council housing, urban renewal and tenancy protection; examine where it went wrong, and develop a new synthesis. In this process, economics has an important role to play, but only if it is of the type which integrates theory with institutional and empirical studies, in a context of general culture. What is needed today in urban economics is not to find some new all-embracing theory, or to refine sophisticated techniques based on crude premises. It is rather to clarify the most basic economic concepts in their application to urban problems, clear away prejudices and muddles dating from the Victorian city, and learn from the experience of differing policies in various countries. This situation is not peculiar to urban economics. As an economist and US Assistant Secretary of Defence once put it:

> The tools of analysis that we use are the simplest, most fundamental concepts of economic theory, combined with the simplest quantitative methods. . . . The reason Ph.D's are required is that many economists do not believe what they have learned until they have gone through graduate school.[9]

REFERENCES: CONCLUDING THOUGHTS

1. *Capitalism and the Permissive Society*, Macmillan, 1963, p. 122.
2. Herman Kahn, *On Thermonuclear War*. Princeton University Press, 1960.
3. Edward C. Banfield, *The Unheavenly City*, Boston, 1970.
4. E. S. Schumacher, *Small is Beautiful*, Blond and Briggs, London, 1973.
5. K. E. Boulding, *Economics as a Science*, New York, 1970, p. 146.
6. Herman Kahn. *The Next 200 Years*. Morrow, 1976.
7. Paul Johnson, *Enemies of Society*, Wiedenfeld and Nicholson, 1977.
8. Kevin Lynch, *The Image of the City*, MIT Press, 1960.
   Ibid – "The Possible City" in L. S. Bourne (ed.), *Internal Structure of the City*.
9. Alan A. Enthoven, 'Economic Analysis in the Dept. of Defence', *American Economic Review*, May 1963.

Index

270